Psychology, Law and Eyewitness Testimony

Wiley Series in

The Psychology of Crime, Policing and Law

Series Editors

Graham Davies
University of Leicester, UK

and

Ray Bull
University of Portsmouth, UK

Psychology, Law and Eyewitness Testimony

Peter B. Ainsworth

University of Manchester, UK

JOHN WILEY & SONS

Chichester • New York • Weinheim • Brisbane • Singapore • Toronto

Copyright © 1998 by John Wiley & Sons Ltd,
Baffins Lane, Chichester,
West Sussex PO19 1UD, England

National 01243 779777
International (+44) 1243 779777
e-mail (for orders and customer service enquiries)
cs-books@wiley.co.uk
Visit our Home Page on http://www.wiley.co.uk
or http://www.wiley.com

Other Wiley Editorial Offices

John Wiley & Sons, Inc., 605 Third Avenue,
New York, NY 10158–0012, USA

WILEY-VCH Verlag GmbH, Pappelallee 3,
D-69469 Weinheim, Germany

Jacaranda Wiley Ltd, 33 Park Road, Milton,
Queensland 4064, Australia

John Wiley & Sons (Asia) Pte Ltd, 2 Clementi Loop #02–01,
Jin Xing Distripark, Singapore 129809

John Wiley & Sons (Canada) Ltd, 22 Worcester Road,
Rexdale, Ontario M9W 1L1, Canada

Library of Congress Cataloging-in-Publication Data

Ainsworth, Peter B.
Psychology, law, and eyewitness testimony / Peter B. Ainsworth.
p.   cm. — (Wiley series in the psychology of crime, policing, and law)
Includes bibliographical references and index.
ISBN 0-471-96931-1 (cloth) — ISBN 0-471-98238-5 (pbk.)
1. Eyewitness identification. 2. Psychology, Forensic.
3. Evidence, Criminal.   I. Title.   II. Series: Wiley series in psychology of crime, policing, and law.
K5483.A77   1998   98–19886
614′ . 1—dc21   CIP

British Library Cataloguing in Publication Data

A catalogue record for this book is available from the British Library

ISBN 0–471–96931–1 (cased)
ISBN 0–471–98238–5 (paper)

Typeset in 10/12pt Century Schoolbook by Saxon Graphics Ltd, Derby
Printed and bound in Great Britain by Biddles Ltd, Guildford and King's Lynn
This book is printed on acid-free paper responsibly manufactured from sustainable forestry, in which at least two trees are planted for each one used for paper production.

To
Edith Ainsworth and June Watson

Contents

About the author

Peter B. Ainsworth is originally from Blackburn, Lancashire. After leaving school he joined Blackburn Borough Police as a cadet and later became a police constable with Lancashire Police. Peter was subsequently seconded to Lancaster University where he obtained a degree in Psychology. He then took up a scholarship to study Psychology and Sociology at Colorado University, USA. Peter returned to the UK in 1977 to start work on his Ph.D. and the following year was appointed lecturer in the Department of Social Policy and Social Work at Manchester University. Peter has remained at Manchester University up to the present time and teaches courses in Applied and Social Psychology. For the past eight years he has taught on the subject of eyewitness testimony at both undergraduate and postgraduate level and has carried out research in this field. Peter's previous book, *Psychology and Policing in a Changing World* (Wiley, 1995), demonstrated the way in which psychology can be applied to the complex world of policing.

Series Preface

The Wiley Series on the Psychology of Crime, Policing and the Law publishes concise and integrative reviews on important emerging areas of contemporary research. The purpose of the series is not merely to present research findings in a clear and readable form, but also to bring out their implications for both practice and policy. In this way it is hoped that the series will not only be useful to psychologists, but also to all those concerned with crime detection and prevention, policing and the judicial process.

Psychology, Law and Eyewitness Testimony provides a valuable and unique introduction to contemporary research in what is simultaneously one of the oldest and most contemporary concerns of forensic psychology: the reliability of the eyewitness. Even today, despite all of the advances in forensic science, such as DNA profiling and computerised fingerprint analysis, most crimes which come before the courts are still resolved by judge and jury balancing the credibility of one witness's account against the assertions of another. Peter Ainsworth's important book provides a lucid and up to date guide to both the strengths and vulnerabilities of the witness. It will be as valuable to the police officer who must conduct an interview with an anxious witness as to the lawyer who must question him or her on the stand.

The topics which Ainsworth discusses: the selectivity of memory; its vulnerability to corruption from preconceived attitudes and subsequent knowledge; the special problems posed by children and those who must try to identify strangers on the basis of a brief glimpse under stress would have been familiar to the turn of the century pioneers like Stern and Munsterberg. They were among the first to stage unexpected incidents before astonished professional audiences to demonstrate the fallibility of eyewitness reports and show that even confident observers could be wrong. However, many of the topics Ainsworth discusses would be novel to these pioneers, such as the use of the Cognitive Interview to assist police officers in questioning witnesses more effectively, the use of voice and smell cues to identification as well as the role of the expert witness in assisting the jury to evaluate conflicting testimony. The psychologist expert is a familiar sight in courts in the United States and some European countries but one which is still rare in the United Kingdom.

As Ainsworth points out, in the United Kingdom, the vagaries of the eyewitness are held by judges to be common knowledge, unworthy of expert opinion. The dangers of just trusting to common sense were dramatically illustrated in a case before the Court of Appeal in February 1998. The Court quashed the conviction for murder in 1952 of a Somali seaman, Hussein Mattan, who had been hanged at Cardiff prison 46 years previously. The main evidence against him was that of eyewitness identification. Only later did it emerge that a second Somalian seaman, Tahir Goss, had also been under suspicion and was subsequently convicted of another murder in the same year under strikingly similar circumstances. One witness to the first murder had reported that the suspect had a prominent gold tooth. Mattan had no such tooth, but Goss did. Such a miscarriage of justice serves as a sobering complement to the literature on the problems of cross-racial identification which figure among a host of relevant findings described in this important book.

We have no doubt that this new work will add to Peter Ainsworth's reputation as an interpreter and guide to the large and often complex research literature in forensic psychology for a wider audience. He has already demonstrated his capacity to write lucidly for professional as well as academic readers in his earlier book in the series, *Psychology and Policing in a Changing World* (1995). Peter started his professional career as a police officer before being tempted into academia and so knows at first hand the problems of eliciting and evaluating witness statements. Perhaps if all those who must deal with witnesses would read his book, tragedies like the Mattan case could be avoided.

GRAHAM DAVIES
RAY BULL

Preface

Eyewitness testimony has now become one of the most researched areas within the field of applied psychology. Over the last 20 years, great strides have been made in understanding the many factors which influence witnesses' memory. Since the publication of Loftus's seminal work *Eyewitness Testimony* in 1979, the field has expanded rapidly and now covers a wide range of issues and topics.

Whilst much of the research has taken place in the laboratory, most psychologists have been keen to demonstrate the importance of their findings in the real world of eyewitnessing. The law is a notoriously conservative institution, often opposed to change and to the introduction of new ideas. Nevertheless, psychologists have had some impact on legal procedures, and have been instrumental in introducing a number of important changes to legal practice. Not least of these have been changes to the way in which child victims and witnesses are treated by the criminal justice system. Psychologists have also made many other valuable contributions, including the development of more effective witness interviewing techniques.

Unlike some research in the field of psychology, there is a very real sense of relevance and applicability to much of the work on eyewitness testimony. This is demonstrated by the fact that today it is becoming increasingly common for psychologists to be called upon to provide expert testimony on the subject of eyewitnesses. The law has not always felt that such testimony is necessary and in the past has often ruled that knowledge about such matters is just a matter of common sense. As this book will show, a significant amount of the research on eyewitness testimony challenges some commonsense notions and shows that jurors may make important mistakes when evaluating the testimony of eyewitnesses.

Whilst a great deal of research has been carried out both in Europe and the USA, there have been few books published which give an overview of the current state of the subject. This book intends to do just that and attempts to provide an introduction to both the area in general, and to the more important topics within the field. It is not intended to be the definitive guide to every piece of relevant recent research, but rather provides the reader with an introduction to many of the more important current areas of interest. The book is written in a non-technical style, in the hope that those outside the field of psychology will be able to understand the material, and to see its relevance.

It must also be born in mind that, at any time, each of us may be a victim of, or a witness to, crime or traffic accidents and thus become eyewitnesses ourselves. Ironically the current author was recently driving home after delivering a lecture on eyewitness testimony. Whilst on the motorway he witnessed a rather serious accident, the exact details of which are still rather hazy! Let us hope that as a result of books such as this we will at least come to acknowledge that memory is fallible and that we may all make mistakes. Recognition of this fact by the criminal justice system might mean that there will be less chance of wrongful convictions in the future. If this is the case, then the work of all the psychologists covered in this book might just have been worth while.

Acknowledgements

A large number of people have contributed towards the completion of this book but unfortunately it is not possible to name all of them individually. However, I would like to thank my wife, Susan, and my delightful daughter, Genevieve, for their understanding of my need to work for very long hours in order to complete this text.

I am particularly indebted to Professor Graham Davies for his patience in reading drafts of each and every chapter. His comments were, as always, extremely helpful. He was able to point me in the direction of much important recent research, and to reassure me during the inevitable periods of despair and despondency! I would also like to thank Chris Hitchen for her reassurance and for her comments on draft chapters. I am also very grateful to Ken Pease for his interest in the book, and for his ever-helpful comments. Despite Ken's very busy schedule, he found time to read the draft and, as always, made some extremely useful suggestions. Thanks also to Bernard Gallagher for his comments on Chapter 9 and to Jackie and Elaine for their continued help and support. Finally, I would like to thank my publishers John Wiley & Sons for providing me with the opportunity to reach such a large audience with this book.

Introduction

There can be few areas of applied psychology which have shown such massive recent expansion as that of Eyewitness Testimony. Following the large-scale development of both theories and models of memory in the 1960s came a recognition that at least some of the research could have practical applications in a number of important areas. Nowhere was this more apparent than in the field of Psychology and Law, and specifically in Eyewitness Testimony.

It is not possible to put a precise date on the birth of this important applied area. However the assertion by Ulrich Neisser that much memory research lacked an applied focus was of great significance. Ulrich Neisser had been one of the main players in the development of Cognitive Psychology. Indeed his seminal work of the same title (Neisser, 1967) represented a milestone in this area, and was required reading for most undergraduate psychology students both in the USA and in Europe in the 1970s. However, by 1982 Neisser had recognised that too much of the massive amount of memory research did not address everyday memory processes or problems. Research was all too often carried out in the laboratory with meaningless material and with little concern for external validity. Rigorous scientific methodology was often seen as more important than practical application. Any members of the public wishing to improve their own memory would have received little practical help from the mass of psychological research which was being carried out in the 1960s and 1970s.

By contrast there was a great deal of interest in understanding why memory was capable of some amazing feats, yet could let people down in frustrating ways. The outcome of a significant number of court cases rested on the accuracy or inaccuracy of the memory of witnesses. Despite the rapid advance of forensic science, and its increasing use in criminal cases, juries were still being primarily influenced by the testimony of eyewitnesses. A number of psychologists (e.g. Loftus, Buckhout) came to suggest that the Criminal Justice System may well have unrealistic expectations of witnesses. Could an eyewitness really be expected to remember every detail of an incident which may have taken place many months or even years earlier? Might witnesses not make mistakes, and if so could psychology offer explanations for such errors? Should defendants be convicted on eyewitness testimony alone? Could children really be good and accurate witnesses? Such questions laid the foundation for the collaboration between psychologists and lawyers which was seen in the 1980s.

Yet there remained many formidable obstacles. Psychologists and lawyers, whilst recognising that cooperation might be fruitful, seemed to be speaking different languages. Lawyers and judges used expressions such as 'beyond all reasonable doubt' whilst psychologists talked of findings being 'statistically significant at the .05 level'. Clearly there was a great deal still to be done if psychologists were to be regarded as having a valuable contribution to make to the legal field. Much more progress was needed before psychologists working in this field would be accepted as expert witnesses in court.

Whilst recognising that there has been this rapid expansion in the last 30 years, it is easy to forget that the investigation of the fallibility of eyewitness testimony started almost a century ago. As long ago as 1909 Munsterberg noted that:

> 'Justice would less often miscarry if all who were to weigh evidence were more conscious of the treachery of human memory.' (Munsterberg, 1909, p. 45)

Some 90 years later judges and juries are still accepting the evidence of eyewitnesses as though such testimony were an objective, factual and indisputable truth. As this volume will testify, the reality is that it is often none of these!

Most witnesses who appear in court have to take an oath. The exact contents of such oaths vary from country to country but in all known cases they ask the witnesses to swear that they will tell the truth whilst giving evidence. In Britain witnesses are asked to say the following words whilst holding the bible: 'I swear by almighty God that the evidence I shall give shall be the truth, the whole truth and nothing but the truth.' Whilst the legal reasoning behind such oaths is obvious, one has to question whether such a statement is realistic. It is obviously in the court's interest to know that the witness is not deliberately telling lies. Indeed, to do so would be to commit the serious offence of perjury or, if collusion is involved, conspiracy to pervert the course of justice. However, where the psychologist and the lawyer would differ would be in the beliefs about human perception and memory. Even the most honest and upstanding of witnesses will inevitably produce their own subjective and personal version of 'the truth'. As we will see in Chapters 1 and 2, human perception and memory are not literal and objective recorders of 'fact'. Rather these processes are personalised and subjective interpreters and recorders of information. Thus the court may honestly believe that the witness is indeed telling 'the truth'. The psychologist may, however, point out the factors which can distort an honest witness's recall of events.

When one considers the other parts of the oath the problem becomes even more pronounced. Is it realistic to expect a witness to tell 'the whole truth'? Such an expectation assumes that witnesses are capable of taking in every small detail of the scene which they witnessed, and of storing these details accurately and fully. But surely this is naive and unrealistic? Humans are simply incapable of taking in all the information which they encounter. Perception is selective in what it attends to, and large amounts of detail simply go unnoticed. Even if a witness notices the key aspects of a scene, he or she will be unable to remember all the information contained therein. What eventually reaches the long-term memory store will be but a small proportion of the amount of information contained within the scene. The amount of accurate information available to the court will be further diminished by the processes of interference and decay. The longer the gap between the event and the court case, the more likely it is that memories will have faded or have been altered.

Similarly, asking a witness to tell 'nothing but the truth' may be a laudable ideal but an unrealistic expectation. Whilst most witnesses may well not lie deliberately, it is almost inevitable that at least some parts of their evidence will be fictitious. As we will see in Chapter 1, human perception works by interpreting stimuli and by making 'educated guesses' about what is actually out there. Most of the time the interpretation will be accurate, but on some occasions it will not. For example, it has been demonstrated that witnesses consistently overestimate the length of time that an incident lasted. Thus if a witness is asked under oath to say how long a robbery took, he or she may well give an 'honest' but inaccurate answer. If a portion of a scene is hidden from view, perception will tend to fill in the gaps so as to allow the person to perceive the scene as a whole. This happens often unconsciously without the witness being aware of the process. The witness will later be unable to distinguish those parts of a memory which were actually witnessed, and those bits which have been imagined in order to fill in the missing detail.

It is thus inevitable that what a witness says in court will be a subjective and incomplete version of 'the truth' interspersed with small portions of fiction. This is not to say that eyewitnesses should never be heard – most cases would be unable to proceed without evidence from eyewitnesses. Rather it will be argued that courts must realise that witnesses are not necessarily the objective tellers of truth which the oath might assume. It is the task of the court to try to separate out the different elements within the witness's testimony. In some cases this may be helped by an expert witness such as a psychologist giving testimony about how human memory works. In the USA this is becoming more and more common, though in Britain it is still relatively rare. However, in many cases jurors may well rely on hunches or 'common sense' to establish the veracity of a witness's testimony. Even here, though, there will be the danger of systematic errors. As we will see later in this book, juries are likely to be impressed by a witness who gives his or her testimony in a very confident way, and to be less persuaded by one who is faltering and unsure. However, this understandable stance is rather spoiled by research which has shown that there is often little correlation between witness confidence and witness accuracy.

It is thus apparent that many of the assumptions which the Criminal Justice System makes about eyewitness testimony are inappropriate. In the rest of this volume it will be argued that only by understanding the psychological processes underlying eyewitness testimony can courts fully judge the testimony of one who has sworn to 'tell the truth, the whole truth and nothing but the truth'. In this respect psychology may have a great deal to offer in assisting courts to decide whether witnesses are likely to be accurate or inaccurate in their testimony. Whilst we may still be some way from being able to discriminate absolutely between the totally truthful and the totally mistaken witness, we know a great deal about the many factors that influence eyewitnesses. As such, psychologists should have an increasingly important role to play in the outcome of criminal trials in the future.

By drawing attention to the way in which witnesses can make mistakes, psychologists may have an effect on the number of wrongful convictions. Any reduction in such convictions will be welcome, not least by those innocent people who may be wrongly convicted. However psychologists might also be able to have an influence on the number of occasions on which the guilty are convicted. If psychologists can recommend techniques which improve the accuracy of witnesses' recall, then this should result in a larger number of perpetrators actually being convicted. As we will see later in the book, psychologists have developed a number of techniques which are designed to improve recall, and in many cases such techniques have proved to be very successful.

This volume will thus address many of the major issues which surround eyewitness testimony.

Chapter 1 deals with the topic of perception and, in particular, considers the subjectivity involved in the process. It is argued that perception is not an unbiased objective system which simply takes in information, but rather is a personalised and subjective process which is subject to a large number of influences. The chapter will consider differences in individual perception, and consider whether the analogy of the video camera is an appropriate way of understanding perceptual processes.

Chapter 2 considers some theories of memory and the implications which these have for eyewitnesses. The chapter does not provide a comprehensive overview of memory theories, but rather concentrates on some of the more important contributions made by psychologists. It also considers whether memory is a permanent store, or whether all memories eventually fade with time. The notion that memories might be transformed whilst in storage is also addressed.

Chapter 3 looks at how witnesses remember events and outlines some of the errors which are likely to be made. It examines a large number of variables which can affect the accuracy of eyewitness accounts. These include features of the event itself, and also differences between individual witnesses. Although we are not yet in a position to be able to say with certainty that a witness is right or wrong, the chapter will help to identify the important factors which contribute to accuracy and inaccuracy.

Chapter 4 develops these ideas further and looks at how original memories might be changed by, for example, subsequent misleading information. The notion that events are somehow fixed in memory is challenged, and it is argued that most memories are subject to some kind of revision over time. The chapter draws heavily on the work of Beth Loftus whose contribution to the field has been invaluable.

Chapter 5 looks at some theories of facial memory, and assesses the implications for the Criminal Justice System. The chapter examines the ways in which facial memory might differ from event memory, and considers the difficulties of facial recall. The effects of interference are also highlighted along with difficulties such as cross-racial identifications.

Chapter 6 examines why and how identifications go wrong and reviews a number of different identification techniques. The chapter also considers whether changes to current identification procedures might serve to reduce the number of misidentifications and subsequent wrongful convictions. This chapter also includes a review of a number of actual cases in which identifications went badly wrong.

Chapter 7 looks at some of the ways in which witnesses might be interviewed in order to obtain the maximum amount of (accurate) information. It reviews the important work of Fisher and Geiselman, and traces the development of the Cognitive Interview Technique. The chapter also looks at the potential obstacles to the use of such techniques and, in particular, the police service's apparent reluctance to embrace fully such novel interviewing strategies.

Chapter 8 examines the vexed question of hypnotic memory retrieval, and considers whether the technique really can enhance witnesses' memory. The chapter considers why hypnosis was greeted with such enthusiasm in the 1970s, but is now treated with much more suspicion. The opposing views of Martin Reisser and Martin Orne are explored and suggestions made for appropriate safeguards.

Chapter 9 looks at children as witnesses and considers recent changes designed to make it easier for child victims to be heard. Although the Criminal Justice System has always been wary of child witnesses, the chapter points out that recent research suggests that this suspicion may well be unjustified. The effect of changes to the rules of evidence concerning children are also considered at length.

Chapter 10 considers whether it might be possible to identify suspects via other sense modalities, dealing in particular with voice recognition. Although research in this area is still at a rudimentary stage, it is argued that identifications by voice are possible, and in some cases entirely appropriate. The notion that blind people may have superior powers of voice recognition is also considered.

Chapter 11 discusses whether psychologists should be appearing as expert witnesses in court and considers the legal and ethical implications of such appearances. Recent legal rulings concerning the admission of expert testimony are reviewed and potential obstacles to such admission are considered. The chapter also examines whether the appearance of psychologists as expert witnesses will enhance or diminish the reputation and standing of psychology as a scientific discipline.

Finally, in the Conclusion, the current status of psychology within the legal system is examined. The chapter also considers the likely future role of eyewitnesses within the Criminal Justice System and looks to the future of psychological research in the area. The need for more realistic studies is explicitly acknowledged.

CHAPTER 1

Perception and the Eyewitness

Like all other animals, humans need to be able to understand and make sense of the world around them. This is achieved through the process of *perception*. Once the sensory organs take in information, perception takes over and tries to make sense of these inputs. In most cases this process occurs without people realising it, and with little conscious effort. When a person looks around a room his or her perceptual processes may tell that person that there are four chairs and a table in the room. The person may perhaps not be aware of a sensory image upon the retina nor of the interpretation of the stimulus then taking place. Yet he or she would have little doubt that his or her perception was accurate and appropriate. If necessary the person could probably identify the material from which the table and chairs were made, and recognise other details of the scene. Most everyday perception appears to be of this kind and goes on with little consideration of the processes involved. Yet, as we will see later, perception is actually quite a complex process involving a number of strategies and techniques.

IS PERCEPTION JUST LIKE A VIDEO CAMERA?

Many people, including some of those in the Criminal Justice System, imagine that perception and memory work just like a traditional (i.e. non-digital) video camera and recorder. The camera (or the eye) is directed towards a scene, the camera takes in what is there and the image is then stored on the videotape. The recording lies there for as long as necessary. When recall is needed the person simply rewinds the tape, presses the "play" button and an exact copy of the original scene is played back. Courts tend to assume that this is indeed how perception and memory work. A witness may appear in court many months or even years after an offence has been committed and be asked to recall every detail, as though replaying a videotape. Such evidence may well be accepted in a similar way to that of an actual videotape being played.

With the ever-increasing use of security cameras, it is increasingly common for video footage (showing what an accused did) to be used in the criminal justice process. Whilst this often produces a convincing case for the prosecution, the evidence may be seen as no better than that of a confident witness who appears in court and gives a detailed account of what he or she believes took place.

Whilst the analogy of the video camera may have some use in understanding how perception works it can actually be quite misleading. The main point to stress is that unlike the human perceiver, the video camera and recorder does not *interpret* the information in any way. Providing there is enough light, the camera will simply record what it "sees" and transfer the image on to a tape. The old adage "The camera never lies" may not be literally true but at least video cameras are not affected by such things as prejudice, stereotypes, and expectations. The video camera (provided it is pointed at the entire scene) does not selectively attend to some parts of the scene and ignore others. The video camera, unlike the human perceiver, will not feel relaxed when looking at one scene and anxious when looking at another.

There are a large number of reasons why it may be misleading to think of perception and memory as similar to video recording. Having said that, there may be some similarities worth bearing in mind. A video camera might be pointed at the wrong part of a scene and thus fail to record some important detail. In a similar way a witness's attention may be so concentrated on one aspect (e.g. a loaded gun) that other details are ignored. Videotapes can be misplaced or misfiled. The original recording can fade with time or be erased. Video recordings, especially those made via a digital camera, can also be tampered with and altered so as to give an altered image. As we will see later, human perception and memory can suffer similar fates.

So if the video camera analogy is misleading how should we see perception? There are a number of views which attempt to explain the process and two of these will here be discussed briefly.

THE PROCESS OF PERCEPTION

Perception has been described as both a *top-down* process and a *bottom-up* process and we will consider these terms here. Bottom-up processes are said to be driven solely by the input itself. We might recognise a chair simply because its physical configuration matches that which we have encountered before (i.e. we have a template for the object "chair"). The object has four legs, a flat seat and a back, and is therefore identified as a familiar object – in this case a chair. However, an individual might also recognise the object by using a more top-down process. The individual might notice that the object is propped up against a table, each side of which has a similar looking object leaned against it. The fact that at the next table people are sitting on these "things" would also lead the person to label the sensory input as a chair. Most everyday perception may well be of the bottom-up type and be accurate. However, as we will see later, many cases of eyewitness testimony involve top-down processing, leading to a more subjective and possibly inaccurate interpretation. Bottom-up processes may well be more appropriate for the perception of simple objects, whilst top-down processes would be used in the perception of more complex events and incidents.

As we will see later, context and expectation can play a major role in perception, affecting the top-down processing of criminal acts, traffic accidents, etc. A person entering a large classroom would probably have no difficulty in recognising a chair. However, a mountaineer encountering such an object on the top of a deserted peak would experience rather more difficulty in labelling the object correctly. Interestingly, the ubiquitous supermarket shopping trolley is invariably recognised irrespective of where it is encountered!

Perception as Interpretation

For now we should return to an earlier point regarding the way in which perception occurs with little conscious effort. Humans may only become aware of the complex process of perception when an input is novel or ambiguous. Let us consider a couple of examples. Suppose a person is seated in the carriage of a stationary train and another train is stopped alongside. One train starts to move but for the first few moments it is not possible to establish whether it is the person's own train that is moving or the one alongside. The reason for this confusion is that the visual information which the person receives is the same whether it is his or her own or the other train which starts to move first. In such circumstances the person may well look out of the window on the other side in order to check if the scenery appears to be moving. Alternatively, the person might check to feel if there is any vibration coming from the train in which he or she is sitting. In either of these cases, the traveller would conclude that it was his or her own train that was indeed now moving.

In recent years there has been a large increase in the number of simulators appearing as arcade and fairground attractions. Such machines allow people to sit in a small container and experience the sensations of riding a roller coaster, being driven in a rally car, etc. Although all those in the simulator know that it is just a simulation, they still experience many of the same sensations they would feel if they were actually in the situation which is being simulated. Indeed such machines can only work if they convince occupants that they are experiencing similar feelings to those which would be felt on the roller coaster itself. Recent advances in the creation of "virtual reality" also mean that many people can experience things which they would not normally be able to. Dreams and drug-induced hallucinations can also make people feel as though they are experiencing things which in reality they are not.

Whilst such states may be considered unrepresentative of most everyday perception, they give insights into the creative and subjective nature of most perceptual experiences. Dreams also provide some insights into perceptual processes. Although we may be aware that dreams are only internally generated images, that does not stop us believing that the dream is a real event at the time that we experience it. Nightmares can be terrifying because they feel very real at the time – only later are we able to work out that the event was imagined. As we are beginning to see, perception is certainly not the straightforward taking in of information which the earlier video camera analogy may have lead us to believe.

As Gregory and Colman note:

"There is, indeed, an intelligence to perception: it involves complex problem solving and does not always get the right answer."(Gregory & Colman, 1995, p. xi)

Human perception should thus be thought of not as an objective, static and totally accurate process, but rather one that is active, creative and subjective. Humans do not simply record chunks of data which they encounter but rather sift it, interpret it subjectively, and then record that interpretation. That our perception is neither objective nor always accurate can be demonstrated by the many visual illusions which appear in psychology books (see, for example, Sternberg, 1996, ch. 4). Space does not permit a detailed discussion of such phenomena here, but one striking example may illustrate the point.

In Figure 1.1 most subjects perceive two triangles in each picture, one with the point to the top, and the other inverted. The inverted triangle is clearly visible in the middle of each picture. If told that these inverted triangles are illusions and do not actually exist, most people would disagree strongly. People can see and even trace the outline of each triangle against the background. However, if one covers up the three incomplete circles in the picture, the triangle mysteriously disappears. Reveal the circles again and the triangle reappears as if by magic!

This curious phenomenon can be explained by reference to the "top-down" model of perception discussed earlier. Perception tries to make

Figure 1.1. (Figure from *Cognitive Psychology* by Robert J. Sternberg, copyright © 1996 by Holt, Rinehart & Winston, reproduced by permission of the publisher)

sense of the information and makes an informed guess as to what the patterns falling on the retina might represent. In this case, the most likely interpretation of the visual image is that there is an inverted triangle on top of an upright triangle which is covering up parts of three circles. Given this interpretation, our brains somehow draw in the lines of the triangle, so that we perceive it quite clearly. If people who had been shown this figure were asked to appear in court and to testify that an inverted triangle really did exist, most would do so happily. Such people would not be lying deliberately, but would be telling what they believed was the truth. No doubt most would even be able to survive intensive cross-examination as to the existence of the triangle.

Bias and Subjectivity in Perception

The sceptical might question the relevance of such visual "tricks" but they do serve to show the truly creative nature of human perceptual processes. Humans tend to make "the best bet" as to what is actually out there in the world, yet do not realise that this is just an educated guess. Let us consider another example. A witness is walking past a bank one day when she sees a masked person with a gun emerging from the bank. The robber runs down the road, into an alleyway and then disappears briefly from view. Seconds later a person runs from the other end of the alleyway into the arms of a passing police officer. If asked to give evidence in court, the witness may well testify that the police without doubt arrested the person whom she saw running out of the bank. Her perception may well have told her that the person whom she saw running into the alleyway "must" be the person who emerged from the alleyway only seconds later. However, this may simply be an example of how perception fills in any missing parts, so as to make a complete picture. It is of course possible that the real robber ran off in a different direction and the man whom the police stopped just happened to be in the wrong place at the wrong time. The point is that the witness would find it hard to accept that her perception of events was not totally accurate and objective.

It has been suggested that the process of perception might be compared to that of an artist painting a picture. The artist uses his or her own interpretation of the scene, translates that into visual imagery, and then creates something unique on the canvas. Ten artists painting the same scene would all produce a slightly different end product. Whilst there would be some common themes across all the pictures, each one would have its own idiosyncrasies and subjective interpretations. Some artists might have chosen to highlight one particular aspect of the scene whilst others may have almost ignored it. Some artists may have sought to create a certain mood or atmosphere in the scene through the use of colour or light and shade. Some of the artists might be more accurate than others in the details which they record.

The artist analogy is perhaps much more useful in understanding perception than that of the video camera. Just like the group of artists, ten people witnessing a bank robbery will all have different interpretations of what took place and thus have slightly different memories. Each witness's attention may well have been directed to a different part of the scene. Some witnesses may have been more fearful than others and thus have been less able to take in details of the event (see Chapter 3). Whilst all witnesses may have overestimated the duration of the event there might well be significant differences in the estimations that they give of how long the robbery took. Thus, whilst all witnesses might agree that there were two robbers, many other details of the event will be in question. A police officer taking statements from all the witnesses may well be unsure which version of events should be believed.

As we will see later, there are many reasons why witnesses might interpret scenes differently. Whilst some features of perception are inherited, most perceptual skills are learned. The newborn baby struggles to make any sense of the world of visual images and sounds. But as humans develop, so does their ability to interpret stimuli in the environment. They learn, for example, that although an object appears to become smaller when it moves into the distance, this is not actually so. They also learn that a bright red ball is still a bright red ball even though it may appear to be a dull brown colour in poor lighting conditions.

Learning, Experience and Perception

Because each human experiences subtle differences in their upbringing, so their perception of events will be slightly different. A child who is raised by parents who are fearful of the world will tend to perceive the world as a dangerous place. Events which may in reality pose little threat will be viewed with suspicion. A person out alone who believes that the city is a dangerous place may well perceive every face he or she meets as that of a potential mugger. Those city dwellers who live with a high fear of crime might react to every ring of the doorbell with suspicion and trepidation. To the lonely rural dweller, the same sound of the doorbell ringing might be perceived as a welcome sound, possibly signalling the arrival of a friend.

If a police officer stands up in court and says "My attention was drawn to the suspect because he was acting suspiciously", what might this mean? Would a civilian viewing the same actions perceive them as suspicious? Because of the nature of their work police officers spend time looking out for people who are (or who are perceived to be) acting suspiciously (see Ainsworth, 1981). Such people may well be stopped and questioned as to their activities. Police officers may be more likely to arrest some people simply because of their demeanour or apparent disrespect for authority (see Worden & Shepherd, 1996). The point is that a police officer walking the streets may well perceive far more 'suspicious circumstances' than would a civilian (Ainsworth, 1981). A person walking in the rain with his or her collar turned up and hat pulled down may be perceived as someone who is simply trying to keep dry – or as someone who is trying hard not to be recognised. A person carrying a can of petrol may be perceived as a stranded motorist by civilians, but be seen as a potential arsonist by a police officer.

Because perception is largely a learned process it draws heavily on personal experience. When a person first arrives in a new town, especially one with an unfamiliar culture, it may be hard to make sense of the many novel visual images. But as the person becomes more familiar with the environment so his or her perception of it becomes less demanding. The person who first arrives in New York may find it hard not to spend a great deal of time looking up at the skyscrapers. The long-term resident may, however, walk the streets with not so much as a single glance skyward. The more familiar a setting becomes, the less time and effort people devote to examining its features. The motorist who witnesses his or her first serious traffic accident may be overwhelmed by the carnage at the scene and find it difficult to make any sense of what has happened. By contrast, the experienced police officer who has dealt with many such incidents will be able quickly to take in all the relevant information and decide on a course of action.

Serious road accidents, assaults and armed robberies are relatively rare. What that means is that for most witnesses it will be their first and only time of experiencing such an event. (see Latane & Darley, 1970). For this reason, processing the inputs may prove difficult, whether from a top-down or bottom-up perspective. Many may simply misinterpret the event, and assume that there is an innocent explanation for what is taking place. As such they will pay little attention to the incident or interpret it inappropriately. Little in their past will have prepared them for such an event, and consequently their perceptual processes may well find it difficult to interpret and then record features of the scene. Such inexperienced witnesses may not express themselves well in court.

Expectations and Attributions in Perception

Following this line of argument, we might ask whether those who have seen a large number of accidents (or robberies) would make much better eyewitnesses than those who witness such an incident for the first time. Whilst experience will mean that a witness will be less fazed by the incident, it is possible that this very experience may lead to distortions in perception. For example, a police officer may have dealt with many accidents caused by "the inexperience of youth". He or she may thus make certain assumptions when attending an accident involving a young person. Psychologists have known for a long time how stereotypes and expectations can come into play when viewing a scene (see Allport & Postman, 1947). The police officer may well reach an inappropriate conclusion when viewing the accident, assuming that the cause is "obvious" when this is not necessarily so. In a personal communication with the author, a Chicago police officer was discussing the causes of traffic accidents and said, "The trouble is that all the young people drive too fast and all the old people drive too slow". There can be little doubt that such a simplistic and stereotypical view would affect this officer's perception of the causes of the accidents he investigated.

One of the consequences of the process of perception is that individuals tend to see (or more correctly perceive) what they expect to see and are inclined not to see what they do not expect to see. One example of this is the number of accidents involving car drivers who pull out of junctions and collide with motor cyclists on the main road. Following such accidents car drivers often utter the inimitable words, "Sorry mate I didn't see you"! However the common nature of such accidents suggests that an explanation might be found in the process of perception. The car driver waiting to pull out of the junction may look both ways and, seeing no cars approaching, believe that it is safe to move out. However, many car drivers may well be looking only for other *cars* approaching. The smaller (and perhaps darker) figure of the motor cyclist may not "register" and the motorist will thus believe that it is safe to pull out. In the past it was the policy of many British police forces to insist that traffic patrol officers must learn their skills as motor cyclists before being allowed to drive traffic cars. Part of the reasoning behind this was that if the officers were to survive as motor cyclists they had to learn to think for the other driver as well as for themselves. The belief was that such training could prove to be invaluable and make car drivers much more aware of the dangers around them.

That people tend to perceive what they expect to see has been demonstrated in many ways. One common method is to show audiences a picture containing an error and to then ask people what they believe they saw. One such example is reproduced below.

When shown this slide the vast majority of people tend to report having seen "I LOVE PARIS IN THE SPRING" and do not realise that "THE" appears twice in the actual picture used. It is often difficult for students and authors to proof read their own material as they tend to see (or perceive) what they expect to see. Thus an error which might be quickly spotted by someone detached from the work will go unnoticed by the writer of the piece. He or she knows what the text should say, and perceives that this is what it actually does say.

The fact that people tend to see (and remember) what they expect to see was demonstrated in a now classic study carried out 50 years ago. In this experiment, Allport and Postman (1947) showed a detailed picture of two men, one black and one white, standing facing each other in a subway train. In the picture, the white man was holding an open razor. The subjects in the experiment were asked to look at the picture and then tell a second person what they had seen. This second person then recounted the details to a third person and so on, until up to six or seven people had been told the details. This is similar to the game of 'Chinese whispers', and was a technique used by an early British psychologist, Sir Frederick Bartlett (see Chapter 2). What Allport and Postman found was that in more than 50% of cases, the final version of the story had the black man holding the razor rather than the white man. This study tends to suggest that some people do indeed perceive what they expect to see (or hear). For some white subjects, stereotyped beliefs would tell them that it was more likely that the black man would have been holding the razor than the white man. Thus in retelling the story, some subjects transferred the razor from the white man's hand to that of the black man.

Allport and Postman's study was carried out more than 50 years ago, and one is left to ponder the extent to which today's witnesses might also fall back on their stereotyped views of the world in trying to remember "the truth". Certainly some more recent studies do suggest that this is indeed the case. In one experiment (Boon & Davies, 1988) people at an airport were asked to listen to a tape recording describing an altercation between a black man and a white man on the London Underground. During the tape it was said that "a knife was drawn out" but no mention was made of which party actually drew the knife. Subjects were asked to recall the details as accurately as possible, and to speak into a tape recorder. Their version of the story was then played to another person and in turn, this person's version told to a third person and so on. At the end of the chain, the stories were examined for accuracy. Of the 16 chains that were produced, 12 did not say which of the two people in the story had been holding the knife. However, the other four all "placed" the knife in the hand of the black man. In other words, 25% of the chain presumed that it was the black man who would have drawn the knife, and none presumed that it would have been the white man. Boon and Davies conclude that even when witnesses are told that accuracy is important (something that did not happen in the Allport and Postman study) "there is a trend for subjects to distort recall for verbally delivered events in attitude specific ways" (Boon & Davies, 1988, p. 55).

Although this study is interesting, it is difficult to assess the exact relevance to eyewitness testimony cases. It is highly unlikely that witnesses would be asked to appear in court to recount a version of events which had been passed on from one person to another, then another, etc. Indeed, most courts specifically prohibit the admission of so-called hearsay evidence. However, in a second study, Boon and Davies found that attitudes can affect perception and memory for material which has been perceived first hand. In this study, subjects were shown a series of five slides depicting an incident similar to that described in the previous tape-recorded story. In the slides, a black and a white man were shown facing each other, and the white man was holding a knife. Boon and Davies needed to be able to separate out those cases where mistakes occurred simply because of memory errors from those where racial prejudice may have caused inaccurate memories. For this reason, a second set of slides was used, showing two white men, as opposed to one white and one black.

Subjects were asked to describe what they had seen by writing an account. The crucial measure was whether subjects correctly ascribed the knife to the hand of the white man, incorrectly placed it in the hand of the black man, or made no such ascription. In addition to the descriptive task, subjects were also given a recognition task, where they were shown a series of slides and asked to say which of these they had seen earlier. In this second task, subjects were in fact shown a slide in which the knife had been switched to the hand of the originally unarmed person. The results showed that there was a powerful influence of racial prejudice on memory accuracy with a significant number of subjects believing (incorrectly) that the knife had been in the hand of the black person.

However, the findings were qualified by evidence of an interaction with the order in which subjects were asked to report. Boon and Davies had chosen to give some subjects the recognition task first, followed by the free recall test, whereas for others the order was reversed. As it turned out, the order was to prove important. When the recognition test was administered first and the recall task second, there was evidence that stereotypes affected memory. When the recognition task was given second, there was less likely to be a difference according to whether the scene contained two white men or one black man and one white.

A third experiment reported by Boon and Davies further showed how attitudes can affect perception and memory. This study dealt with attitudes towards police actions during the British miners' strike in 1085. Subjects' attitudes towards the strike and the policing of it were first measured. Subjects were then shown a photograph taken during the strike of a mounted police officer, baton raised, advancing towards a female. Subjects were later asked to identify which of a series of six drawings was most like the photograph they had seen originally. The drawings were all slightly different, the main variation being the degree to which the police officer was shown in a threatening pose. The results showed that there was an interaction between attitudes towards the miners' strike and memory for the picture. Those who supported the police's actions were more likely to choose a drawing which showed the police officer as less threatening, whereas those who were hostile to the policing of the strike tended to pick out a drawing which showed the police officer's actions as more threatening.

We can see from these studies that attitudes and stereotypes can indeed affect perception and memory (see also Diges, 1988). When asked to apportion blame for an incident, the influence of prejudice and stereotyping is even more obvious. Another classic study carried out in the 1950s examined the way in which students viewed the actions of their own sports team, compared with the actions of their opponents (see

Hastorf & Cantril, 1954). Students from Princeton and Dartmouth Universities were each asked to watch a film of a game of American Football played between teams from the two colleges. The game contained a large number of fouls and resulted in quite serious injury to at least one player. The students were asked to watch the film and to note down the number of fouls committed by each team. Despite watching exactly the same film, the two sets of student subjects came up with very different versions of reality. For example, the Princeton students reported having seen on average 9.8 fouls committed by the Dartmouth team. By contrast, the Dartmouth students claimed on average to have seen only 4.3 fouls committed by their own team.

There are many similar cases where the actions of others are perceived or interpreted in different ways, depending upon the observer's own views. The actions of the football referee who awards a controversial penalty in the last minute of a game will be cheered loudly by one set of supporters but greeted with derision by the opposing fans. It is unlikely that any amount of supporting evidence will convince each set of supporters that their version of the truth is not correct! This view was supported by some recent work by Boon and Davies (1996). In this study subjects from both an English and a Scottish University were recruited and asked to watch a number of incidents extracted from an England v Scotland football match. Having watched the incidents, subjects were asked to judge each one according to who was at fault, and to recommend an appropriate action (e.g. sending off one player, etc.). Measures were also taken of each subject's level of support for one team or the other. The results showed that there was a significant relationship between subjects' support for a team, and their performance on the perceptual rating task. Not surprisingly, strong support for one team was associated with a tendency to judge incidents in favour of that team, and against those of the opposing team. In other words, team allegiance affected perception, not randomly, but in a self-serving way. One implication of this finding is the suggestion that:

> "...motivational forces do play a significant role in the interpretation of information to the extent of materially altering experience at the time of encoding." (Boon & Davies, 1996, p. 162)

In other words, witnesses appearing in court may genuinely believe that they are giving an objective recollection of an incident when in reality they are giving a story based upon a biased and self-serving interpretation.

This research may have direct relevance to the area of eyewitness testimony. There are many cases where such subjective interpretations will be crucial. Suppose a fight breaks out between two men outside a pub and the incident is witnessed by a large number of people. One of those involved in the fight subsequently appears in court accused of assault. He claims that he was only acting in self-defence, and that the other person attacked him. The outcome of the case rests largely on the testimony of those witnesses called to give evidence. It may well be that their version of the incident is as subjective as was that of the American college students referred to above. If one of those involved in the fight was known to the witnesses then this would undoubtedly affect their perception of his actions. If the accused was a friend of the witnesses then his actions are more likely to be seen in a positive light. Conversely, if the accused is known as a troublemaker and is disliked by the witnesses then the same actions are likely to be perceived and remembered very differently. Whilst in this example the bias may be understandable and obvious to the court, there are many cases where more subtle forms of prejudice may cloud both the judgement and the memory of a witness. One such example is provided in a study carried out by Duncan (1976).

Duncan was interested to see whether actions committed by a person of one race might be perceived differently from the same actions carried out by a member of a different race. His subjects watched a videotape of an altercation between two people. The altercation became gradually more heated until eventually one person pushed the other. After viewing the incident, Duncan's subjects were asked to describe what they had seen. All the subjects in the study were white American college students. In fact, Duncan used a number of different versions of the videotape with different groups of subjects. In one version, the person who pushed the other was white, but in another version he was black. The videotapes were otherwise identical.

The subjects were asked to say whether the behaviour of the person who pushed the other could best be described as "playing around" or as "violent behaviour". When the perpetrator was white, only 13% of subjects chose to label the actions as "violent behaviour". However, when the perpetrator was black, some 70% labelled the behaviour in this way. This difference is staggering considering that the subjects saw the exact same actions, with only the race of the perpetrator altered. The implications of such a study have profound implications for eyewitness testimony. If Duncan's subjects were all to appear as witnesses in a real criminal case, their version of "the truth" would clearly be affected by whether the defendant was black or white. Some recent cases (e.g. the trial of O.J. Simpson) suggest that members of the public may be divided on ethnic lines when it comes to assessing the likely guilt or innocence of a black defendant.

CONCLUDING COMMENTS

We can thus see that perception is not the simple, objective and reliable process which courts seem to assume. Because perception is creative and subjective it is inevitable that people will make mistakes in their perceptions, and that different people will emerge with very different versions of events. Courts should thus perhaps be a little wary of the confident witness who claims proudly, "I know it's true – I saw it with my own eyes." As we will see later, such a witness's confidence may be misplaced.

CHAPTER 2

Theories of Memory and the Eyewitness

All creatures require some kind of memory. Almost every function which humans perform each day requires them to have a memory system upon which they can draw. Whilst people may often be heard to say that they "have a terrible memory", in reality most of their memory is probably functioning perfectly adequately. Even people who claim that "they cannot remember a thing" still seem to be able to cook their meals, stop at a red traffic light, pick the children up from school or whatever. None of these would be possible if they had no memory. Whilst there are cases of people who have memory problems caused by damage to parts of the brain (see Baddeley, 1995) most other memory problems are of a much less serious nature. When failures do occur, they can be of two main types, i.e. a failure to recall information, or a failure to recognise something or someone as familiar. In this chapter we will look at some models of memory which help to explain the issues addressed in this book. It is not the intention to offer a complete overview of memory theories, but rather to offer an insight into some representative and relevant contributions which psychologists have made. The interested reader may wish to consult sources such as Baddeley (1990) for a more comprehensive review of human memory research.

MEMORY FAILINGS

There are a very large number of ways in which memory can "let us down". People may well enter a room and forget what they went in for; they might fail to remember the name of the person they have just met; or they may forget the last thing on the shopping list. Whilst these failures can be very frustrating, their consequences are of only momentary significance. However, when we consider memory "failure" in the realm of eyewitness testimony, the consequences can be much more serious. The Criminal Justice System places a very heavy emphasis on the role played by eyewitnesses and, as such, the role of memory is crucial.

Many criminal trials last a long time and involve a large amount of technical evidence. In deciding such cases, the jury may well go along with the testimony of the most important eyewitness. A confident and credible eyewitness can have a very large degree of influence on jurors (see Chapter 11). In a complex case which lasts for weeks, the image of a poised, confident and likeable eyewitness may stick in jurors' minds and have a disproportionate influence on the ultimate decision. Whilst a judge may implore a jury to consider all the evidence in the case, this would seem unrealistic. Human memory was not designed to take in, store, and then recall vast amounts of complex information accurately and objectively.

Human memory is selective and subjective. Humans pay attention to only a small amount of the mass of information around them at any one time. Whilst you are reading this book, you are (probably) unaware of the sounds going on outside the room, the temperature, the pressure of your shoe on your foot or whatever. In the same way that an eyewitness will pay attention to some aspects of the incident and ignore others (see Chapter 3), a jury will also be selective as to which parts of the case they concentrate upon and thus feel are the most important. Research has shown that humans generally find it much easier to remember information that is meaningful to them, and less easy to remember that which is more obscure (see Baddeley, 1990). The intricacies of a complex business fraud, or the mechanics of DNA profiling, will be beyond the comprehension of many jurors and may thus be paid comparatively little attention. However, a confident witness who claims to have seen the defendant holding "the smoking gun" will form a lasting impression. In psychological terms, such evidence will tend to produce a stronger memory trace.

THE IMPORTANCE OF MEMORY IN CRIMINAL CASES

Whilst the number of "scientific" aids used in crime detection has increased rapidly over recent years, there is still a heavy reliance upon the more traditional evidence of an eyewitness. Any new "scientific" evidence has to be tested at length before it will be accepted in a court of law. The scientists will need to prove that their findings are not open to doubt and that they can be "proved" scientifically (see Chapter 11). No such conditions apply to the human eyewitness. Providing that the court accepts that the witnesses *could* have seen what they claim to have seen, their testimonies will tend to be accepted, almost uncondi-tionally. Whilst the defence lawyer may try to suggest that a witness could be "mistaken", it will generally be impossible to *dis*prove his or her testimony. Courts appear to like eyewitnesses, especially those who appear to be sure of their "facts". As Leippe (1994) notes:

> "dozens of important articles and books on eyewitness testimony have begun by emphasizing the central, indeed pivotal, role that eyewitness tes-timony plays in criminal cases. … An eyewitness report, confidently deliv-ered, has swayed many a jury." (Leippe, 1994, p. 385)

However, it will be argued below that this faith may be misplaced. Indeed one might go so far as to argue that if eyewitness testimony were a new form of evidence that was being introduced to the court for the first time, it might well be disallowed. As we will see, human memory can be fraught with so many biases and inaccuracies that it is perhaps surprising that it is ever allowed in court! The rigour that is applied when a judge is considering whether to accept modern "scientific" evi-dence is largely absent when the evidence of an eyewitness is presented.

LABORATORY VERSUS REAL WORLD STUDIES OF MEMORY

Because memory is such an integral part of humans' ability to function in the world, it is not surprising that psychologists have spent a great deal of time studying the subject. Unfortunately (for the purposes of this book) a large amount of the research has been carried out in the psychological laboratory and with little obvious concern for everyday memory problems and difficulties. Researchers have tended to be scrupulous in attending to the scientific design of their experiments (i.e the internal validity) whilst failing to address the question of relevance and applicability outside the lab (i.e the external or ecological validity). In 1982, Neisser went so far as to suggest that "If X is an interesting or socially significant aspect of memory, then psychologists have hardly ever studied X" (p. 4). This implied challenge has been answered more recently by some psychologists who have turned their attention to real world problems. For example the study of individuals' recall of signifi-cant events in their own lifetime is now examined under the heading of autobiographical memory.

One problem with memory research is that "memory" is not a single entity. Whilst all memory processes involve the taking in, storing and retrieval of information, this hides a bewildering array of different tasks which the human memory is expected to perform. Great Britain in the 1990s has seen a massive growth in the area of trivia quizzes and the like. These involve people being asked to recall large amounts of (by definition) trivial information. Those performing well on such tests can win money and prestige as reward for their "good memory". Some become almost addicted to these quizzes and spend most of their time acquiring more and more "facts" to add to their memory. Should we admire such people for having "very good memories" or should we regard them as "sad" because they seem to have nothing better to do with their lives? Whatever the answer, many might argue that such people have "good" memories and might thus make "good" eyewitnesses. However, this assumes that skill in one area of memory automatically applies to all others. Would we be totally surprised if we learned that the person who has just won a top television quiz show always forgets her husband's birthday? Or that the eminent science professor always leaves his umbrella on the bus?

The point is that even those who appear to have a "good" memory probably have some deficiencies in their memory processes. For most people the roles of attention and meaning are all important. The science professor may well remember a vast number of complex scientific formulae which would mean nothing to the average person in the street. The wine buff may be able to recall the exact smell and taste of the last great bottle that she opened; whereas most people could not even remember the name on the label. Because meaning has such an important influence on memory, some psychologists have tried to understand and measure it, whilst others have sought to eliminate it in the name of scientific rigour. One researcher from the latter school was Herman Ebbinghaus.

EBBINGHAUS AND THE SCIENTIFIC STUDY OF MEMORY

Ebbinghaus was by no means the first person to try to study memory – scholars in many ancient cultures had paid the subject a great deal of attention. However, Ebbinghaus is credited as having attempted the first *scientific* study of memory. Many before had argued that because memory was so subjective and depended upon the meaning of the material to each individual, it would be almost impossible to study memory "scientifically". Ebbinghaus chose to try to analyse memory by deliberately removing the role of meaning. He chose to construct long lists of "nonsense syllables". These were 3-letter combinations such as GUK, NOV, VUL, etc. He then gave subjects (including himself) lists of these to memorise and tested their recall some time later. Ebbinghaus's reasoning was that if the nonsense syllables had no meaning to any of his subjects, then all should find the task equally difficult.

Whether we should applaud or denigrate Ebbinghaus's particular approach is open to debate. On the one hand, he might be praised for at least attempting to study memory in a scientific way – but he might also be accused of carrying out a rather pointless exercise. If meaning is so important to memory then to try to rule it out renders the results of the studies literally meaningless. Such a debate is still found today, with some psychologists believing in the sanctity of the scientific method, whilst others argue for more relevance and ecological validity (see Tollestrup, Turtle & Yuille, 1994, and Chapter 11 of this book).

Whilst many have been critical of the early work of Ebbinghaus, some of his findings have stood the test of time. For example, he was able to show just how rapidly most forgetting occurs. Testing subjects less than an hour after an original learning session, Ebbinghaus found that his subjects had to spend over 50% of the original time taken to relearn material. If subjects had taken 10 minutes to learn a list of nonsense syllables, they typically had to spend at least 5 minutes relearning the list even one hour later. In most criminal cases, investigating police officers will take a statement several hours, or even days after the original incident, thus almost guaranteeing that a significant amount of detail will be missing.

One interesting finding from Ebbinghaus's work was the discovery of what became known as the "Serial Position Effect". This was the phenomenon whereby subjects whose memory was tested immediately after they had read a list of words, tended to remember those at the beginning and end of the list more often than those which occurred in the middle. Whilst the reason for this was not obvious to Ebbinghaus, later research (to be discussed later) went some way to offering an explanation. Such findings have interesting implications when witnesses observe a long-lasting and very complex crime. The early parts may well be better recalled than those in the middle. Similarly, a jury may well recall issues raised early on in the trial and in the judge's summing up more clearly than material presented in the middle.

BARTLETT AND MEMORY FOR MEANINGFUL MATERIAL

If Ebbinghaus's work can be described as scientific but irrelevant, perhaps the opposite could be said of the work of one early British psychologist, Sir Frederick Bartlett. Bartlett was particularly interested in how legends and folk tales were passed on from generation to generation, and set out trying to understand such processes. Bartlett quickly realised that in order to study memory it was nonsensical to try to eliminate the role of meaning to the individual. This was, of course, the very thing which Ebbinghaus had attempted to do. Bartlett realised that meaning and interpretation play a crucial part in the memory process. One need only think how much easier it is to memorise material which is interesting and meaningful than it is to try to learn something which has little appeal, or which makes no sense to us.

Bartlett was able to show that if material is unfamiliar, or is from a different culture, humans have great difficulty in remembering details accurately. Bartlett found that his subjects did not simply try to learn the material exactly as it was presented. Rather, subjects tended to translate and interpret the material, and to assimilate it into their own pre-existing schema of the world. Two of the techniques Bartlett used were *Serial Reproduction* and *Repeated Reproduction*. In the former, Bartlett would read a story to a subject, who would then have to repeat the story to a second person and so on until up to 10 people had each heard and retold the story. Bartlett found that although the amount of material declined with each retelling, the story itself often changed in detail and in emphasis due to differing interpretations of the subject matter. When Bartlett chose a story taken from a different culture (*The War of the Ghosts*) his English subjects had great difficulty in making sense of the material. Consequently, they often reinterpreted the story using their own particular frame of reference or "schema". The final version of the story thus became much more typical of a Western event than one taken from a different culture. Given Bartlett's work it is perhaps not surprising that many courts do not allow so-called "hearsay evidence" (see Boon & Davies, 1988, discussed in Chapter 1). Hearsay evidence is that which a witness has heard another person (not the defendant) say.

If the reinterpretation of material is understandable given the large number of different subjects, we might not expect to find the same sorts of results using Bartlett's other method, that of Serial Reproduction. In these studies, subjects were asked to recall information shortly after hearing it, then again after one hour, again after say for four hours and so on up to several weeks after the original presentation. Although Bartlett noted that the amount of retained material declined over time, he was more interested in what happened to the bits that remained. Just as with the Repeated Reproduction Method, individual subjects invariably translated and reinterpreted material and "remembered" a version that was often far removed from the original.

By today's standards, some of Bartlett's research might be criticised for its somewhat naive methodology (see Baddeley, 1990). However, his work did offer valuable insights into memory processes. Although carried out over 60 years ago, the research showed quite clearly that memory does not work like a tape recorder. If this were the case we could offer little explanation for the extraordinary transformations which occurred in the stories told by Bartlett's subjects. Bartlett was able to show that humans rarely sit back and try to learn material in a rote fashion. Rather they actively engage with, interpret, and alter the material in order to make more sense of it. Bartlett saw memory as essentially reconstructive in nature. The notion that witnesses can be objective recorders of "the truth" would not sit easily with Bartlett and other psychologists who subscribe to the schema theory of memory (see, for example, Rumelhart, 1975).

MODELS OF MEMORY

During the 1960s psychologists started to produce models to illustrate how memory processes might work. A number of such models were produced and refined, the best known being Broadbent's Filter Theory and the Atkinson–Shiffrin Buffer Model. What both these models had in common was a belief that memory was not a unitary phenomenon but rather could be divided up into a number of separate components. The researchers imagined some kind of a Short-Term Memory system, in addition to a Long-Term Memory.

Broadbent's Filter Theory

This theory recognised that the human brain was incapable of attending to and analysing all of the information which bombarded the sense organs at any one time. He thus emphasised that there was a filtering system which allowed humans to attend to those aspects which were important, and to filter out those stimuli which were less important or irrelevant. Thus when reading this book most people would be unaware of the ambient temperature in the room, the pressure of their wristwatch on their arm, the distant sound of a bird or aeroplane, etc. Information about all of these may well be entering the sense organs, but is quickly dismissed so that the person can concentrate on the task in hand.

Interestingly, Broadbent and other researchers found that the filter does not work in a complete on/off fashion. For example, when concentrating on a particular task, a person may well shut out the sound of voices in the background. However, if one of the voices utters the person's own name, the filter may well switch attention to this sound and away from the immediate task. One technique which Broadbent used was to play tape-recorded messages into one ear of his subjects, and have them shadow (i.e. repeat out loud) these messages. He would then introduce a second (different) message to the other ear. When tested later, subjects could remember hardly anything about the information being fed into the non-shadowed ear. Broadbent concluded that humans were by and large unable to attend to two things at the same time. However, some have criticised this view for being rather simplistic. For example, most people can read a book and listen to music at the same time; or drive a car and hold a conversation simultaneously. Allport, Antonis and Reynolds (1972) suggested that one reason that subjects could remember little of the unshadowed message was that both this and the other information were presented via the same sense modality, in this case the ears. Allport and colleagues had subjects view pictures at the same time as they were shadowing material presented in their ears. In this case, subjects scored a 90% correct performance on a later picture recognition task. When watching a film, most people find it relatively easy to watch the action on screen and listen to the dialogue at the same time. However, if the film is in a foreign language and subtitled, viewers may have more difficulty in watching the action and reading the subtitles at the same time.

Although there have been many criticisms of Broadbent's early work, it is true that humans do find it necessary to filter out a large proportion of the information entering the sense organs. This does not, however, mean that everyone attends to the same stimuli or that they filter out the same bits. As we saw in the previous chapter, perception is selective and based on each individual's personality and background. For example, many people would simply filter out all traffic noise and pay it little attention. However, the keen car enthusiast may notice the distinctive sound of an American V8 engine and pay particular attention to that vehicle. Such a person may, however, be so busy admiring the sight and sound of the vehicle, that he or she fails to notice that the driver is hooded and is carrying a shotgun! Broadbent's theory might again lead us to question whether it is realistic to expect witnesses to tell "the whole truth".

Broadbent believed that a selective filter was necessary because humans were not perfect information-processing machines. Rather, they had a limited capacity and could process only a small amount of material at any one time. The filter was necessary to avoid the system becoming overloaded. It was thought that some information about the many stimuli emerging from the environment was stored very briefly in a sensory "buffer". Information about one of these stimuli was then selected for further attention (or processing) by passing through the filter.

Broadbent made an important distinction between Short-Term Memory and Long-Term Memory, and this distinction was further emphasised in the work of Atkinson and Shiffrin (1971).

The Atkinson–Shiffrin Buffer Model

This model conceptualised memory as a three-stage system. Information entering the sense organs was first held very briefly in a sensory store. If attended to, the information was then passed on to the Short-Term Memory store. The Short-Term Memory (STM) could hold a limited amount of information for up to about half a minute. After this time it was either displaced by new information or, through rehearsal in the STM, passed into the Long-Term Memory (LTM). The "Buffer Model" was so called because the STM was thought to have a protective buffer which prevented the LTM from trying to deal with too many bits of information at the same time (see Figure 2.1).

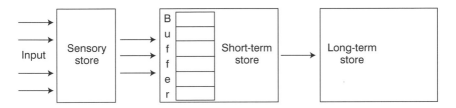

Figure 2.1   Model of memory (adapted from Atkinson & Shiffrin)

The capacity of this memory store was said to be 7 plus or minus 2 "chunks" of information. Thus, if people were briefly trying to memorise a telephone number, they would tend to have little difficulty if the number contained 5 or 6 digits. However, if the number was 11 or 12 digits long, most people would have great difficulty in storing such information accurately in the STM. The reason why the capacity was referred to as "chunks" of information rather than single units is that humans often join together small bits to form a larger "chunk". The obvious example of this is the combining of strings of letters to form words. Thus, whilst most people could probably hold a string of only about 7 letters in their STM, they could also hold 7 words, each of which might contain a large number of individual letters. But no matter how the information is "chunked" most humans have difficulty holding more than 7 or 8 items in the STM. For this reason, most witnesses who claim to remember accurately a very large number of words spoken by an accused may not be being totally honest.

The distinction between STM and LTM was important, because Atkinson and Shiffrin believed that information could only be placed into the LTM if it was first "rehearsed" in the STM. The longer a memory trace spent in the STM the more likely it was that it would be stored permanently in the LTM. This view offered a neat explanation for one of the phenomena discovered by Ebbinghaus many years earlier. Readers may recall that Ebbinghaus highlighted the "Serial Position Effect". This was the curious finding that items at the beginning and end of a list were more likely to be remembered than those in the middle. The explanation which the Atkinson–Shiffrin model offered was that those items at the beginning of the list spent longer being rehearsed in the STM than those which came later, and were thus more likely to enter the LTM store. (This was referred to as the Primacy Effect.) Those items which appeared at the very end of the list were also more likely to be recalled because they were still in the STM, and so could be accessed directly from there (the so-called Recency Effect). The Recency Effect is generally found if subjects' memory is tested immediately after they have been presented with material. However, if they are distracted for a short time and then tested, the recency effect is less likely to be observed (see Baddeley, 1990).

As with Broadbent's Filter Model, the Atkinson–Shiffrin Buffer Model attracted a great deal of attention when it was first published. It offered neat explanations for a number of interesting memory phenomena including the Primacy/Recency Effect highlighted above. The Atkinson–Shiffrin model was also claimed to offer an insight into a phenomenon known as retrograde amnesia. This is a type of memory failure sometimes found when a person has been involved in an accident and has been rendered unconscious. Such people often claim to have little memory for anything that happened immediately before the accident. Atkinson and Shiffrin believed that this curious phenomenon could be explained by their model of memory. Because the person was rendered unconscious, they did not have sufficient time to process or rehearse information entering the STM during the last few seconds or minutes just before the accident. Consequently, the details never really entered the LTM store. Whilst this is an interesting explanation, it is not necessarily the only or indeed the correct one. For some people, the memory may actually be in their LTM store, but they are unable (or unwilling) to recall it because of the painful associations. We must also bear in mind that not all people who become unconscious appear to suffer from retrograde amnesia.

Whilst the Atkinson–Shiffrin model aroused much interest, it also started to attract critics. One immediate problem concerned the way in which information was supposedly passed from the STM to the LTM. According to Atkinson and Shiffrin's original idea, providing that information was in the STM long enough (or often enough) it should "automatically" be transferred to the LTM store. However, common sense tells us that this is not necessarily the case. If the theory is correct, information about items which humans encounter almost every day should be stored accurately in the LTM. Thus the exact appearance and details of banknotes should (in theory) be held in each human's LTM store. But if people are asked to describe such items in detail, they generally have great difficulty.

DEPTH OF PROCESSING

One way in which this problem could be resolved was proposed by Craik and Lockhart (1972). They suggested that the length of time that an item spent in the STM was not necessarily important. What was important was what the individual did with the information when it was in the store. Craik and Lockhart emphasised the importance of the depth of processing which the information underwent. Thus, if an individual attended only to the superficial characteristics of an item of information, it would be unlikely to become a lasting memory in the LTM store. Conversely, if the person processed the information at a deeper level – for example, by analysing it in a more meaningful way – then it would be more likely to be remembered later. Thus Craik and Lockhart presented subjects with words which they would be later asked to recall. However, before each word, they were asked a question which would encourage subjects to process the word at a certain level of processing. For example, subjects might be asked if the word appeared in capital letters, or they might be asked a question about the word's meaning. Their results showed that the deeper the level of processing demanded by the question, the more likely it was to be recalled subsequently.

This notion could have important implications for eyewitness testimony. If witnesses merely look at a suspect, a getaway car or whatever, then they might be less likely to remember many details later. On the other hand, if they process the information carefully, and really think deeply about it at the time, then they will be more likely to have an accurate and detailed knowledge in the memory store.

WORKING MEMORY

In more recent years, the distinction between STM and LTM has been seen by some psychologists as less important than early researchers had thought. Having said that, it is not the case that psychologists now see memory as a unitary system. In particular, researchers such as Alan Baddeley have introduced the notion of a working memory which deals with simple everyday memory tasks such as mental arithmetic (see Baddeley, 1986). The concept of working memory bears some resemblance to that of the STM, but Baddeley argues that it fulfils some different functions from those envisaged by Atkinson and Shiffrin. One obvious example of working memory is in the performance of mental arithmetic. If a person is asked to multiply 15 by 7, he or she may do this by first multiplying 5 by 7, remembering the answer, carrying 3 forward, multiplying 1 by 7 and adding the 3 to this to then end up with the answer (105). The process is actually more difficult to describe than it is to perform! However, this relatively simple task relies on the person holding small pieces of information in his or her working memory whilst the next bit of the problem is being worked out.

Baddeley believes that working memory comprises an attention coordinating system known as the Central Executive. Two auxiliary systems are envisaged, namely the Visuo-spatial Sketchpad (used for setting up and manipulating visual images) and the Articulatory Loop (which holds and utilises inner speech). One of the best ways of illustrating the concepts is by asking people to work out how many windows there are in their current house. People will first form a visual image of their home and then count the windows as they imagine walking through the house or imagine looking at it from the outside. The Visuo-spatial Sketchpad allows the person to set up and manipulate a visual image, whilst the Articulatory Loop allows subvocal counting. The whole operation is overseen by the Central Executive.

Baddeley suggests that humans will experience some difficulty in trying to perform two tasks at once, if each uses the same part of the system. Thus driving a car and listening to soft music may pose few problems. However, driving a car and trying to rehearse a mental map may pose more difficulty, as both would require the services of the Visuo-spatial Sketchpad. Similar problems are encountered when people are asked to perform two tasks simultaneously, each of which requires the use of the Articulatory Loop. Thus, trying to read and learn a list of words whilst at the same time repeating one word over and over again will pose great difficulty. Baddeley has identified some people who suffer from memory difficulties which stem from an inability to perform simple phonological coding of the type just described.

The Three Stages of Memory

So far we have considered a number of theories explaining the workings of memory. However, memory may actually be better thought of as three separate but closely interrelated tasks, i.e. the acquisition of information, the retention of information, and the retrieval of material previously learned. As we have seen above, memory can fail because of problems at any of the three stages. In Chapter 1 we saw some of the ways in which perception can distort memories, and in this chapter we have considered some influences on the other stages of memory. As we will see in Chapters 3 and 4, there is potential for memory inaccuracy at each of the three stages in the process, and each can affect eyewitness accounts in different ways.

CONCLUDING COMMENTS

It is obvious from the theories and views examined in this chapter that not all psychologists agree on the exact nature of memory, or even on how it should be studied. Like many fields of human research it seems that the more we learn, the more we realise that there is much still to be learned. Having said that, we know a great deal more about memory today than we did a hundred years ago. Most psychologists no longer see memory as a single entity, but as a complex interlocking and interrelated set of functions. Whilst there may not be agreement on the exact nature of memory, there is a recognition that memory is a great deal more than a simple objective recording of information. The assumption made by the Criminal Justice System that witnesses will "tell the truth, the whole truth and nothing but the truth" appears to be naive, simplistic and unrealistic. Courts need perhaps to recognise the complexities of human memory, and to be aware of its many failings. As we have seen in this chapter, psychologists already possess a great deal of knowledge which would benefit courts in their deliberations about the likely veracity of witnesses' stories. We will see in the following chapters how theorising about memory processes has offered insights into some of the more common eyewitness memory failings.

CHAPTER 3

Memory for Events

The two most common tasks that an eyewitness will be called upon to perform are either to recall details of an incident (known as event memory) or to identify the face of a person seen earlier (known as facial recognition). Although such tasks share some characteristics in the processes of perception and memory, there are also some differences between event memory and facial memory. For this reason, the two will be dealt with separately, dealing in this chapter with memory for events.

Event memory forms a very large proportion of eyewitness accounts. Although the visual identification of a suspect is dramatic, most eyewitness testimony is concerned with reporting details of an incident. It is thus perhaps surprising that the majority of research on eyewitness testimony has concerned itself with the identification of suspects rather than the study of event memory *per se*, (see, for example, Sporer, Malpass & Koehnken, 1996; Cutler & Penrod, 1995). Some of this material will be reviewed in Chapters 5 and 6.

Whenever a crime occurs, the police or other authorities will be keen to establish just what happened. Every serious road traffic accident or crime will be investigated so that the facts surrounding the case can be established and, where warranted, the appropriate people prosecuted. Despite the increased use of video surveillance equipment, most crimes and traffic accidents occur unseen by the police. On attending the scene, the police will need to talk to victims, question others involved in the incident, and take statements from any independent witnesses. Although physical evidence will be gathered at the scene, the police will rely heavily on what witnesses tell them in order to establish just what did happen. Even if it appears obvious that one party is to blame for, say, a serious car accident, the Crown Prosecution Service may well choose not to prosecute if there are no independent witnesses. However, as we saw in the previous chapter, witnesses are not necessarily the reliable reporters of fact which the justice system might assume. In this chapter we will start to look at some of the factors which make certain events easier to remember than others, and to consider why some witnesses tend to perform less well than others. These two variables are usually referred to as *Event Factors* and *Witness Factors* and we will consider each in turn. Although the two will be dealt with separately, it should be acknowledged that there will inevitably be an interaction between them.

EVENT FACTORS

Common sense would tell us that some incidents will be easier for witnesses to remember than others. The trivial may well be paid scant attention and so leave little in the way of a reliable memory. Conversely, we might expect the most serious incident to have a dramatic impact on a witness, and to leave an indelible and reliable memory trace. However, as we will see later, this is rather too simplistic an explanation. An extremely dramatic incident may in fact so traumatise a witness that he or she can give little information to police investigators, at least immediately following the incident.

Exposure Time

Traffic accidents are often over in a matter of seconds, yet the police will expect witnesses to give detailed statements. Some crimes, such as a handbag snatch, might also take only a second or two. Witnesses may say: "It was all over before I realised what was happening." Other crimes may last for several minutes or even longer. In general, psychological research would support the commonsense notion that the longer a witness has to study an incident, the more will be remembered. However, we are here talking about the difference between a witness having a second or two to take in information, compared with one who has several minutes. In a crime such as kidnapping or a siege, the incident may well last for several days and the witness/victim would hardly be expected to remember every detail of the entire incident.

One interesting aspect concerning exposure time is the fact that witnesses appear routinely to overestimate the length of time that a crime incident took. In one study (Loftus *et al.*, 1987) subject witnesses were shown a videotape of a simulated bank robbery. Among other questions, subjects were asked to estimate the length of time that the robbery took. The average estimate given was two and a half minutes when in reality the robbery took only 30 seconds. This overestimation of event duration could be important when assessing a witness's credibility. Earlier we mentioned that people seem to believe that the longer witnesses have to view a scene, the more likely they are to be accurate in their memory. If witnesses overestimate the length of time they had to view a scene by a factor of up to five, then a false impression may be created in the minds of jurors evaluating such testimony.

Crime Seriousness

One important variable which could affect the quality of eyewitness accounts is how serious the event was, and the impact it had on the individual. The commonsense view may well be that the more serious the crime, the better will be the witness's memory. However, as with many aspects of eyewitness testimony, things are not quite as straightforward as this. As we saw in Chapter 1, stimuli need to be novel and interesting enough to attract attention in the first place. However, a particularly distressing incident may lead a witness to literally turn away in horror, and to take in relatively little information. There are two problems for psychologists who wish to study the relationship between crime seriousness and memory:

1   For obvious ethical reasons psychologists can never recreate the impact and trauma which a serious crime will have on an individual.
2   The impact which the crime has on a victim may be different from the impact it has on an uninvolved eyewitness. This is an important point as almost all laboratory based studies will rely upon testing the memories of uninvolved witnesses as opposed to victims.

For these reasons, we should bear in mind that extrapolating directly from the laboratory to the "real world" is not a simple exercise. As Tollestrup, Turtle and Yuille (1994, p. 159) note:

> "An overdependence on laboratory research and field simulations has left this field with a potentially distorted rather than comprehensive picture of eyewitnesses."

Nevertheless, there have been a number of studies which shed some light on the relationship between crime seriousness and memory. In one British study, Clifford and Hollin (1981) showed groups of subjects an interaction between a man and a woman. There were two versions of the film, one involving violence (the woman was forced against a wall and had her handbag stolen) and one non-violent (the woman was simply asked for directions by the man). Clifford and Hollin found that those who were shown the violent film were significantly less accurate and less complete in their memories than those who had watched the non-violent event.

In a similar study in the USA, Loftus and Burns (1982) showed groups of subjects a film of a bank robbery. Half were shown a version of the film which had a particularly violent ending (a young boy was shot in the face), whereas the other half were shown the same robbery but without the violent ending. When later questioned about the incident, those who had been shown the violent version were again less accurate and less complete in their reporting of details of the incident. Loftus and Burns found that it was not only memory for the violent parts of the film which was affected. They reported that memory for some details which occurred two minutes before the shooting was also affected. Loftus and Burns suggest that the trauma associated with seeing the shooting may have interfered with the processing and storing of earlier non-violent details. As we saw in Chapter 2, if people do not have the opportunity to rehearse or process information as it enters their short-term (or working) memory, it may not reach the long-term memory store.

Such findings do seem to contradict the simplistic notion that the more serious a crime is, the better it will be remembered. People who are victims of serious crime or who are involved in a near fatal traffic accident may believe that they will "never forget this day as long as they live", such was the effect on their lives. However, whilst the impact of the event may well stay with the person for ever, the exact details of the incident may not be well remembered.

Some authors have suggested that we should view the memory task as no different from any other with respect to the amount of stimulation which is required to elicit a good performance. The Yerkes Dodson law was established as long ago as 1908. It stated that stimulation affects performance in a curvilinear manner. Insufficient stimulation will cause insufficient arousal which in turn will lead to a poor performance. But too much stimulation will produce too much arousal, which will also lead to a poor performance. If we apply the Yerkes Dodson law to memory performance, then we would expect that an incident which produces too little or too much stimulation would result in comparatively poor recall. Conversely, an incident which produces an optimum amount of stimulation should lead to a better memory performance, i.e. more complete and more accurate recall.

Although we are here primarily concerned with stimulation at the time that the incident occurred, we need also to consider the amount of stimulation at the time that the material is recalled. Appearing in a criminal court as a witness can be a daunting and nerve-racking ordeal for most people. Under such conditions of overstimulation, the Yerkes Dodson law would predict that memory performance would also be impaired.

Returning to the notion of severity of impact, we must bear in mind that event seriousness is not something that is easy to quantify objectively. For many people, being the victim of a burglary or robbery will occur only once in a lifetime and as such the incident will have a very large impact. However, for some inner city residents, such incidents are almost an everyday occurrence and will have much less of an impact on the individual. Only recently has the importance of repeat victimisation been recognised by criminologists (see Pease, 1996).

The perceived severity of an event will also vary according to whether one is considering the impact on the victim or on an uninvolved bystander/witness. Trying to establish whether victims or uninvolved witnesses will provide better information is not, however, straightforward. For example, a victim who is literally closer to the action might observe far more detail than the casual observer across the street. However, the victim is also more likely to experience greater arousal or stress than the witness which may impair his or her ability to recall accurately. In one study using archival (as opposed to laboratory generated) data, Tollestrup, Turtle and Yuille (1994) found that witnesses were no better than victims in correctly recalling hair colour. However, rather curiously, witnesses were significantly more accurate than victims in their descriptions of facial hair!

In another recent paper, Thompson, Morton and Fraser (1997) have produced some evidence which suggests that even following a particularly harrowing experience, witnesses do not necessarily show evidence of motivated forgetting. In this case, psychologists studied the accounts given by survivors of the *Marchioness* river boat sinking. This was a particularly distressing case in which a pleasure boat sailing on the River Thames was struck by a large dredger; 51 people died as a result of the collision and a further 80 survived. In examining the statements made by some of the survivors, the researchers found that the witness survivors appeared to have fairly accurate memories for some details of the incident. Although the statements were taken many months after the sinking, it was found that most people had accurate memories for details such as who they were sitting next to when the disaster occurred. The researchers conclude that:

> "Despite restrictions in both the sample and the date (sic) which might have served to inflate the apparent frequency of traumatic amnesia, motivated forgetting appears to be extremely rare in a natural disaster."
> (Thompson, Morton & Fraser, 1997, p. 615)

We will return to the notion of traumatic amnesia later in the book, though it is worth noting at this stage that other recent research has begun to question notions such as repression and motivated forgetting first proposed by Freud.

Weapon Focus

One way in which crime seriousness might be measured is by categorising events according to whether a weapon was or was not used. In cases where a weapon is present, arousal is likely to be greater, if only because those present will have a greater fear for their personal safety. Studies have found that when a weapon is used, those present tend to pay a great deal of attention to the weapon, and less attention to other events and people at the scene. In one of the first laboratory studies to examine this topic, Loftus, Loftus and Messo (1987) found that the presence of a weapon interfered with witnesses' ability both to recall information about the incident and to recognise those present at the scene. Part of the problem is to do with attention. Not surprisingly, those who have a gun pointed at their heads tend to focus a great deal of attention on the gun itself, rather than on other things in the room or on what the person holding the gun happens to be wearing. Some studies which have monitored the eye movements of victims of crimes involving weapons have shown that this is indeed the case. A meta-analysis (i.e. a combined reanalysis of a large number) of weapon focus studies has shown that in almost all cases the phenomenon does occur, and that it interferes with both description and identification of the person holding the weapon (see Steblay, 1992). Although most studies of weapon focus have used a gun as the stimulus, one study found similar results when subjects were confronted with a syringe (Maass & Koehnken, 1989).

Most of the evidence for the existence of weapon focus is drawn from laboratory-based studies. However, one study using archival data from actual cases of robbery did not offer unequivocal support for the notion. Contrary to the trend established in the laboratory, Tollestrup, Turtle and Yuille (1994) found that witnesses to weaponless crimes provided significantly less detailed descriptions than did those who witnessed crimes where weapons were used. In addition, victims (who would presumably feel more personally threatened than witnesses) tended to provide better descriptions than did non-involved witnesses.

This curious finding is difficult to reconcile with the results of the laboratory-based studies. However, the situation is further complicated when one learns that in the Tollestrup study, witnesses and victims of crimes in which weapons were used were less likely to be able to identify a suspect later. It appears that whilst witnesses and victims of real crimes involving weapons may be able to offer more in terms of descriptions, they perform less well when asked to try to recognise the perpetrator in, say, a line-up. Tollestrup, Turtle and Yuille speculate that, in serious cases involving weapons, the police may push the witness for more information, and the witness may provide some more detail. However, it would appear that this information may be trivial or inaccurate, and so not help in any subsequent recognition task. An alternative explanation is that witnesses may feel intimidated or fearful when attending an actual ID parade.

Tollestrup, Turtle and Yuille do not seek to dismiss the results of laboratory-based studies which have demonstrated the weapon focus effect. Rather they conclude that the presence of a weapon has complex effects on the memory of witnesses and victims. The authors suggest that:

> "... researchers of eyewitness memory must be cautious about generalizing results from one context to another. This caution should be exercised not only when applying laboratory or field simulation findings to actual eyewitnesses, but also when applying findings based on actual eyewitnesses to other eyewitnesses." (Tollestrup, Turtle & Yuille, 1994, p. 158)

We can thus see that trying to make predictions as to which crimes will be remembered best is not an easy task. Whilst a number of important variables have been identified, it is not possible to make absolute predictions. Because we cannot know how much stress a given situation might produce in a given witness, it may prove difficult to advise a court on such matters (see Stern & Dunning, 1994).

Although we sought to make a distinction between event factors and witness factors, it is obvious that the two sets of variables interact to a large degree. Having said that, we will now consider some individual variables which are associated with good or poor eyewitness performance.

WITNESS FACTORS

In the same way that not all events will be remembered with equal accuracy, some witnesses will inevitably provide more detailed and more accurate information than will others. Unfortunately, in most crimes, the police do not have the luxury of being able to choose the best witnesses to help in any prosecution. A significant number of crimes will have only one witness – the hapless victim. As such, the police will have to make the most of what they have and do all they can to elicit as much information as possible (see Chapter 7).

Whilst a number of relevant factors have been identified, it is still not possible to make absolute predictions as to whether a given witness will or will not be accurate on any given eyewitness task. As we saw in Chapter 2, memory is a very complex process. As such, a witness who performs well on a test of event memory may not necessarily do so well on a face recognition task. We must also bear in mind that there will be an inevitable interaction between the type of memory task and the type of person. For example, a very stressful crime may have a more dramatic effect on an already nervous witness. A calmer and more self-confident witness may handle the stress of such an event better, and be able to recall far more detail.

Age

It has long been recognised that memory performance alters with age. Some have suggested that age is in fact the most important individual variable to affect memory performance generally (West, Crook & Baron, 1992). Both the very young and the very old generally do less well than young or middle-aged adults. Having said that, it does appear that early psychologists such as Piaget may have underestimated children's ability to remember. More recent research suggests that whilst children may offer less information than adults when first asked, further delicate probing can often elicit as much information as the average adult might provide. Criminal Justice Systems have traditionally been reluctant to admit the testimony of children, believing that the memory of children cannot be trusted, that children may fabricate stories and may be very easily led (see Chapter 9). Whilst some of this scepticism persists, children's evidence is today much more likely to be accepted than was the position only 15 years ago (see Davies, 1992). Whether or not children can be trusted to give accurate testimony has become a major concern with the increasing number of allegations of child sexual abuse. In many such cases, prosecutions can only take place if the court is prepared to accept and believe testimony from very young victims. The issue of child witnesses is a major area of research at present, and some of the research findings will be reviewed at length in Chapter 9.

As regards witnesses at the other end of the age spectrum, there may again be a stereotype about memory ability. Some (including those in the Criminal Justice System) may well believe that old people generally make unreliable and often confused witnesses. However, whilst evidence suggests that some older people may perform less well than young adults, this is by no means inevitable. With the demographic changes currently taking place in most Western societies, there is an increasing number of older people in the population. As Yarmey (1996) points out, this will inevitably mean that more and more elderly people will be appearing as witnesses, and that courts need to be made aware of their likely abilities. Unfortunately, the vast majority of research on the effects of age on eyewitnessing ability has tended to look at younger, rather than older people. As such, our knowledge of the elderly's likely ability is incomplete.

Reviewing much recent research, Yarmey highlights a number of important factors which must be borne in mind when considering the testimony of older people. Firstly, ageing affects both hearing and eye-sight, and as such the elderly are more likely to make mistakes at the acquisition stage of memory. The elderly also tend to need more time to integrate information, and have difficulties if their attention is divided between two or more tasks. Yarmey also believes that the elderly are more likely to make errors in identification tasks, and to make false identifications. Having said that, he does not believe that we should sim-ply dismiss elderly witnesses as a group; rather, he argues that, as with all other witnesses, credibility should be judged in terms of all the per-sonal and situational factors which might affect accuracy. Those suffer-ing from conditions such as Alzheimer's disease will have cognitive deficits which will grossly interfere with memory abilities. However, the majority of older people will show comparatively little impairment and their testimony might be no less valuable than that of a young adult.

Yarmey does acknowledge that the elderly can pose special difficul-ties. However, he has suggested a number of ways in which the police might be able to get the best from elderly witnesses. These suggestions include: not asking leading questions; the use of a narrative interview style, rather than using set questions; acknowledging that the elderly may be slower to respond to questions, and be more cautious; using sequential (as opposed to simultaneous) line-up presentations so as to avoid distraction (Yarmey, 1996, p. 274).

Before moving on from the influence of age, we must bear in mind one important point. The vast majority of psychological research, including that on eyewitness testimony, is carried out in the laboratory using undergraduate students as subjects. Given that the average age of these subjects will be between 18 and 21, the findings might not easily be generalised to those in other age groups.

Occupation

Here again, we might reasonably expect to find that members of some occupational groups perform better as eyewitnesses than others. Groups such as police officers, security guards, and intelligence officers might be presumed to be more accurate and more complete in their recall of factual information. That such a presumption exists has been supported by some research (see Loftus, 1984a; Leippe, 1994). This assumption means that the word of a police witness may be presumed to be more accurate than the word of a civilian witness. However, it is rather more difficult to find good research evidence to support the belief that police officers are more accurate. Comparatively few studies have examined the effects of occupation *per se* on the quality of eyewitness accounts. One early British study (Ainsworth, 1981) found that police officers might be no better than civilians at spotting offences taking place. However, in this study it was found that police officers tended to be more suspicious in their perceptions, and were prone to label perfectly innocent incidents as possible criminal offences. This finding was in line with some earlier studies (e.g. Tickner & Poulton, 1975).

In a study with a little more realism, Clifford and Richards (1977) found that police officers were able to give better descriptions of a person who asked them for directions than were civilians. However, the same superior performance was not found when the interaction with the other person was much briefer. (In this case asking for the time, rather than directions.) Clifford and Richards suggested that police officers may well process information differently from civilians because of the training they have received.

Part of the supposedly superior memory performance of police officers might simply be a question of attention. Most people walking down the street are on their way to some specific appointment, and as such they will be paying relatively little attention to incidents around them. By comparison, police officers tend to be walking down the street with the specific purpose of looking for criminal activities or suspicious events. As such, they are much more likely to take in and be able to recall details. Police officers may also pay more attention to specific details of a suspect's appearance than might a civilian (see Yuille 1984). Because a significant part of a police officer's time may be spent collecting information and having to recall details, his or her performance may appear superior to civilians on some memory tasks. However, it must be borne in mind that police officers are human, and as such are subject to all the possible distortions of perception and memory which apply to all other humans.

Confidence

One reason that members of a jury might be more convinced by testimony given by police officers is that they will tend to give their evidence with more confidence and authority than would most civilians. Giving evidence in court is an almost everyday occurrence for police officers, and as such they become practised in the art of appearing "sure of their facts". It would seem only a matter of common sense to assume that the more confident a witness appears to be, the more likely he or she is to be accurate in his or her recollections. In fact, the area of witness confidence is one where psychology does not simply "prove the obvious" but in fact challenges a widely held view. There is no simple linear relationship between confidence and accuracy. It is by no means inevitable that the more confident a witness is, the more reliable his or her testimony is likely to be. Loftus (1979, p. 101) summarises this complex issue thus:

"... although there are many studies showing that the more confident a person is in a response, the greater the likelihood that the response is accurate, some studies have shown no relationship at all between confidence and accuracy. In fact, there are even conditions under which the opposite relation exists between confidence and accuracy, namely, people can be more confident about their wrong answers than their right ones ... one should not take high confidence as any absolute guarantee of anything."

There is further evidence that even when jurors are aware of the many factors that might affect the truthfulness of eyewitness accounts, they still tend to be heavily influenced by the confidence with which testimony is given (see Cutler & Penrod, 1995, pp. 236–238). For this reason many psychologists, including Cutler and Penrod, have argued in favour of the admission of expert testimony on these matters (see Chapter 11). They believe that it can only help to discourage jurors from attending to inappropriate cues when trying to decide on the likely accuracy of eyewitness accounts.

Personality Characteristics

Psychologists have developed literally hundreds of different personality tests in order to identify individuals' traits and behaviour patterns. Unfortunately the exact relationship between personality variables and eyewitnessing ability is not easy to establish (see Kapardis, 1997, ch. 3). Whilst some studies have shown a slight correlation between personality variables and memory for faces, the results might not be so easily applied to event memory (see Davies, Ellis & Shepherd, 1981; Hosch, 1994; Narby, Cutler & Penrod, 1996).

The one area where a relationship might exist is with trait anxiety or neuroticism. Clearly some people have lower general levels of anxiety than do others. Some people appear nervous and worried most of the time, whereas others appear laid back and unruffled by even moderate amounts of stress. It would thus seem reasonable to speculate that a very nervous or overly anxious person might make a poorer witness than would a more stable person. The assumption might be that nervous people would be so preoccupied with their own worries that they would fail to pay enough attention to events in the outside world. Unfortunately it is difficult to establish whether such a simplistic link does exist. Although some studies have shown a slight link between trait anxiety and facial recognition accuracy (Bothwell 1991; Shapiro & Penrod, 1986) it is difficult to say whether even these slight effects apply to event memory. The fact that anxious people tend to narrow their focus of attention and to have an inward focus would suggest that they may fail to encode some aspects of the external environment. However, in the absence of good experimental evidence on this subject, this remains rather speculative.

Kapardis (1997, pp. 49–52) has reviewed a large number of studies dealing with personality variables and eyewitnessing. His review suggests that whilst some personality variables might be relevant, in most cases any differences are only slight, and the effects are not always consistent. It should also be noted that most studies looking at personality variables have been concerned with facial identification rather than event memory.

One reason why the effects of personality variables are hard to quantify is that they inevitably interact with event factors such as crime seriousness. Very anxious or neurotic individuals may well make poor witnesses if they are victims of a serious crime. However, they may make better witnesses if they are uninvolved bystanders when a relatively minor crime takes place. By comparison, the laid back personality may cope much better with the stress of a personal attack, but may fail to even notice the minor crime taking place across the street.

Gender of Witness

If nothing else, psychologists should surely be able to say something about whether men make better witnesses than women, whether the reverse is true, or whether there are no significant differences. To the possible frustration of the reader the answer is unfortunately not so clear. Many of the studies examining gender differences have been concerned with facial memory and facial recognition rather than event memory *per se*. Of these studies, some differences have been found, but the differences are often only slight. Shapiro and Penrod (1986) carried out a meta-analysis of eyewitness studies and found that females tended to perform slightly better on facial identification tasks than did males, but that they also tended to make more mistakes.

Shepherd (1981) cited 17 experiments which revealed a gender difference in facial recognition, with females usually performing slightly better than males. Unfortunately, Shepherd also cited 18 experiments where no such sex difference was found, making it somewhat difficult to draw any firm conclusions. MacLeod and Shepherd (1986) found that where gender differences did exist, they covaried in a complex way with the type of question, for example: action details versus descriptive details; statements relating to the self, the victim, the accused or peripheral details; incidents involving injury versus those that did not. Sporer (1992) has reported that although females tend to give less wordy verbal descriptions of other people, their statements contain just as many important details.

It has been suggested that where sex differences are found, this may partly be accounted for by differential focusing of attention between males and females (see Powers, Andriks & Loftus, 1979). To take one example, males might be more likely to have an interest in fast cars than might women. Thus if memory was tested by asking subjects about a sports car which had appeared in a film, males may perform better and thus appear to have better recall. Conversely, women might be more likely to pay attention to the clothes and hairstyles of people appearing in the film. Thus if memory were tested by asking for information about these items, the performance of the females would be judged to be superior to that of the males. Some support for this notion was provided in a study by Davies *et al.* (1996). However, these authors conclude that it would be inappropriate for police officers to presume that males will always be better witnesses than females with regard to descriptions of motor vehicles. Rather, they suggest that police officers should ask witnesses about their knowledge of, and interest in, motor vehicles. Those who show the greatest prowess in this area are likely to be more accurate, irrespective of gender. Another point to bear in mind is that males are far more likely than females to suffer from red-green colour blindness. Thus as a group, males are more likely to make errors when asked to describe the colour of cars, etc.

As with many such factors, we are talking here in terms of overall trends rather than specific instances. It must be acknowledged that many men have no interest at all in cars, and that many women have little interest in clothing fashions! However, there is a serious point here. Although overall it may be difficult to prove the existence of sex differences, males and females may bring different skills to eyewitnessing tasks. Males and females may be superior in different aspects of the task, but may perform similarly in other areas. One reason why some studies have shown apparently contradictory findings in the area of sex differences is that the tasks which subjects were being asked to perform were often different in different studies. Those studies which have shown an apparently superior performance by men have tended to use rather stressful stimulus material. Studies examining memory for less stressful events have tended to show less difference, and in some cases better performances by women.

The interrelationship between sex differences and eyewitness testimony can thus be seen to be complex. As with the other individual differences discussed in this chapter, making predictions of the likely accuracy of any particular individual's testimony is fraught with difficulties and dangers. This is unfortunate as courts would dearly love to hear psychologists state with confidence that Witness A will be telling the truth, whereas Witness B will not. Having said that, psychologists may still be able to help the court by advising jurors to ignore those eye-witness characteristics which are *not* necessarily correlated with accuracy (see Chapter 11). The most obvious example of this is in the area of eyewitness confidence. As we saw above, jurors may be well advised not to make the simple assumption that confidence is automatically correlated with accuracy of testimony.

CONCLUDING COMMENTS

The picture painted here would appear to be a pessimistic one, with psychologists apparently unable to make exact predictions as to the likely accuracy or otherwise of individual witnesses. However, by drawing attention to factors such as weapon focus, and the effect of stress on memory, psychologists can also be of value to all those charged with decision making within the Criminal Justice System. As has been pointed out earlier, individual and event factors often interact in complex ways which make absolute predictions difficult. Nevertheless, psychologists can still advise courts on the many factors which will diminish or heighten the likely accuracy of eyewitness reports. If psychologists' contributions reduce the number of false convictions by a mere 1%, then their advice will surely have been worth while.

CHAPTER 4

Changes in Original Memories

So far in this book it has been argued that memory can be both unreliable and incomplete. We saw in the previous chapter that there are a large number of factors which might affect a person's memory. Most of the elements identified were concerned with individual and event factors which affected memory, primarily at the acquisition stage. However, we need also to consider inaccuracies which might occur as a result of transformations of the memory during the retention period.

For many years it was believed that the two major problems which eyewitnesses might encounter were incorrect or biased perceptions, and the simple forgetting of information. However, more recently it has been recognised that changes can occur in the original memory as a result of new information, or even as a result of the type of questioning to which a witness is subjected. As Loftus (1979, p. 54) has noted: "Time alone does not cause the slippage of memory. It is caused in part by what goes on during the passage of time." In this chapter we will start to look at some of the ways in which original memories can become altered, to the point where the recovery of the original uncontaminated memory becomes almost impossible. We will examine in some depth the invaluable contributions made to this area by Beth Loftus and her colleagues.

Loftus was by no means the first person to bring the transformation of memories to our attention. Indeed, Sir Frederick Bartlett highlighted the phenomenon as long ago as the 1930s (Bartlett, 1932). Bartlett noted that whilst people often did simply forget material, of more interest was the fact that many subjects showed significant changes in their original memories. Often these changes or transformations took place without the person being aware of them. In one study, Bartlett showed to subjects drawings of men from different branches of the armed services. Some time later he tested their memory for the original pictures and discovered an interesting phenomenon. Subjects often exhibited changes in their memory, and recalled a face which was rather different from the original. Bartlett suggested that his subjects held a stereotype as to what the average soldier, airman, etc., looked like, and that this stereotype had become interwoven with the original memory. This particular study was carried out at the time of the First World War, which may well have intensified the effects. The influence was so strong that when some subjects were shown the original picture again, they simply refused to believe that it was the same one that they had seen originally.

Whilst Bartlett's contribution made interesting reading, it was not until the 1970s that research interest in the transformation of memories really took off. Loftus and her colleagues were particularly interested to discover whether witnesses might have their original memories altered by the introduction of deliberately misleading information. She investigated this by conducting a series of classic studies which will be discussed below.

THE INTRODUCTION OF NON-EXISTENT OBJECTS

Loftus's early work examined whether it might be possible to introduce a non-existent object into subjects' memories. Many of her experiments involved showing student subjects a film or a series of slides depicting traffic accidents. After viewing the films/slides, subjects were typically asked a series of questions, at least one of which contained deliberately misleading information. Some time later, subjects were recalled to the laboratory and asked further questions about the accident. One such study is described in Loftus (1975). Subjects in this experiment were shown a film depicting a car accident and then asked questions about some of the details. Half the students were asked the neutral question: "How fast was the white sports car going while travelling along the country road?" However, the other half were asked the question: "How fast was the white sports car going when it passed the barn while travelling along the country road?" This second question was deliberately misleading as there was in fact no barn on the country road in the film. However, when subjects were asked one week later whether they had actually seen a barn, some 17% of those who had earlier been misled answered "Yes". This compared with less than 3% of those subjects who had not been asked the misleading question.

It would thus appear that even casually mentioning a non-existent object during the course of questioning can increase the chances that a person will later recall having "seen" the non-existent object. Loftus claims that the phenomenon occurs equally outside the laboratory as well as inside. In one study (cited in Loftus, 1979, p. 61) a fake theft was staged at railway stations and witnesses (who did not know that it was not a real theft) were asked about what they had seen. The supposed victim claimed that her tape recorder had been stolen from her bag. One week later subjects were asked a number of questions, including what the tape recorder looked like. Over half the subjects happily provided a description although there were significant differences in the descriptions given. The results make very interesting reading because in reality none of the witnesses had ever actually seen the tape recorder which was alleged to have been stolen. Although the supposed victim claimed that her tape recorder had been stolen, in reality the "thief" was seen merely reaching into the bag, pretending to remove something, and then pretending to hide an article under his coat. Those subjects who described the tape recorder were doing so despite the fact that none of them had ever seen the tape recorder that was supposedly stolen one week earlier! Because some witnesses' memory can be so easily altered, it is important that police officers do their best not to distort memory through the use of (mis)leading questions (see Ainsworth, 1995, pp. 20–21).

COMPROMISE MEMORIES

Loftus went on to examine the impact of misleading questions further. In one study (Loftus, 1977) subjects were shown a series of 30 colour slides depicting a car–pedestrian accident. A red Datsun car was shown approaching a junction, turning right, and whilst doing so colliding with a pedestrian crossing the main road. At this point a green car was shown driving past the scene but not stopping. After viewing the slides, subjects were asked a series of questions, including one which mentioned the colour of the vehicle which had driven past the scene. However, half the subjects were asked a deliberately misleading question, suggesting that this car was in fact blue rather than green. Others were asked a neutral question which did not mention a colour. Some 20 minutes later, subjects were asked to pick out the colour from a colour wheel containing 30 different shades. Loftus found that subjects who had been given the misleading information tended to choose a blue or bluish-green colour. Those who had been given no such information tended to pick a colour nearer to the original shade of green. In terms of memory theory, the results of this study are quite interesting. They suggest that information which enters via one sense modality (in this case visually) can be altered by information presented via a different modality (in this case auditorily).

In another study (Loftus, 1975) students were shown a three-minute videotape in which a group of eight noisy demonstrators disrupted a professor's lecture. After viewing the video, subjects were asked a series of questions, the crucial one of which introduced misleading information as to how many demonstrators there had been. Half the subjects were asked, "Was the leader of the four demonstrators who entered the classroom a male?", whereas the other half were asked, "Was the leader of the 12 demonstrators who entered the room a male?" One week after viewing the videotape subjects returned and were asked further questions about the videotape. The crucial question was: "How many demonstrators did you see entering the classroom?" Those subjects who had earlier been asked the question about 12 demonstrators reported on average that they had seen 8.9 people. However, those who been asked the question about four demonstrators, reported on average 6.4 people. Loftus' suggests that her subjects had produced a compromise memory – what they reported was a compromise between what they saw originally (i.e. eight) and what they were later told (either four or 12). This study again suggests that investigators who interview witnesses should be extremely careful not to introduce new information to the witnesses.

Compromise memories are an interesting phenomenon which are not easily explained. Indeed the very notion challenges one well-established theory of forgetting, i.e. interference theory. Interference theory posits that people forget details of an event because something else that they learn prevents the original from being remembered – the new knowledge interferes with the ability to recall the original, and instead the person is likely to recall only the new information. However Loftus and others have found repeatedly that compromise memories can occur (see also Belli, 1989). Such memories are neither the original nor the new version, but a blend of the two. As Hall, Loftus and Tousignant (1984, p. 140) acknowledge:

> "... compromise memory is a puzzling phenomenon. We suspect that compromise memory, as well as some other instances of change in recollection, may best be explained in terms of changes in underlying memory traces."

We will return to this issue later.

ALTERATIONS IN MEMORY

The last two experiments reviewed suggest that compromise memories can occur. However, in many cases witnesses will not have the opportunity to compromise between the original memory and subsequent information – they will either be right in their answers or they will be wrong. As we saw earlier in the study of the barn, subjects either reported seeing a non-existent barn or they did not. Loftus conducted a number of studies in which she set out to deliberately introduce new and substantively incorrect details to subjects' memories. In these cases it was not so much a compromise as a fundamental alteration of the original memory.

One such study is reported by Loftus, Miller and Burns (1978). Some 200 subjects were recruited for this experiment and were shown a series of 30 colour slides depicting a car–pedestrian accident similar to that in the colour study reviewed above. The car approached a main road, turned right and collided with a pedestrian who was crossing the road. Half the subjects saw a slide which showed a "Stop" sign at the junction, whereas the other half saw a slide which showed a "Yield" sign. After viewing the slides subjects were asked a number of questions, including one which was crucial. Half the subjects were asked, "Did another car pass the red Datsun while it was stopped at the stop sign?" However the other half were asked the same question, but with "yield sign" inserted rather than "stop sign". Crucially, for some of the subjects the type of sign mentioned was the same as the one which they had seen earlier (i.e they were given consistent information). However, for others the type of sign mentioned was different from that originally seen (i.e they were given misleading information).

Almost half an hour after viewing the original slides, subjects were asked to look at a series of pairs of slides, and to decide which slide in each pair they had seen before. One such pair showed the red Datsun stopped at either a Stop sign or a Yield sign. The results made interesting reading. Of those subjects who had been given consistent information, 75% correctly chose the same slide which they had seen originally. However, of those who had been given inconsistent (i.e. misleading) subsequent information, only 41% chose the correct slide. This result suggests that people who are given misleading information perform less well than someone who was merely guessing at the answer (where we would expect a 50% success rate).

Is Alteration of Memory Inevitable?

Whilst the results of studies such as these make fascinating reading, two aspects of the experiments require further comment. Firstly, it would seem that not all subjects who are given misleading information have their memories altered. The experiment where subjects were told about a non-existent barn resulted in some 17% of people believing that they had seen a barn. However, one could report these results in a rather different way, by emphasising the fact that over 80% of subjects were *not* misled despite attempts to do so. Indeed there would appear to be no studies in which 100% of subjects have had their memories altered. It would seem that many of the variables identified in the previous chapter come into play here, with both event factors and witness factors having an effect on just how manipulable memories are. The implication would seem to be that the more certain a witness is of his or her facts, the more difficult it will be to alter that witness's memory.

The second point concerns the type of information which researchers have attempted to alter. The studies cited above have been concerned with altering peripheral, and, one might say, trivial details. These peripheral details may well be paid little attention compared to the central details in the slides or videotape. For example, in the Stop/Yield sign study, Loftus may not have achieved quite such dramatic alterations in memory if she had attempted to convince her subjects that it was a large yellow bus, rather than a red Datsun car, which had struck the pedestrian!

This issue was addressed in one study by Dritsas and Hamilton (1977). In their research, subjects were shown a videotape containing three industrial accident scenes. After watching the videotape, subjects were asked a series of questions about the incident. Dritsas and Hamilton found, firstly, that subjects' memories for central details were far more accurate than were their memories for peripheral details. In the former case, subjects were accurate on 81% of occasions compared with 47% when asked about peripheral details. The researchers also looked at how misleading information might alter memories for central as opposed to peripheral details. They found that the misleading information affected memory for peripheral details on 69% of attempts. However, when questions concerned more central details, the misleading information produced change on less than 50% of occasions. Loftus, Miller and Burns (1978) confirmed the finding re central v. peripheral details, but have argued that this is not because there was no original memory at all. The reason for the change in memory has instead been explained thus:

> "... recollections of peripheral details are vulnerable to alteration by postevent information because subjects often fail to attend to discrepancies concerning such peripheral details." (Hall, Loftus & Tousignant, 1984, p. 136)

Whatever the reason, the results do seem to suggest that alteration of memory is more likely for the less central features of any given scene. However, as we will see later, Loftus has still been able to show that in some circumstances even memory for more important central features of an incident can be altered.

The Type of Questioning

The Loftus studies reviewed above have shown that in certain circumstances a proportion of witnesses appear to have their memories altered by the introduction of misleading information. However, Loftus was also interested to learn whether memories might be altered by more subtle and less deliberate means. Specifically she set out to examine whether the wording of the questions which witnesses are asked might affect their memory. One of her best-known studies involved having subjects watch a videotape of a car accident (Loftus & Palmer, 1974). After viewing the videotape subjects were asked a series of questions, including one concerning the speed of the vehicles at the time of the impact. The question specifically was: "About how fast were the cars going when they hit each other?" In fact Loftus and Palmer altered one crucial word in the question, with different groups of subjects being asked a slightly different question. The word "hit" in the question was replaced by a series of alternatives, i.e. "smashed", "collided", "contacted" and "bumped". The results showed that the altering of just this one simple word in the question led to different estimates of speed. At the two extremes, those subjects who were asked the question containing the word "contacted" produced an average estimate of speed of 30.8 mph. However, those subjects who were asked the same question, but containing the word "smashed" to describe the impact, produced an average estimate of 40.8 mph.

The subject of question wording is an important one to bear in mind. Whilst questions which deliberately lead a witness are forbidden in most courts of law, such controls do not exist when a police officer is interviewing a witness (see Ainsworth, 1995, pp. 20–26). Leading questions are those which suggest a certain answer in the question itself. Thus a question such as "He was driving too fast wasn't he?" would be disallowed in court. However, the leading of witnesses can occur in a much more subtle way than this crude example suggests. For example, a witness might be asked the question, "How far away was the car when the boy stepped into the road?". An alternative wording might be, "How close was the car when the boy stepped into the road?". Neither of these would be considered leading questions, but each might produce a slightly different estimate of the distance. The resulting answer might be important – if the police believe that a driver had ample time to react, but still hit the pedestrian, they may be more likely to recommend a prosecution for careless driving.

Loftus provides many other examples of how subtle alterations in the wording of questions can lead to differences in answers (see Loftus, 1979, pp. 94–97). However, until such time as interviews with witnesses are routinely tape recorded, we can only speculate as to the number of occasions on which witnesses' answers have been manipulated by the wording of questions. It is interesting to note that in those cases where interviews with victims and witnesses are now routinely video recorded (i.e. cases of alleged child sexual abuse), some prosecutions have failed largely because of the way in which the questioning has been conducted (see Chapter 9).

Returning to the "Smashed/Hit" experiment briefly, we should note one further aspect of the study. Some of those who took part in the experiment returned to the laboratory one week later and were asked a further series of questions. The crucial question was: "Did you see any broken glass?" In fact there had not been any broken glass at the scene, but Loftus and Palmer reasoned that some subjects might assume there to have been broken glass following the severe impact. The researchers were particularly interested to know whether the previous questioning of the witnesses might affect their "memory" of whether there had been any broken glass. What they found was that those subjects who had been previously asked the question about cars having "smashed" into each other were more likely to claim that they had seen the non-existent broken glass. In fact 16 (out of 50) claimed to have done so. However, for those subjects who had previously been asked the "hit" question, only seven (out of 50) claimed to have seen the glass.

Loftus argues that, in the above examples, subjects have two separate sources of information. They have their original memory for the incident plus any subsequent "external" information. However, she argues that:

> "Over time, information from these two sources may be integrated in such a way that we are unable to tell from which source some specific detail is recalled. All we have is one 'memory'." (Loftus, 1979, p. 78).

This view is helpful in understanding how subsequent information might affect memory. However, as we will see later, it is a little too simplistic a notion, and there are in fact a number of theories as to why recall of the original (uncontaminated) memory can prove difficult.

The Timing of Misleading Information

As we noted in Chapter 2, memory can fade rapidly with time and a person's recollection for an event can become more and more hazy. However, an interesting question that might arise concerns the timing of any subsequent misleading information. If a person was given misleading information immediately after viewing an incident, would it have a greater or lesser effect than if it were given just before the person was questioned later about the incident? This issue was addressed by Loftus, Miller and Burns (1978). In this study, some subjects were given misleading information immediately after viewing a series of slides of a car accident and were then tested one week later. A second group was given the misleading information one week later, i.e. immediately before being tested. In the former case, subjects answered correctly in just over 50% of cases. However, those subjects who were misled just prior to being tested, were correct in only 20% of cases. Loftus argues that, in those subjects misled immediately after the incident, memory for both the original incident and for the misleading information will have faded with time. However, for those who were misled just before being interviewed, the misleading information will be more salient or fresher in their mind, and will be more likely to be recalled than the original memory. This appears to be an example of the "Recency Effect" highlighted in Chapter 2 and has clear implications for the way in which witnesses are interviewed and for the timing of such interviews.

SOME REASONS WHY MEMORY CHANGE MIGHT NOT OCCUR

There is thus clear evidence that memory change can occur in certain circumstances, but that this is by no means inevitable. Since Loftus's early work, researchers have been keen to establish some of the factors which are associated with the likelihood that memory will be altered. Hall, Loftus and Tousignant (1984, p. 135) suggest one important principle:

> "Recollections can change only if the subject does not immediately detect discrepancies between postevent information and memory for the original event."

When subjects are presented with misleading information they may simply dismiss it as unreliable. Alternatively, the subjects may label the new information as different from the original, encode it separately, and so not alter their original memory. This might partly explain why memory for peripheral details is easier to alter than memory for more central components.

One possible reason for the apparent memory change is the fact that subjects would have no reason to suspect that they might be given misleading information. They might reasonably expect that the person conducting the experiments knows the true facts, and so would only give out correct information. This view has been supported by researchers such as McCloskey and Zaragoza (1985) who suggest that many of the findings reported by Loftus have more to do with the "demand characteristics" of the experiments rather than memory alteration *per se*.

If faced with a slight discrepancy in a peripheral detail subject, witnesses may well come to trust the new information (which comes from what is presumed to be a reliable source) rather than rely on a hazy recollection. In support of such a view, it is interesting to note that Loftus and her colleagues have shown that simply warning subjects that they may be about to encounter misleading information reduces the likelihood that they would be influenced by such information (Greene, Flynne & Loftus, 1982).

A second principle which tries to explain the erratic and unpredictable nature of memory change is that:

> "Change in recollections for an original event occurs only if a postevent experience restores memory for the original event to an active status." (Hall, Loftus & Tousignant, 1984, p. 137)

Loftus believes that a distinction should be drawn between active memory and inactive memory. The distinction appears similar to that made by Baddeley between working memory and long-term memory (described in Chapter 2). Loftus believes that if the original memory lies dormant in the inactive long-term store, then new information will not affect it. Only when the subject reactivates the original memory and recalls it into their active (working) memory is it likely to be altered.

ARE ORIGINAL MEMORIES REALLY LOST FOR EVER?

Throughout the discussion so far, we have tended to assume that when memory change occurs, the original is lost for ever and only the new modified memory remains. This is the view generally adopted by Loftus (see, for example, Loftus & Hoffman, 1989), but is not one with which everyone agrees. Early critics such as Bekerian suggested that the original memory might still exist, but that the problem was accessing it (see Bekerian & Bowers, 1983). To date a number of quite distinct theories have been put forward to explain memory transformations, and these will be considered below (see Fruzzetti et al., 1992, for a further review of these theories).

Loftus's theory as to why transformations appear to take place has been labelled the *alteration hypothesis*. As we saw above, it is believed that the original is not recovered simply because it no longer exists. The original has been altered or transformed into a new memory (sometimes a compromise memory) to the point where the original is lost for ever. Loftus supports this view by reference to the fact that giving subjects large incentives for trying to recover original memories, using hypnosis, or even allowing subjects a "second guess" leads to little success (Loftus & Hoffman, 1989). Similarly, witnesses who have been misled are often just as confident in their (wrong) answers as those who have not been misled and thus answer correctly (Loftus *et al.*, 1989). A dramatic example of how powerful the new altered memory can become is provided by Loftus & Ketcham (1991). In this true case, a woman who had been raped was pressurised to provide the name of her rapist. She eventually gave the name of the husband of a work colleague. The man was convicted, although shortly afterwards the real rapist was caught and confessed fully to the crime. Despite being confronted by the obviously true confession of the second man, the victim maintained that it was the first man who had raped her. It would appear that, over time, her memory for the real rapist's face had become altered in such a way that it proved impossible to recover.

If Loftus's alteration hypothesis is correct then there are serious implications for police investigators. The view would be that if a witness has been given any further information about an incident, their original memory is likely to be contaminated. It would thus be important for police officers to establish whether a witness has discussed the incident with others or whether he or she has seen reports in the media, etc. The police officer must also be very aware that his or her own form of questioning may itself serve to contaminate an original memory (see Ainsworth, 1995a).

An alternative view is provided by the so-called *coexistence hypothesis*. As the name implies, this theory suggests that both the original and the modified memory coexist within the memory system, and that each is capable of being recovered. Supporters of this theory point to the fact that it is sometimes possible to recover some parts of an original memory, even after misleading information has been presented (see Bekerian & Bowers, 1983; Christiaansen & Ochalek, 1983). Supporters argue that although it does often prove to be all but impossible to recover an original memory, this does not in itself prove that the original memory no longer exists. Rather, they suggest that the failure should simply be seen as a (possibly temporary) retrieval difficulty. The problem here may be that recent memories are often more easily accessed than are more distant recollections. This is similar to the so-called "Recency Effect" discussed in Chapter 2. The coexistence hypothesis is slightly more optimistic about the possibilities of recovering original memories than was Loftus's view. It implies that police officers interviewing witnesses should try to persuade witnesses to put themselves mentally back at the scene, rather than just try to recall all they can about the incident. This is a topic to which we will return in Chapter 7.

A specific form of the coexistence theory has been proposed by Morton, Hammersley and Bekerian (1985) and labelled the *Headed Records Theory*. This theory suggests that information is represented in memory units called "Records" and that each unit is headed by an access key or "Heading". These headings allow the recovery of a memory by describing the information that is held in the record. In some ways, the system envisaged is similar to a filing cabinet or a computer directory (or folder). Providing that each file is labelled correctly, and contains the desired information, then recovery of the material should be easy.

When searching for a particular memory, the person tries to match a description of the record to an appropriate heading. However, it is suggested that not all "files" are equally accessible. Specifically, Morton and colleagues believe that the misinformation effect occurs when the headed record for the original information is less accessible than the headed record for the misleading information. In other words, the person may have two different memories, one of which is more recent and thus "nearer the surface" or more salient than the other. Because the person cannot distinguish between the headed record for the original and the misleading information they make the mistake of only ever recovering the most recent version of events. This view again suggests that police officers may be more likely to retrieve the original memory if they are careful and specific in their questioning of witnesses (see Chapter 7).

A further explanation which has been offered is concerned with *Source Misattribution*. This theory suggests that subjects are fooled by misleading information because of confusion about the true source of information. According to the theory, the misinformation effect occurs because a subject confuses the source of the original information and that of the misleading information. Thus the source of the misleading information is attributed (incorrectly) to the originally witnessed event. According to this view, a witness who hears another witness describe what the driver of a car said to him, may subsequently come to believe that his memory is based on having heard the conversation first (as opposed to second) hand.

As with the Headed Records Theory, Source Misattribution Theory can explain why subjects are more likely to recall the misinformation as opposed to the original. Because the former is more salient in the memory, it is presumed to be from the originally witnessed event. Followers of this theory have attempted to deal with the misinformation problem by adopting a source monitoring approach. In this, subjects are encouraged to think about and monitor the source of any information which they recall. The results of such studies have been somewhat mixed, but appear to show that even when subjects are instructed to monitor carefully the source of information, they are still vulnerable to misleading information (see Weingardt, Toland and Loftus (1994) for a review of such studies). As was suggested earlier, the problem is at least partly caused by the fact that subjects are not always able to recall correctly the source from which any particular piece of information derived (Lindsay, 1994).

Some of the problems associated with source misattribution might be avoided if those charged with the duty of interviewing witnesses are at least aware of the phenomenon. Instructions to a witness to think carefully about the source of his or her "original" memories may have some effect. Questioning each witness as to other sources of information to which he or she has been exposed may also help to identify those who are more likely to experience source misattribution difficulties.

CONCLUDING COMMENTS

As we can see, there are a number of theories which go some way towards explaining the misinformation effect, though no one view may be totally correct. Some (e.g. McCloskey & Zaragoza, 1985) have even argued that the effect itself is not so much a real phenomenon but more an apparent one. They argue that many subjects in the Loftus studies may well not have had an original memory at all, and so their memory is not so much altered by new information as created. As noted earlier, they also suggest that subjects in the studies may simply be responding to the particular demands of the experiment, and be giving the answer which they think the researcher wants.

Such radical views have not gone unchallenged, and some researchers who have used a more sophisticated experimental design still report evidence of the misinformation effect (Belli, 1989; Tversky & Tuchin, 1989; Lindsay, 1990). Needless to say, this is an issue which is likely to be debated for some time to come. After reviewing a considerable amount of recent research, Fruzzetti and colleagues draw the following conclusion:

> "... the research addressing the permanence of memory trace has, over the past decade, yielded results to support multiple hypotheses. The question of whether or not the original trace of critical information is altered has not been unequivocally answered, and the debate rages on. Future research must further delineate the conditions that are conducive to such memory interference." (Fruzzetti *et al.*, 1992, p. 34)

What we can say is that memory is malleable, and in a significant number of cases, can be altered. Whilst we are not yet in a position to specify the exact conditions under which a witness will or will not experience alterations in memory, we are right to be cautious about witnesses' statements. Because eyewitnesses do appear to have difficulty in separating out originally witnessed information from any subsequent "facts" we can never be sure which memory they are drawing upon at any one time. For this reason, it is important that witnesses are interviewed in ways which will not add to their potential confusion (see Chapter 7). In serious criminal cases it is not uncommon for witnesses to have to wait a year or more before being asked to testify in court. This suggests that there will be a large number of opportunities for witnesses to be given, and perhaps accept, misleading information.

Academics may long debate the relative merits of the "alteration" or "coexistence" hypotheses. For an accused person the only important question may be: "Might this witness be mistaken in his or her account?" From the evidence reviewed in this chapter it would appear that witnesses can quite easily have their memories altered, often without their being aware of the fact. Indeed, in an interesting variation of the usual misinformation study, Weingardt, Toland & Loftus (1994) report that subjects who have been given misleading information are often still willing to bet money on their memory being correct! For this reason we should again exercise caution before accepting unconditionally the evidence of one who swears to "tell the truth, the whole truth and nothing but the truth".

No discussion of altered memories would be complete without at least a mention of the so-called "False Memory Syndrome". This is the scenario in which a person who has no previous recollection of an event having taken place may suddenly produce an apparent memory for the incident. Such sudden discoveries invariably occur while the person is undergoing some form of therapy or counselling. Some therapists claim that these revelations demonstrate the Freudian notion of repression and that the recall is evidence of a real memory. However, many psychologists disagree strongly with such suggestions and argue that those "memories" are merely confabulations which in some cases may have been encouraged by the therapist. The issue has produced heated debate, and in some cases has divided the academic community. The evidence currently available suggests that many of these so-called recovered memories are in fact fabrications, with little basis in fact. In addition, the notion that unpleasant memories are invariably repressed has been challenged. We will return to this topic in Chapter 8.

CHAPTER 5

Facial Memory and the Eyewitness

So far in this book we have looked at a large number of ways in which witnesses' memory may be incomplete or inaccurate. Most of the research covered has dealt with the attempted recall of the details of an event or incident. We have seen that good recall is essential if the police are to build up an accurate picture of the circumstances surrounding a particular incident. However, perhaps the most dramatic task which a witness may be called upon to perform is to describe or to identify an alleged perpetrator. If a witness is unable to describe a perpetrator's appearance comprehensively and accurately then the police will be much less likely to apprehend the offender. More worryingly, if a witness makes a mistake and incorrectly identifies an innocent person, the consequences are even more serious (see Chapter 6). The Devlin Committee (Devlin Report, 1976) noted that in 1973 there were some 347 cases in England and Wales where eyewitness testimony was the only evidence against an accused. In 74% of these cases the accused was convicted. In half of these cases, there was only one eyewitness. Brandon and Davies (1973) cited some 70 cases in which eyewitness testimony was the main factor in the conviction of an innocent person. In this chapter we will thus start to consider some important aspects of facial recognition and consider ways in which recognition may differ from recall. The thorny question of mistaken identifications will be addressed in some detail in Chapter 6.

THE DIFFICULTIES OF FACIAL RECOGNITION AND IDENTIFICATION

One of the most dramatic illustrations of the difficulties of facial recognition and identification was provided by Buckhout (1980). In this study a short film of a staged purse snatch was shown on television. In the film, a man was seen to run towards a woman in a hallway, grab her purse and knock her to the ground. The man then ran towards the camera so that viewers could see his face clearly. After seeing the film, viewers were shown a line-up of six men who resembled the assailant and were asked to phone in to a special telephone number if they thought that they could identify the perpetrator. Viewers were told specifically that the attacker might or might not be in the line-up (in reality he was). Over 2,000 calls were received from viewers who thought they could identify the robber, and some 14.1% correctly picked out person number two from the line-up. To put that figure a different way, over 85% of viewers were unable to pick out the correct person, a result that was worse than would have been expected by chance. This figure is particularly worrying when one considers that those people who did phone in were presumably fairly sure that they could identify the perpetrator. It might reasonably be presumed that viewers who were unsure would be less likely to phone in at all.

RECOGNISING AND RECALLING FACES

Facial recognition is a task which we tend to take for granted and yet is a complex process requiring a great deal of cognitive effort. As Bruce (1988, p. 2) has noted:

> "Although potentially reliable keys to identity, faces form a class of objects whose recognition poses a far from trivial problem of visual pattern classification ... faces form a rather homogeneous set of patterns in which there may be very subtle differences between one individual's face and the next."

Most people would have no difficulty in recognising the face of a close relative or good friend even after a very long delay (see Bahrick, Bahrick & Wittlinger, 1975). However, if asked to describe the person's facial features accurately, many would struggle. Thus facial recall and facial recognition may involve slightly different cognitive tasks. The attempted recall of facial features may even have an affect on a person's ability subsequently to recognise that face. Schooler and Engst-Schooler (1990) conducted a number of studies in which groups of subjects viewed a videorecording of a staged crime. One group was then asked to provide a verbal description of a face seen in the video, whilst a second group was asked to form a visual image of the face, and a third group was given no instructions. Each group of subjects was then shown a photospread containing the face seen earlier in the video and was asked to pick out the person. Rather surprisingly, the researchers found that those subjects who had first been asked to provide a verbal description of the person tended to perform less well in the recognition task than each of the two other groups. The difference in performance was found for time intervals of up to two days between the presentation of the face and the subsequent recognition task.

One interesting footnote to this study was that the difference between the groups was not found when subjects were given only a short period of time to study the photospread. More recently, Schooler, Ryan and Reder (1996) have suggested that although verbalisation of facial details can interfere with future recognition accuracy, this is not inevitable. They note that in many circumstances verbalisation does have a negative effect, but in others it can make little difference, or even have a positive effect.

These findings seem to challenge the notion that a witness who can provide a good verbal description of a suspect will be more likely to pick out the person's face in a photospread or identification parade (see Pigott & Brigham, 1985). It is thus surprising to learn that courts sometimes direct jurors to give greater weight to witnesses whose verbal descriptions match the perpetrator's appearance and who then pick out the person in an identification parade. There is a tendency to assume that because a suspect matches the description provided by a witness, then he or she must be the guilty person. However, as we will see in the cases highlighted in Chapter 6, this is a rather naive assumption. The fact that the police have arrested someone who matches the witness's verbal description is not in itself proof that the right person is in the dock. Verbal descriptions are often so vague as to be of little use to those trying to identify a suspect. Verbal descriptions may also contain a number of inaccuracies which may simply be carried forward to the identification process. For example a witness may recall incorrectly that a perpetrator had long greasy hair. The police may use this information to arrest a suspect who has similar hair and put him on an identification parade. If the witness then picks out the suspect this may simply prove that the witness is being consistent (but wrong), not that the police have the right person in custody.

It would appear that facial recall and recognition are not governed by exactly the same rules as other memory processes (see Bruce & Young, 1986). However, many of the variables which affect event memory will also be relevant when considering facial memory (see Chapter 3). Thus, things like exposure time, retention interval, prior knowledge and expectations, misleading suggestions and stress might all affect facial recall and recognition.

If asked to describe the physical features of one's own house, this may well prove easier than if one were to be asked to describe the physical features of a good friend's face. People may well be able to recall hair colour, and perhaps the person's size, but little else. However, if the person came across the friend in even the most crowded street, it is unlikely that he or she would go unrecognised.

Facial recognition can perhaps best be seen not as one process but several. On encountering a face a person needs to decide at least three things:

1. Is the face familiar, i.e. is it one which the person has encountered previously?
2. In what way is the face familiar, i.e. how does the person know the face and from where?
3. What is the name of the person whom he or she recognises as familiar?

Mistakes can be made at any of these three stages. People may simply fail to recognise the face of a familiar person as one which they have encountered previously. Perhaps, more embarrassingly, the person may believe that they recognise a face, greet the person warmly, and only then discover that the face is actually that of a complete stranger.

People may also recognise a face as familiar but be unable to recall how they know the person or from where. This type of difficulty seems more likely when the face is encountered away from the usual context. Thus a work colleague might be recognised instantly when encountered around the office, but be more difficult to place when seen on a foreign holiday. In such a circumstance the person may make a mistake and mislabel the face as, say, that of someone who just happens to be on the same package tour. Similarly, television personalities will be recognised instantly when hosting their regular game show, but be more difficult to place when seen out shopping. When a person is mislabelled, the phenomenon is sometimes referred to as unconscious transference and, as we will see later, can have grave consequences for those mislabelled.

Perhaps the most common difficulty in facial recognition is the scenario in which a person recognises another as familiar, may even recall where the person was seen, but cannot recall the person's name. Once again, the difficulty may be in the form of a simple failure to recall the name, or may be a mistake in that the person attaches the wrong name to the face.

These types of error are surprisingly common, yet other types of failure which might be anticipated are much rarer. For example, it is unlikely that many people will have experienced the scenario in which they are able to recall a person's name, but not their facial appearance. This again suggests that facial memory may involve different processes than object memory. Bruce and Young (1986) have provided perhaps the best-known model of facial recognition and some features of this will be discussed briefly below.

A MODEL OF FACIAL RECOGNITION

The first point that Bruce and Young make is that the analysis of facial expression and facial speech is independent of facial recognition. In other words, it is possible to recognise the expression on someone's face even if we have never encountered that particular face before. Both psychologists and social anthropologists have highlighted the universality of facial expression across all cultures – a person who is happy smiles, whether he or she is from Britain or Borneo. Similarly, a person can generally understand what another is saying by watching lip movements, irrespective of whether the face is familiar. However, it should be noted that if a person is first encountered with only one expression, a subsequent change in expression will hinder later recognition. Thus if a person was very sad on the first occasion when we encountered his or her face, we may have problems identifying that person if he or she is happy when we meet for a second time (see Bond & McConkey, 1995). This has implications for eyewitness identifications, as a person committing, say, an armed robbery may be experiencing different emotions (and so have a very different facial expression) compared to when he or she is having a drink in the pub.

Although a face encountered many times is more likely to be recognised than one which is seen only once, there are more subtle differences. For example, a face encountered in different poses is more likely to be subsequently recognised than one seen from only one angle. If only one pose is seen, then a three-quarter view would appear to offer the best chance of future recognition. Research has suggested that the human' brain has two types of facial recognition cells. One type responds to a frontal view, whilst the other responds to a profile (see Perrett *et al.*, 1986). When a three-quarter pose is encountered, this tends to lead to the firing of both types of facial recognition cell. Given this information, it is perhaps surprising to learn that most police forces still take a frontal pose (and perhaps an additional profile) rather than a three-quarter shot.

On the subject of brain cells it is interesting to note that some people who have suffered damage to certain parts of their brain subsequently experience great difficulty in recognising familiar faces. One such condition is that of prosopagnosia, which is experienced by some who have suffered damage to the right hemisphere of the brain. People with this condition recognise a face as a face but are unable to tell whether it is familiar or unfamiliar. Thus a person who is unfortunate enough to suffer prosopagnosia may be unable to recognise the face of someone whom he or she has known for many years, and will treat each encounter with that face as a novel experience. In one rather bizarre case of prosopagnosia, a sufferer who took up sheep farming was able to distinguish between the faces of his sheep, but not between different human faces! (See McNeil & Warrington, 1993). Needless to say, sufferers of prosopagnosia would tend not to make good eyewitnesses. There are other conditions which also make facial recognition difficult (Dolan *et al.*, 1997; Moscovitch *et al.*, 1997) but these will not be discussed here.

Bruce and Young suggest that when people encounter a face, they must first decide whether it is familiar or unfamiliar. A familiar face triggers what Bruce and Young call a "face recognition unit". In some cases, "recognition" proceeds no further than this and the only thing that the person knows is that the face is one which seems familiar. However, for many encounters, recognising the face as familiar may also trigger what Bruce and Young refer to as "person identity nodes". Such clues may indicate how one person knows another, and also where he or she has encountered the other previously. Once these steps have been passed, the viewer may then be able to put a name to the face.

When studying faces, people tend not to look at each feature equally. There is a tendency to concentrate on certain parts of the face and virtually to ignore others. Studies which have examined the eye movements of people viewing faces show that more time is spent studying the hair not only in terms of its colour and style, but also how it affects the outline of the face. Next to be examined tend to be the eyes, with features such as the mouth, lips and chin receiving comparatively little attention. Witnesses may thus tend to be accurate in describing a suspect's hair, but the dimpled chin or turned up nose may go completely unnoticed. For this reason witnesses who view a robbery in which a criminal's only disguise is the wearing of a hat, may experience significant difficulty in recognising the person later.

Although the order in which people examine different facial features is reasonably well established, there are some exceptions. For example, if the face being viewed has one unusual or distinctive feature, then people tend to concentrate on this. In perceiving faces and other objects in the environment, the viewer may well concentrate on the most salient feature and ignore the less distinctive aspects (see Chapter 1). Thus the reader may recall that Barry Manilow has a rather large nose or that Jimmy Hill has an unusually long chin. However, it may be more difficult to recall the hair style or eye colour of these two individuals. One should also bear in mind that not all individuals will attend to exactly the same aspect of the faces which they encounter. For example, a dentist may first notice a perpetrator's teeth, and be able to give a detailed description of the person's jaw shape and dental features.

Some faces are, of course, more distinctive than others. For this reason it could be claimed that some faces are inherently memorable whilst others are instantly forgettable. Shepherd and Ellis (1973) found that attractive faces were more likely to be remembered than unattractive ones. Light, Kayra-Stuart and Hollander (1979) suggest that faces which stand out in some way are much more likely to be recalled and later recognised than "average" or more usual faces. Goldstein and Chance (1981) suggested that distinctive faces may evoke more arousal in the viewer and may even be stored differently from normal faces. The police may experience great frustration when a witness can do no better than describe a person's face as "average" or "normal". Unfortunately, it does appear that faces which have no distinctive features are difficult both to describe and to recognise. It is interesting to note that in 1976 the Devlin Committee recommended that judges should advise a jury that a defendant's nondescript appearance might reduce the likely validity of any identification.

CROSS-RACIAL IDENTIFICATION

If one follows the argument about distinctive faces then it might reasonably be presumed that faces from another race would be more easily remembered than those from a person's own race. Such faces would certainly command greater attention because they would tend to stand out from the crowd. However, most psychological research tends to suggest that this is not the case (Shepherd, 1981; Chance & Goldstein, 1996). In fact one fairly consistent finding from eyewitness testimony studies is that faces from another race are more difficult to recall and recognise than are those from the person's own race. Bothwell, Brigham and Malpass (1989) reviewed a number of previous studies on the other-race effect, and concluded that it was a significant factor in many eyewitness identification cases. They suggest that the other-race factor can account for between 10 and 12% of the variance in performance in face recognition studies. Their views are supported by other researchers (e.g. Shapiro & Penrod, 1986) although some have sought to play down the influence of the other-race effect (see, for example, Lindsay & Wells, 1983).

The problem with cross-racial identification seems to stem partly from inappropriate encoding strategies. People tend to use face-encoding strategies which have proved to be effective in the past. Thus a white person viewing the face of another white person may pay close attention to hair colour and texture and perhaps eye colour. However, for the white person viewing a black face, such a strategy may prove to be inappropriate (see Ellis, Deregowski & Shepherd, 1975). In most black faces, hair colour and eye colour tend to be uniform. Thus if a witness were to concentrate on these aspects of the face, he or she would later have great difficulty in picking out the person from an array of faces from the same race. It might be presumed that faces from some races are inherently more difficult to distinguish than faces from other races. However, this appears not to be the case. Studies which have compared the difference between faces within a number of different racial groups show that there is a similarity in the absolute number of distinguishing features (see Goldstein, 1979).

Chance and Goldstein (1996) provide a comprehensive review of the other-race effect and suggest that there are two other possible explanations. Firstly, ethnic attitudes might impair or enhance people's recognition of faces of other racial groups. Secondly, differential amounts of experience or familiarity with other groups might modify the person's face perception and/or memory processes.

They conclude that:

> "... although attitudes towards other groups may influence the degree and quality of contact with them, no straightforward relationships between attitudes and memory occur." (Chance & Goldstein, 1996, p. 170)

These researchers believe that limited prior experience with faces of a different race leads to difficulties with perceptual and memory processes. They suggest that experience with any class of events leads to changes in how new instances are handled. When faces from a familiar race are encountered, established schemata or internal representations allow people to process the data efficiently and effectively. However, when faces from a less familiar race are encountered, processing and differentiation between faces becomes more difficult. This problem is compounded by the fact that through the process of stereotyping, humans tend to assign more similar characteristics to members of other groups than they do to members of their own (see Brown, 1986).

It would thus seem that people viewing faces from a different race do not pay enough attention to those features which would later help them to distinguish between one face and another. A white person who has had little contact with non-whites, may recall little about a black face other than its distinctive colour. However, such detail will be of little help to a police officer trying to establish the identity of a black offender.

If the problem of cross-racial identification stems from inappropriate encoding strategies, then one might reasonably ask whether training could reduce the difficulty. Unfortunately, the evidence is that training leads to little improvement in people's ability to recognise faces. For example, Woodhead, Baddeley and Simmonds (1979) report three studies in which people's recognition accuracy was evaluated both before and after a three-day training course. In two of the studies reviewed, no improvement was found after the training, and, in one, the level of correct identification even went down. Malpass (1981) has offered two possible explanations for these findings. Firstly, he suggests that, for most people, the learning of faces is such a well-established skill that it is difficult to change. Secondly, the type of training used in studies such as that of Woodhead and colleagues may be inappropriate for improving facial recognition. Following this line of argument, Malpass looked at four different types of training course and assessed each one's effectiveness. Unfortunately, the results showed that no one type of course was better than any other and, if anything, recognition performance tended to fall rather than improve after training. Ellis (1984) has speculated that Malpass's discouraging results may be due partly to the fact that each type of training lasted only 12 hours. It is possible that longer training courses may have had a more beneficial effect.

INTERFERENCE IN FACIAL MEMORY

In Chapter 3 we saw how easy it can be to alter a person's memory for an event through the use of leading questions or through the introduction of misleading information. Researchers have been keen to establish whether the same transformations can occur in facial memory. If facial recall and recognition are somewhat different from event memory, then we might reasonably presume that they are less likely to be altered by subsequent information. In reality, research shows that facial memory may be just as vulnerable to alteration as other kinds of memory. As long ago as 1932, Bartlett showed that the longer a facial image is stored in memory, the more likely it is to undergo some kind of transformation. Shepherd, Davies and Ellis (1978) showed that simply attaching a label to a face can produce an alteration in memory. In this latter study, subjects were allowed to view a photograph of a male face for some 30 seconds and were later asked to construct a Photofit of the face. However, half the subjects were told that the face was that of a lifeboat captain decorated for bravery, whilst the other half were told that the face was that of a mass murderer. Shepherd found that the two groups of subjects tended to produce slightly different Photofit pictures. For example, those who had been told that the face belonged to a mass murderer, produced a face which was judged to be less intelligent looking and more cruel and unpleasant.

In a series of studies, Loftus and Greene (1980) showed that misleading information about faces can be incorporated into memory. In their studies, subjects saw a target face live, in photographs, or on film, and were then exposed to misleading information about some feature of the face. Subjects typically overheard what appeared to be another witness providing some detail about the face. In some cases this was deliberately misleading – for example, when a target person had straight hair but was described as having curly hair. In other cases, a detail was introduced which had not been present in the target face – for example, a person might be led to believe that the target had a moustache, when in fact he did not. Loftus and Greene showed that a significant number of subjects could be misled in this way.

Interestingly, the results were similar when memory was tested by asking for the recall of facial details and when facial recognition was tested. In one study, subject witnesses viewed a scene which contained one particular man as a central figure within it. The subjects then read an account of the scene which suggested (incorrectly) that the man had a moustache. A few minutes later, subjects were asked to try to identify the man from a photo array of 12 men, six of whom had a moustache, and six of whom did not. Sixty-nine per cent of subjects who had been given the misleading information incorrectly selected a photograph of a man with a moustache. By contrast, only 13% of subjects who had not been given the misleading information chose a face with a moustache. Research such as this study by Loftus and Greene may offer an explanation for some cases of mistaken identification (see Chapter 6).

Thus although facial memory may be slightly different from event memory, it is by no means immune from the effects of interference and misleading information. It is interesting to note that, in the Loftus and Greene studies, the misleading information was sometimes introduced via a different sense modality from that in which the original face was encountered. For example, in one study the original face was presented visually, but the misleading information was presented verbally. However, the results were similar to those experiments where the misleading information was presented via the same sense modality on both occasions. This suggests that even if facial images are encoded or stored differently from other memories, they are still susceptible to subsequent misleading information.

One interesting footnote to the Loftus and Greene study is the fact that witnesses' susceptibility to misleading information was affected by the format of the question which contained the misleading detail. Specifically, the researchers found that misinformation embedded in a complex question was significantly more likely to alter memory than if the same information was contained within a more simple question.

UNCONSCIOUS TRANSFERENCE

We saw earlier that people can make mistakes in identifications because they recognise a face as familiar, but then incorrectly recall where they know the face from. Thus an eyewitness may come across a familiar face several days after a crime, and mislabel it as that of the perpetrator. The process may even lead to a witness labelling an innocent bystander at the scene of a crime as the perpetrator. In such cases the witness may recognise the face as familiar, correctly associate it with the scene of the crime, but incorrectly label it as the face of the perpetrator. The effect of such an error can be the conviction of a genuinely innocent person. One well-known case of unconscious transference was cited by Houts (1956). In this incident, a railway booking clerk was held up at gunpoint and his money stolen. The clerk was later asked to attend an identity parade and the person he picked out was a local man. However, that person was able to prove categorically that he was nowhere near the scene of the crime at the time of the robbery. When trying to establish the reason for the mistake, the booking clerk admitted that, unlike all the others on the parade, the "suspect's" face had appeared familiar and this was why he had picked him out. It emerged that the "suspect" was in fact a sailor from a local camp who had bought tickets from the clerk on a number of occasions. The clerk had thus correctly recalled that this person's face was familiar but incorrectly associated it with the robbery.

A number of researchers have examined the phenomenon of unconscious transference (see, for example, Loftus, 1976; Gudjonsson, 1992) and pointed to the potential problems which can result. Unfortunately, there is no easy way of establishing the frequency of the occurrence objectively. As with other cases of mistaken identification, some instances may never come to light. In the case cited by Houts above, the mistake was recognised because the suspect was able to provide a cast-iron alibi. However, it seems reasonable to presume that there will be other cases in which the suspect may not be so fortunate and be unable to prove that a mistake has been made.

Not all researchers agree that unconscious transference is a major factor in wrongful convictions. Ross *et al.* (1994a, p. 81) note that:

> "To date there are only a handful of studies on unconscious transference and the findings are mixed, providing weak and inconsistent support for the existence of unconscious transference."

However, some recent research (Ainsworth, 1995b) suggested that the problem can occur following the media's reporting of an incident. In this study, subjects were asked to read a short passage from a local newspaper and were told that they would later be asked questions about the report. The article was concerned with a number of serious sexual assaults in the Manchester area. In addition to the text, the article contained two pictures. One picture was a Photofit of a suspect in the case, whilst the other was a photograph of a "good samaritan" who had intervened and prevented a possibly serious assault. One week later, and without prior warning, subjects were asked to try to pick out the face of the suspect from an array of six pictures. Subjects were divided into three groups. One group was shown an array containing the Photofit picture of the suspect, a second group was shown an array containing the picture of the good samaritan, and a third group was shown an array containing six foils but neither of the two pictures encountered earlier. The results showed that the group who were shown the array containing the real suspect picked out the correct picture on almost 40% of occasions. However, the group who were shown an array which did not contain the suspect, but did contain the picture of the good samaritan, incorrectly identified this face as that of the suspect in almost 50% of cases. In other words, the chances of the good samaritan being incorrectly identified were about the same as the chances of the real suspect being correctly identified.

These results do tend to suggest that, in certain circumstances, unconscious transference can pose real difficulties. Over 20 years ago, Brown, Deffenbacher and Sturgill (1977) also showed that this can be a serious problem. In their study subjects first viewed a number of targets "live" and then studied a photo array. This array contained photographs of the criminals seen earlier, plus a number of other "innocent" suspects. After a gap of four to seven days, subjects viewed a live line-up and were asked to say whether each person in the line-up had been one of the criminals seen earlier. The parade contained three different types of person: some were the "live" criminals seen earlier, some were those whose photographs had been seen earlier in the photo array, and some were foils not encountered previously. Brown and colleagues found that although subjects could generally discriminate between those faces which had and had not been seen earlier, they were incapable of discriminating between those which were of the real criminals (seen "live" earlier) and those whose photographs had been seen in the subsequent photo array. Subjects thus appeared to be very good at recognising familiar faces, but very poor at identifying when and where the face had been encountered previously.

There has been comparatively little research carried out on the effects of the media's reporting of crime on witnesses' recall (see Ainsworth, 1995a, Ch. 11). However it seems likely that such reporting can both cause an alteration in memory, and, in some cases, lead to unconscious transference. If one considers television programmes such as *Crimewatch UK*, which shows reconstructions of actual crimes, the potential for confusion is quite large. Viewers may well begin to believe that the actor who plays the part of the perpetrator is in fact the real suspect in the case. One can only speculate as to the number of occasions on which such actors have been later identified as perpetrators by viewers. On at least one occasion, a viewer phoned into the *Crimewatch UK* studio to report that a person shown in a reconstruction had been recognised. This apparently helpful gesture was, however, misplaced as the caller in fact named the actor who had played the part of the perpetrator in the reconstruction rather than the real perpetrator! (Personal communication, Professor Graham Davies). Although programmes such as *Crimewatch UK* serve a very useful purpose in eliciting new information on unsolved crimes, they may also sow confusion in the minds of witnesses. Hall, Loftus and Tousignant (1984) suggest that any new information about a suspect's appearance may actually lead to an alteration in a witness's original memory. As we saw in Chapter 3, it may be all but impossible for a witness to recall the original facts (or in this case the original face) once some new information has been encountered.

CONCLUDING COMMENTS

In this chapter we have seen some of the difficulties associated with facial recall and recognition. Although facial recognition may involve some different skills than other kinds of memory tasks, it is still prone to errors. In the next chapter we will start to consider why some of these errors might occur, focusing in particular on photospreads and identification parades. We will also see the possible consequences of witnesses' mistakes, i.e. the wrongful conviction of the innocent.

CHAPTER 6

Mistaken Identifications

In the previous chapter we saw some of the problems of facial recall and recognition and considered a number of ways in which difficulties can arise. In this chapter we will look in more detail at mistaken identifications and review some commonly used identification procedures. It is hoped that by studying such procedures, and by examining the occasions on which things have gone wrong, recommendations can be made which might reduce the number of mistaken identifications.

When the Criminal Justice System gets it wrong and an innocent person is convicted there is, understandably, a great deal of concern. Many of those both within and outside the system might agree with the oft quoted adage that "it is better that one hundred guilty men go free than that one innocent man is convicted". However, the reality is that things can and do go wrong and that some innocent people do end up in prison. One such case highlighted by Wrightsman (1991) is that of Father Bernard T. Pagano. Pagano was accused of having committed a number of robberies in the state of Delaware, USA. These crimes were distinctive as the robber frequently apologised to his victims during the crime, resulting in the perpetrator being labelled as the "Gentleman Bandit". The police published a composite picture of the robber based on the witnesses' descriptions and an anonymous caller suggested that the drawing resembled Father Bernard T. Pagano, the assistant pastor of a Catholic church in Bethesda, Maryland. Despite protesting his innocence, Pagano was arrested and subsequently charged with the crimes. At his trial no fewer than seven victims positively identified him as being the robber. Apart from the eyewitness testimony, there was little other evidence linking Pagano with the crimes, but as each witness identified him, a conviction looked increasingly likely.

However, during Pagano's trial a man who was already serving a sentence in prison came forward and confessed to the crimes. He was some 15 years younger than Pagano, but was otherwise very similar in appearance. This man was subsequently charged with the crimes and Pagano was released. However, one is left to wonder how seven different witnesses could all have mistakenly identified Pagano as the robber.

It seems likely that if the real robber had not come forward when he did, Pagano would have been convicted and have served time in prison. Logie, Baddeley and Woodhead (1987) suggest that the chances that a member of the public will correctly identify a person from a facial reconstruction are almost negligible, yet the police persist in using this tactic.

In most cases, eyewitness misidentifications represent a double failure of the legal system: not only is an innocent person convicted, but the guilty person is still at liberty and free to commit further crimes. Putting an exact figure on the error rate is, however, very difficult (see Huff, 1987). Prisons contain a large number of people who claim to be innocent, though it is almost impossible to identify what proportion of these claims are genuine. It is also likely that a number of those who are acquitted at court may in fact have committed the crimes of which they were accused. Huff (1987) conducted an impressive survey of a large number of people involved in the Criminal Justice System in the USA. He found that over 70% of those surveyed believed that the error rate with regard to convictions was less than 1%. A further 20% of respondents believed that the rate was somewhere between 1 and 5%. From this study, Huff concluded that perhaps only 0.5% of cases result in the wrongful conviction of an accused. This figure might appear reassuringly low, but in real terms it is in fact quite worrying. Cutler and Penrod (1995) point out that even if the error rate is as low as 0.5%, some 7,500 people in the USA will be erroneously convicted of a serious offence each year.

There are many ways in which things can go wrong, but the incorrect identification of a suspect is perhaps one of the leading factors. Huff (1987) estimated that eyewitness error was an important factor in almost 60% of the 500 cases of wrongful conviction which he studied. Many recent successful appeals against conviction have centred upon questionable identification procedures.

As was noted earlier, there are a large number of documented cases where apparently well-intentioned witnesses have made mistakes and an innocent person has been convicted (see Cutler & Penrod, 1995; Sporer, Malpass & Koehnken, 1996; Wagenaar, 1988). In May 1974, following a number of celebrated cases of wrongful conviction, the British Home Office appointed Lord Devlin to chair a committee to examine identification procedures. The committee's report was published in 1976 and its main recommendation was that cases where identification was the only evidence against an accused should not normally proceed. If prosecutions did proceed then they should lead to failure. Devlin also recommended that if such cases were brought to court, the judge should be bound to warn the jury of the dangers of conviction on identification evidence alone. Commenting on his report in 1982, Lord Devlin noted that:

"Like most official reports, most of its recommendations have been officially ignored." (In Shepherd, Ellis & Davies, 1982, p. vi)

Devlin believed that whilst some psychological research had addressed issues of eyewitness misidentifications, it was difficult to draw conclusions from this largely laboratory-based work. Indeed, Devlin concluded in a rather pessimistic tone:

"It has been represented to us that a gap exists between academic research into the powers of the human mind and the practical requirements of courts of law, and the stage seems not yet to have been reached at which the conclusions of psychological research are sufficiently widely accepted or tailored to the needs of the judicial process to become the basis for procedural change." (Devlin Report, 1976, p. 71)

Clifford and Bull (1978) took issue with this view and set about trying to demonstrate that the results of psychological research were in fact both relevant and applicable. In the 20 years since the Devlin Report's publication, a massive amount of research has been carried out into the problem of mistaken identifications, and some relatively minor procedural changes have been introduced. However, Devlin's main recommendation was not implemented, and some accused are still being convicted almost exclusively on the basis of eyewitness testimony. Despite a significant amount of psychological research to the contrary, there remains a view in some legal circles that well-intentioned and confident witnesses are unlikely to be mistaken. Jurors may also be convinced by such testimony and convict an innocent accused.

Such a case was highlighted by Cutler and Penrod (1995). Shaun Deckinga was accused of robbing a number of banks in the state of Minnesota. A rather blurry picture of the robber had been shown on local television and a caller had named Deckinga as the culprit. Although there was a small amount of circumstantial evidence, Deckinga was convicted mainly because three bank tellers who had been robbed identified him as being the perpetrator. The three tellers all said that they were either positive or fairly sure that they had identified the right man and this had a significant impact on the jury. One juror is quoted as saying, "He was identified: that's what made the biggest impression on most of us. The tellers said he did it" (quoted in Cutler & Penrod, 1995, p. 4). In this case, the trial judge refused permission for the defence to call an expert witness (Steven Penrod himself) to talk about identification evidence, and Deckinga was convicted of two of the robberies. However, whilst Deckinga was in jail, another almost identical robbery was carried out and a clearer picture of this robber was sent to law enforcement officials. One prison guard identified the robber as

Jerry Clapper, a former inmate. Clapper was arrested and admitted committing a number of robberies including those for which Deckinga had been convicted. As a result, Deckinga was released from prison.

A recent case in Britain (described in *The Guardian*, 25 February 1993) further highlights the problem. In October 1992 a London taxi driver was abducted at gunpoint, and a bomb placed in his cab. Under threat, the driver was told to take the bomb to Downing Street (the Prime Minister's residence) and to leave it there. The cab was driven to Whitehall where the bomb exploded. Patrick Murphy was arrested for the crime despite pleading his innocence. He was so sure that his mistaken arrest would quickly be rectified that he declined the offer of legal representation, and agreed to take part in an identification parade. Three people, including the abducted cab driver, picked Murphy out from the parade and the Crown Prosecution Service commenced proceedings against him. However, Murphy believed that at the time of the hijacking he had been at a meeting of Alcoholics Anonymous. He was in fact able to produce eleven witnesses who were willing to testify that he had been at the meeting at the time, and so could not have committed the crime. Faced with this evidence the CPS agreed to drop the charges against Murphy.

In all of the cases highlighted above, it would appear that mistakes were made and that witnesses simply got it wrong. But it might be reasonable to ask how, in each of these cases, could a number of different witnesses each make a mistake and identify the wrong person. As we saw in Chapter 5, facial recognition and identification is a complex process fraught with potential difficulties and problems. Even so, we might reasonably presume that witnesses who are confident in their identifications are unlikely to be completely wrong. However, despite what jurors might believe, there is often little correlation between witness confidence and witness accuracy (see Chapter 3).

Some explanation for mistaken identifications might be found in the procedures which are used to try to identify a suspect. For this reason we will turn now to an examination of the most common identification procedures and assess the advantages and disadvantages of each. We will see that each procedure may contain biases which might partly explain some of the mistakes made by witnesses.

PHOTOFITS AND OTHER FACIAL COMPOSITE SYSTEMS

When a witness sees, but does not recognise, a perpetrator committing a crime, he or she may be asked by the police to try to provide a detailed description of the assailant. However, as we saw in the previous chapter, most witnesses will not find this easy. A number of techniques have been developed in an attempt to assist witnesses to produce a description or an image of a suspect. The best known of these is the Photofit system, which was first published in the UK in 1970. In this method, the witness firstly provides a verbal description of a suspect's features. A trained operator can then use this description to direct the witness to a number of alternatives for each facial feature. Thus there may be 30 alternative chin shapes and the witness can choose the one which best matches that of the perpetrator. Proceeding in this way, the witness and operator are able to build up a picture which is a general likeness of the perpetrator. Once built up, minor amendments can be made to the composite face until the witness is satisfied with the general result.

More recently other systems similar to the Photofit have been developed. These include the *Minolta Montage Synthesizer, Mac-A-Mug, Identi-Kit III* and *EFIT*. All serve a similar purpose, but use computer databases and/or graphics packages to assist in generating images. None of the systems is claimed to produce an exact photographic facsimile of a suspect, but all are designed to produce a type likeness. Thus a Photofit picture in itself does not normally allow investigators to make a positive identification of a suspect; rather it allows them to recognise the sort of person they are looking for, and possibly to rule out a number of suspects whose appearance is completely different from that of the Photofit. Although the Photofit and subsequent systems have their uses, they are not a panacea for the many difficulties encountered by eyewitnesses trying to provide descriptions. One difficulty is that witnesses tend not to perceive a face as a collection of attributes, but rather as a whole image (see Deffenbacher, 1989). Thus, as we saw in the previous chapter, asking a witness to provide accurate details of individual features may be unrealistic.

An alternative to the Photofit method is to employ an artist to construct a drawing of a face which matches the description provided by the witness. This method may be seen as less scientific than some of the other techniques used, but it does allow more flexibility. In addition it enables the artist to translate and record some of the less tangible impressions which a witness may describe. For example, a witness may recall little detail of an assailant's individual facial features, but may say that the attacker had a rather ugly and menacing appearance. The artist may be able to produce an image which represents this and the witness then be asked to amend or add to the picture to provide more detail. Some police forces employ artists on an ad hoc basis, whilst others train their own officers in the skills needed. Because of this wide variation in practice, evaluations of the method as a whole have proved difficult.

Many of the methods described above are in use today in a number of different countries. However, there have been comparatively few evaluations of the usefulness of the various techniques, and in particular few attempts to establish whether one method is inherently better than any other. As Kapardis (1997, p. 246) notes:

"Evaluation data on the operational effectiveness of face composites is rather scarce. Despite what some police members may think, the available empirical evidence indicates that such face composites only contribute to the apprehension of offenders in a small minority of cases."

Research has identified that any system is only as good as its operator, and that skilled operators may have more success than unskilled. Good communication between the witness and the operator also appears to be an important factor. However, research to date does not allow psychologists to recommend one technique unequivocally. As Shepherd and Ellis (1996) point out, each technique has both advantages and disadvantages but none produces successful identification rates anywhere near to 100%. Perhaps we should therefore acknowledge that whilst the techniques can be useful, they also have their limitations. We should also be aware that the interaction between the witness and a Photofit operator or artist may interfere with an original memory and make its subsequent recovery even more difficult (see Lindsay et al., 1994).

MUGSHOT FILE INSPECTIONS

If a witness's description is insufficient to allow an identification to be made, he or she may well be asked to inspect the so-called "mugshot file". This is a collection of photographs of people who have come to the notice of the police and who have previous convictions for offences similar to the one under investigation. The thinking behind this procedure is that witnesses who are unable to provide a detailed description of an offender may still be able to recognise the person if they see his or her face again. Indeed it may be quite common for witnesses to claim that although they cannot recall specific details of an offender's appearance, they would certainly recognise him or her if they saw the face again.

Although useful, there are a number of problems associated with the use of mugshot files as a form of identification. Firstly, the files only contain photographs of those people who have previously come to the notice of the police. If an assailant has no previous convictions for a particular type of crime, his or her photograph will not be available for inspection. In theory this should mean that a witness will simply report that the attacker's face is not present in the mugshot file. However, in the real world of criminal investigation, witnesses may be encouraged to peruse the files again and feel pressurised to pick out someone from the large number of photographs. This strategy is obviously inappropriate, especially when one considers some research which suggests that the more photographs a witness examines, the more likely it is that he or she will pick out the wrong person (see Davies, Shepherd & Ellis, 1979; Ellis *et al.*, 1989). Wells (1988) recommended that witnesses should be asked to examine no more than 50 mugshots at any one time. This may, however, be impractical in real-life identification attempts where the police may have a very large number of photographs on file, and would find it difficult to edit out some suspects. It should also be borne in mind that some types of crime are very rare and thus police mugshot files would contain relatively few photographs. By contrast, other types are much more common, and the police files might contain literally thousands of photographs.

This latter fact has prompted some researchers to try to develop an alternative to the traditional mugshot search. In a normal mugshot inspection procedure, a witness may have to search through literally hundreds of photographs in an attempt to identify an assailant. Much of this effort will be wasted as many photographs will bear little or no resemblance to the assailant. An alternative is to have each offender's features rated on a number of dimensions and the data stored on a computer database. A witness may then be asked to provide similar ratings of the particular suspect, and a list of offenders matching these criteria can be produced from the database. Such a procedure may result in the witness perusing a much smaller number of photographs than in a normal mugshot search.

These procedures are in their infancy, but early results are encouraging (see Shepherd & Ellis, 1996, p. 109). One should, however, bear in mind that this development can only work if the witness's memory of facial features is accurate and if the assailant's appearance today is similar to when his or her mugshot photograph was taken. As we have seen in previous chapters, it is not uncommon for witnesses to be mistaken in their beliefs as to what they think they saw. No computer program can compensate for the fact that a witness may actually be completely mistaken in his or her memory of an important facial feature. Such a mistake may mean that although an assailant's face is on the database it is never presented to the witness for inspection.

If the police have a suspect in mind, they may be tempted to try to draw the attention of the witness to this person in the files. Such dubious practices would, of course, be frowned upon but may go unrecorded in the case file. If mistakes are made at this stage, it may not be so easy to rectify them later. Once an assailant has supposedly been identified, the police may be unlikely to consider the possibility that a mistake has been made and will be reluctant to consider other lines of enquiry. As has been pointed out elsewhere, by labelling a person as a suspect the police may subsequently reinterpret any further information about that person or any actions which he or she performs (see Ainsworth, 1995c). Although an accused should only be seen as the *alleged* perpetrator until his or her conviction, in the eyes of the police, guilt may be presumed at a much earlier stage and information reinterpreted to fit the picture.

In this connection, the police may decide that a witness who picks out a suspect from the mugshot files should later be asked to try to pick out the person from a photo array, or from a formal identification parade. However, as was pointed out in the previous chapter, such a procedure is inherently flawed. Witnesses will tend to want to appear consistent in their decisions, and thus will be likely to pick out from the photo array or ID parade the same person whom they picked out from the mugshot files. This tendency was demonstrated in an interesting study by Brigham and Cairns (1988). These researchers found that if subject witnesses made an incorrect identification from the mugshot files, this error would be carried forward to the photo array, and witnesses would pick out the same (incorrect) photograph. Conversely, subject witnesses who incorrectly rejected the target face in the mugshots tended also to incorrectly reject the target in the subsequent photo array. Various other writers have pointed out that a witness who picks out the same person from a subsequent photo array or ID parade may simply be demonstrating consistency rather than accuracy (see Cutler & Penrod, 1995, p. 107). It would be naive and entirely inappropriate to assume that because a witness picks out the same person twice, it is somehow twice as likely that he or she is correct.

Lindsay *et al.* (1994) have pointed out that although mugshot searches do pose some difficulties, they can serve some useful purpose. In their studies they found that a variety of mugshot procedures each allowed witnesses to eliminate a very high proportion of the photographs presented, and to reduce the pool of possible suspect photographs to a much more manageable number. Lindsay *et al.* (1994) also point out that mugshot file searches have some advantages over other identification procedures. For example, because mugshots are presented sequentially, the witness will tend not to make relative judgements. This is in contrast to, say, an identification parade where all faces can be examined simultaneously and the one which most resembles the suspect is chosen. This is an important point to which we will return later in the chapter.

Lindsay *et al.* also point out that, unlike selection at an identification parade, the witness can pick out more than one person as a possible suspect; the police can then investigate the suspects and decide which person is most likely to be the perpetrator. Lindsay *et al.* (1994) do draw attention to the fact that a mugshot identification in itself should not be used as proof of a person's guilt and so may still protect the innocent. However, as was pointed out earlier, there is a danger that the police will see such an identification as positive proof, try to build a case against this person, and disregard any alternative hypotheses.

FORMAL IDENTIFICATION PROCEDURES: SHOW-UPS

The police will tend to use mugshot searches on those occasions when they have little idea as to who may have committed a particular crime. There will, however, be many other cases where the police do have an idea of the person who has probably committed a crime, but require confirmation of this suspicion. There will be other cases where the police are absolutely convinced that a particular individual is responsible for an offence, but need further proof before proceedings can be brought. In these circumstances, the police will use one of a number of methods to ascertain that the suspect is indeed the person who committed the crime. These techniques include formal identification parades, photospreads, and what are referred to as "show-ups". In this latter case, a witness will be allowed to see a suspect (live or in a photograph) and will then be asked whether the person is indeed the perpetrator.

Show-ups are the most simple and yet least satisfactory form of identification, as they are likely to lead to a large number of misidentifications (see Kassin, Ellsworth & Smith, 1989). Unlike ID parades or photospreads, showups tend to put pressure on a witness to identify a particular individual. Witnesses, especially those who are victims, may be highly motivated to try to identify an assailant, and if given a choice of only one suspect may be more likely to claim that they do recognise the person as the perpetrator. This tendency may be exaggerated if the police pressurise the witness or lead him or her to believe that this is the right person, but only require the witness to confirm this formally (see Wagenaar & Veefkind, 1992).

Perhaps surprisingly, witnesses who are given only one choice of suspect (for example, via a photo show-up) are not necessarily very accurate. In one study (Yarmey, 1992) witnesses were shown a photograph of a person with whom they had interacted only 2 minutes earlier. Only 57% of such witnesses correctly identified the photograph as being that of the person just encountered. Interestingly, those subject witnesses who were shown a photograph which was not of the same person whom they had met earlier correctly rejected the picture on 87% of occasions.

This study suggests that whilst show-ups may be suggestive and biased they may not even lead to a high level of correct identification (see also Gonzalez, Ellsworth & Pembroke, 1993). Having said that, Yarmey is quick to point out that his research should not be interpreted as offering tacit approval for one-person show-ups. It would appear that in the Yarmey study little pressure was put on witnesses to identify the person seen earlier. In the real world of criminal investigation, this may not be the case (see Wrightsman, 1991, p. 138).

Despite the obvious shortcomings of show-ups and the inherent dangers of misidentification, courts do not necessarily ban such procedures. In America, show-up evidence is often allowed, providing that the identification is otherwise reliable. As Lipton has noted recently:

"Perhaps the bottom line with showups, as with all identifications, is that even if the identification procedure is suggestive, it will be allowed so long as it is 'reliable'." (Lipton, 1996, p. 17)

The legal status of show-ups is not, however, straightforward. Courts in New York and Illinois tend not to allow such procedures, whilst other American states only permit such evidence in specified circumstances. In Britain, show-ups are discouraged but not necessarily banned. In one case (Rogers, 1993) the Court of Appeal ruled that an identification in which two witnesses were taken to view and identify a single suspect was acceptable. Judges in this case pointed out that it would make criminal investigations very difficult if the police had to arrest every person who matched a witness's description, and then put him or her on an ID parade. For this reason, the "show-up" identification was considered appropriate in this case and was accepted.

One particular form of a show-up is where a witness formally identifies an assailant in court. Whilst giving sworn testimony, witnesses may, for example, be asked: "Do you see the man who assaulted you in court today?" Most witnesses will have little difficulty with this, as the accused will be the only person in the dock, or be the person seated at the side of the defence counsel. The Devlin Committee (1976) suggested that courtroom identifications served little evidential purpose and should only be used in cases where the identity of an accused was not in doubt. In the USA, courtroom identifications may still be allowed but may be ruled inappropriate in some circumstances (e.g. where the defendant is the only black person in the courtroom, or where the witness had failed to pick out the accused on a previous ID parade). Lipton (1996) tells of a number of lawyers who have tried to counter the biases inherent in courtroom identifications. For example, some attorneys have instructed a confederate to sit next to them in court and told the accused to sit elsewhere in the courtroom. Whilst psychologists might not disapprove of such tactics, American courts do not generally condone such practices. In one case, a defence attorney was cited for contempt of court for trying such a ploy (United States v. Thoreen, 1981; cited in Lipton, 1996, p. 17).

Dock identifications are clearly unfair and should never be accepted as the only evidence of identification. In an interesting case cited by Wrightsman (1991, p. 139), an accused by the name of Richard M. Nance was identified as the perpetrator in court by a burglary victim. However, as the accused was already labelled as the defendant and was wearing a bright orange jail suit, this could hardly be viewed as an objective and fair identification. In a rare case where a courtroom identification went wrong (cited by Wrightsman, 1991, p. 139), two US Park Police officers pointed to the defence attorney rather than the accused as being the person they had earlier seen committing an offence. The misidentification appears to have been partly caused by the fact that, for the second police officer's testimony, the defence attorney had moved his notepad and papers in front of the accused and instructed him to make copious notes!

PHOTOSPREAD IDENTIFICATIONS

We have seen that mugshot searches and single show-ups are not particularly good ways of testing a witness's identification accuracy. Both systems are flawed and can lead to a significant number of misidentifications. An alternative and theoretically better method is the so-called photospread. This resembles a traditional identification parade in that the witness has to try to identify the suspect from an array of faces. Such a procedure may well be used when the police have a particular suspect in mind but require the witness to confirm their suspicions by identifying the suspect. Unlike traditional identification parades, the suspect is not viewed live, but rather his or her still photograph is shown along with other similar photographs. The witness is instructed to inspect the photographs and, if anyone is recognised, to state who it is and from where he or she knows the face.

Photospreads clearly have advantages over a single photograph show-up, as they force the witness to look at a number of choices and to reject a number of possible alternatives. Photospreads may also be more desirable than mugshot inspections as the witness will have a much smaller number of photographs to examine, and each photograph should at least resemble the description of the suspect. Photospreads may also have an advantage over live identification parades if a witness is particularly nervous and is likely to be intimidated by the presence of the alleged perpetrator (see Ainsworth & King, 1988). For this reason, photospreads may be seen as preferable to ID parades when the witness is a young child.

Photospreads do, however, have a number of disadvantages. Firstly, the fact that a witness has to examine a static photograph of a person whom he or she originally saw "live" may lead to difficulties (see Cutler *et al.*, 1994). This may be a particular problem if the suspect's appearance has changed since the photograph was taken, or if the photograph is a poor-quality black and white frontal shot. The exact construction of photospreads will obviously vary from case to case but most countries impose safeguards to try to ensure that the procedure is as fair as possible. For example, in Britain there are a number of rules which specify the format of photospread identifications. One such rule states that the photospread must contain not less than 12 photographs, and that each foil should be of roughly similar age and appearance to the suspect (see Shepherd, Ellis & Davies, 1982).

Psychologists have attempted to assess whether photospreads are an appropriate method of attempting to identify a suspect (see Cutler *et al.*, 1994). A number of studies have shown that in certain circumstances photospreads can produce accurate results. However, the procedure can also lead to both a failure to recognise a target person and to misidentifications. Many early laboratory-based studies showed that subjects could be quite good at identifying a face which they had seen earlier. However, many of these early tests were somewhat lacking in ecological validity as subjects were asked simply to recognise the actual photograph which they had seen earlier. In real criminal cases, the witness would of course have first viewed the target person live and might then be asked to identify him or her from a still photograph.

The other problem with many early studies was that the target person's picture was always present in the subsequent line-up. Again in the "real world" there would be at least some occasions when the real suspect's photograph was not in the array. Studies have shown that children in particular may have great difficulty when faced with a so-called "target absent" array (see Yuille, Cutshall & King, 1986; Davies, Stevenson-Robb & Flin, 1988). For these reasons it has not always been possible to make predictions as to the likely accuracy of witnesses' photospread identifications in the real world. After reviewing a large number of studies, Cutler *et al.*, (1994) conclude that photospreads produce identification performances which are similar to those found with both videotaped and live identification parades. However, these writers warn that it would be naive to presume that photospreads should thus be seen as no worse than conventional, live ID parades. We must bear in mind that many of the studies on which Cutler's findings were based involved subjects merely trying to recognise a photograph which they had seen earlier. As most genuine witnesses will have seen a real live, walking, talking, moving suspect, photospreads may not be quite so effective as identification parades.

A further problem when trying to evaluate photospreads is the fact that the level of difficulty incvitably varics from one study to another. Some studies have, for example, used a small number of foils all of which bear comparatively little resemblance to the target face. At the other extreme, some studies have used a much larger number of foils all of which are quite similar to the target person. There are other important variables which will determine identification accuracy. These include the length of time a person had to view the target face, and the length of time that has elapsed between viewing the face and being tested for recognition (see Shepherd, 1983). For these reasons it is not possible to make a definitive statement as to the likely accuracy of identifications employing photospreads. Although a large number of variables have been examined, only the retention interval (i.e the time between viewing and testing) seems to emerge consistently as an important variable (see Cutler & Penrod, 1995, p. 110).

If there are large differences in the laboratory-based studies, then there may be even more variation in those real criminal cases in which photospreads are used. Whilst variations do occur in laboratory studies, researchers are at least able to control many of the important variables. In real criminal investigations, such luxuries are rarely possible. For this reason there may well be important differences between the results of laboratory studies and the likely results in the real world.

Although, as noted earlier, some authorities lay down strict guidelines as to the conduct of photospreads, there will be inevitable variations in practice. Those charged with the duty of solving crimes may be tempted to make a witness's task easier by, for example, choosing foils whose appearance is distinctly different from the target (see Wagenaar, 1988, p. 119 for an interesting example of this). Others may even resort to giving hints to a witness who is experiencing difficulty! Some witnesses who had earlier picked out a suspect from a mugshot search may later be asked to pick out the same photograph from a photospread. The vast majority of witnesses will, of course, pick out the same photograph, though, as noted earlier, this certainly does not mean that they are accurate (see Brown, Deffenbacher & Sturgill, 1977; Gorenstein & Ellsworth, 1980; Read, 1994).

Many of the conditions which apply to the fair conduct of photospreads also apply to the conduct of identification parades. For this reason we will now consider some of the ways in which identification parades can produce both accurate and inaccurate results.

IDENTIFICATION PARADES (LINE-UPS)

Identification parades provide perhaps the most dramatic example of the way in which a witness might be called upon to identify a perpetrator. Traditional ID parades involve the witness viewing a line-up containing the suspect, plus a number of foils (or distracters) whose appearance should be roughly similar to that of the suspect. In Britain at least, legislation requires that the foils should be of similar age, height, general appearance and position in life as the suspect (see McKenzie, 1995). As was pointed out earlier, ID parades may have advantages over mugshot searches or photospreads as they allow a witness to see the suspect live and even to observe a varied sample of his or her behaviour. However, ID parades are also fraught with many potential dangers and the conduct of the parade itself can lead to misidentification (see Ross, Read & Toglia, 1994, chs 8–11). For this reason, ID parades have been the subject of a great deal of psychological research, some of which will be summarised briefly below.

One line of research has examined whether the number of foils on an ID parade might affect the accuracy of any identification (see, for example, Malpass & Devine, 1983; Nosworthy & Lindsay, 1990). It is perhaps surprising to learn that there is wide variation in the number of foils used on different parades. Authorities in Britain recommend that at least seven foils should be used, whilst in the USA the minimum number generally accepted is five. Many other countries do not specify an absolute minimum number. The issue would appear to be an important one, as theoretically the more foils there are on the parade the less likely it is that the suspect will be identified. If the parade contains only four people, then the suspect has a 25% chance of being identified by the witness – if it contains 10 people then the chances fall to 10%. The crucial point is that a line-up should be of such a size that the probability of a chance identification of an innocent suspect is relatively low. Having said that, as Wells et al. (1994, p. 229) note:

> "There is no threshold number below which the dangers of false identification are significant and above which they are not."

Research suggests that it is not necessary to have a very large number of foils present in order to make any identification fair. Wells et al. (1994) recommend that a line-up should contain at least five foils plus the suspect. There is, however, some debate as to whether the number of foils on a parade should be seen as an appropriate measure of fairness (see for example, Brigham & Pfeiffer, 1994).

Perhaps the number of people in the line-up is less important than its composition. As with photospreads, the similarity of the foils to the suspect may be a crucial determinant of whether or not a witness is able to identify the perpetrator. Thus although a line-up might contain five foils, it would hardly be considered fair if the appearance of two of these foils was completely different from that of the suspect. The effective (as opposed to the actual) size of such a line-up should thus be measured as three rather than five (see Brigham & Pfeiffer, 1994, for a detailed discussion of this notion). Some of the variation in hit rates across research studies can be accounted for by the similarity or dissimilarity of foils to the target person. Psychologists and legal authorities may both recommend that only appropriate foils should be used, but it is rather difficult to determine exactly what might be considered appropriate or inappropriate.

Perhaps the crucial question is: *how* similar to the suspect does a foil need to be before he or she should be included? Should the police select as foils only those whose appearance matches the original verbal description given by the witness, or should they select foils whose appearance is similar to that of the actual suspect on the parade? Whilst there will be some overlap between these options they will not necessarily lead to the same foils being chosen. There are further complications which also deserve some comment. For example, if a suspect has an unusual or highly distinctive appearance it will be difficult to find appropriate foils. Most police forces now hold lists of people willing to act as foils and can select from a fairly large pool. (This is a marked improvement on previous practice where, in some cases, off-duty police officers were used as foils). However, there will still be occasions when it will prove difficult to find suitable and appropriate foils.

A further complication concerns the amount of detail which a witness might provide in describing a suspect. A witness who provides a very vague description of a suspect may be faced with an ID parade which contains people of widely differing appearance. However, a witness who provides a very detailed description of a suspect may face a parade of people whose appearance is remarkably similar. Thus, paradoxically, a witness who provides the best verbal description of a suspect may face a much more difficult task than a witness with a more vague recollection.

The choice of foils for any identification task is thus of crucial importance. The police may wish to make the witness's task as easy as possible by selecting foils whose appearance differs in some significant way from that of the suspect (see Lindsay, 1994a). At the other end of the spectrum, a suspect's legal representative may try to ensure that the parade contains only those foils whose appearance is very similar to the accused. A number of criminal cases have involved lengthy legal debates as to whether an identification parade was or was not fair. Despite the vast amount of psychological research examining the subject, it is still not possible to establish clear and unequivocal criteria as to what exactly constitutes a fair or unfair identification task. Having said that, many countries do now have guidelines as to the conduct of ID parades. Such guidelines may have eliminated some of the more questionable tactics used in the past, but as some recent cases of wrongful conviction have shown, there is still room for bias and error to creep in.

A further problem with ID parades concerns the witness's attitude towards the parade. Many "witnesses" will in fact be victims and as such may be highly motivated to try to pick out their assailant. If the assailant is on the parade then this motivation may serve to increase the likelihood that a correct identification will be made. However, if the real assailant is not on the parade the witness may still want to try to help the police to solve the case, and as such may identify someone. The police will probably have arrested a suspect who matches the description given by the witness. As such the witness may survey the line-up and identify the person who comes closest to his or her memory. Research in the laboratory has suggested that when faced with a "target absent" ID parade, subject witnesses often pick out someone rather than admit that they cannot identify the person seen earlier. Laboratory studies may thus underestimate the number of occasions on which real witnesses identify a person on the parade even though the true target is not present. Subjects in laboratory-based simulated crimes will generally have significantly less motivation than a victim of an actual crime. Even those studies which have used a life-like crime simulation have still tended to use subjects who are uninvolved bystanders rather than crime victims.

In theory, witnesses are expected to look at each face in the line-up individually and to decide whether or not it is the face of the perpetrator. In practice, witnesses may well survey the line as a whole, and discount each of those present one by one, until only one person is left. Thomson (1995) has described the process as similar to a multiple choice exam question. The witness may not be totally convinced that this person is the real culprit, but may feel that he or she is the most likely person from those presented on the line-up. In recognition of this tendency, witnesses in Britain and in many other countries, are warned that "The person who you saw may or may not be on the parade." However such a warning may not completely override the tendency for a highly motivated witness to try to pick out someone from the parade. If the witness were simply guessing then there would be an equal chance that he or she would pick out one of the foils. However, as we saw earlier, some foils may be so dissimilar from the target that they can be rejected easily. Thus, even on an eight-person line-up the chances of the witness picking out the (innocent) suspect may be much greater than one in eight.

One way in which some of these problems could be addressed is to prevent the witness from viewing the whole parade at the same time. Under this idea, witnesses would be simply asked to look at a number of faces sequentially. As each face was presented the witness would have to say whether or not the face was that of the perpetrator. This procedure may be a somewhat subtle shift from the normal format, but may represent a significant improvement. Identification parades are ostensibly to establish whether or not a witness can recognise the face of a person who has committed a specified crime. Sequential presentation makes it much more likely that this is the decision that will be made. In the traditional identification parade, the witness can make a different kind of decision, i.e. which person on the parade looks most like the person who committed the crime? Sequential presentations may well reduce this tendency towards identification by default. There is now considerable research evidence to suggest that sequential presentation does indeed reduce significantly the number of misidentifications (see Cutler & Penrod, 1995; Thomson, 1995). Despite this, most countries appear reluctant to adopt such a procedure.

Wells *et al.* (1994) have proposed that, as an alternative to sequential presentation, a witness might be asked to examine two parades, one in which the suspect is present, and one in which he or she is not. This procedure would again reduce the chances that a witness may make an informed guess rather than consider each face separately. Interestingly, this suggestion was considered by the Devlin Committee (Devlin Report, 1976) but ultimately rejected.

A further problem with ID parades concerns the actions of the suspect. A suspect is allowed to choose his or her own position in the line, and the suspect (or his or her legal representative) can make limited challenges to the composition of the parade. However, the suspect has little further control over proceedings and may well feel extremely nervous about the whole procedure. It would certainly be reasonable to assume that his or her mental state will be somewhat different from that of the foils on the parade. Unlike the suspect, the foils have absolutely nothing to lose by their presence (in fact they will probably be paid) and so may appear much calmer, confident and composed.

A witness who is undecided as to whether or not the assailant is on the parade may notice these subtle differences in non-verbal behaviour and pick out the one person whose demeanour differs from the rest of the participants on the parade. One might cynically ask whether this is a problem, as the real suspect deserves to "sweat". However, an innocent suspect who has been wrongfully detained by the police may also be very nervous about attending the parade, knowing that his or her liberty is at stake. This anxiety may be construed as guilt by a witness and result in the nervous yet innocent suspect being picked out as the culprit. Similar problems may arise if a suspect has been detained for several days, been deprived of sleep and generally been made to feel vulnerable by investigating officers. Such actions may serve to make the suspect stand out from others on the parade and again lead the witness to believe that this person must be the guilty party.

If suspects are nervous about identification parades, witnesses may also have anxieties about the procedure. Many will have suffered at the hands of an attacker, and will be understandably nervous at the prospect of perhaps seeing the person again. Witnesses may also experience some anxiety about whether they will be able to identify the right person on the parade. Fear of failure may be heightened when coupled with a strong desire to see the attacker brought to justice. Witnesses may also fear reprisals from their attacker, and may have been threatened or intimidated before attending the parade. Some of these problems might be addressed if witnesses saw a videotaped (as opposed to live) identification parade. Such procedures have been used in some countries and early findings suggest that this test medium yields results similar to live parades (see Cutler *et al.*, 1994).

One British piece of research (Ainsworth & King, 1988) looked at real witnesses who attended ID parades in northern England and asked them about their experience. One interesting finding from this survey was that witnesses who admitted to being nervous about attending the ID parade were significantly less likely to pick out the suspect than were witnesses who did not admit to being nervous. Similarly, those witnesses who admitted that they feared reprisals were significantly less likely to identify the suspect than those who did not have such fears. These findings do suggest that there would be some benefit in trying to calm anxious witnesses and in trying to reassure them as to the likelihood of reprisals. Information about witness protection programmes may also help to reassure the victim or witness and make their task slightly more bearable. Despite the research showing the link between stress and inaccurate recall (see Chapter 3), very few practical steps are taken in an attempt to make the witness's task less stressful.

The Ainsworth and King research was carried out at a time when one-way screens were not routinely used and the witness had to be in the same room as the alleged perpetrator. This fact can only have added to the witness's feelings of anxiety over the procedure. It is not so long ago that witnesses in Britain were told that if they did see the perpetrator on the parade they should indicate who he or she was by tapping him or her on the shoulder. One can only guess at the amount of stress that such an instruction would generate in the witness, especially if the crime had been of a personal or sexual nature.

The Ainsworth and King study established that part of witnesses' anxieties stemmed from their ignorance of procedures. Significant numbers of witnesses said that it would have been helpful to have some notes of guidance, explaining in advance what was expected of them. Such notes may well be helpful, but their contents may come under scrutiny by defence lawyers keen to establish any evidence of bias in the procedures. A number of researchers have pointed out that simply telling a witness that the culprit *is* in the line-up leads to higher rates of mistaken identification (see, for example, Cutler, Penrod & Martens, 1987). However, as Kapardis (1997, p. 253) notes:

> "On the basis of the existing empirical evidence, we can conclude that a biassed instructions effect has indeed been demonstrated but the way it operates is not as simple as first thought."

CONCLUDING COMMENTS

It can be seen from this chapter that psychologists have made valuable discoveries with regard to some of the reasons why mistaken identifications occur. Drawing on this research, a number of psychologists have made proposals as to how identification parades might be better conducted. Space does not permit a detailed review of all of these proposals, but the interested reader may wish to consult Wells *et al.* (1994) and Wagenaar (1988, ch. 3). The latter source provides a fascinating insight into how things went wrong in one particular high profile case in which John Demjanjuk was mistakenly identified as being "Ivan the Terrible" (see also Sheftel, 1996). Wagenaar claims that there can be few cases in history in which so many basic rules of identification procedures were broken. Yet the court in Cleveland which allowed Demjanjuk's extradition to Israel refused to allow expert testimony on eyewitness identification. The court in Jerusalem which found Demjanjuk guilty allowed the defence to call such an expert, but then declared that "the testimony was irrelevant because the surviving witnesses could not make mistakes" (Wagenaar, 1988, p. ix). Demjanjuk's successful appeal against conviction served only to highlight the dangers of criminal courts' reliance on identification procedures which are fundamentally flawed or at least highly suspect.

CHAPTER 7

Improving Witness Recall

Throughout this book we have seen that eyewitnesses are not always the reliable reporters of fact that the courts might like to believe. We have noted that witnesses routinely distort information, fail to encode certain aspects of a scene, fail to recall all that they witnessed, and make mistakes in what is retrieved from memory. As we saw in Chapters 3 and 4, there are a large number of both witness and event factors which can affect the likelihood that a witness's recall will be accurate and comprehensive. However, psychologists have now started to focus attention on whether anything can be done to improve recall through the way in which witnesses are interviewed.

Most witnesses will be interviewed initially by a police officer who will try to obtain as much relevant information as possible. However, only recently have police forces come to recognise that the way in which witnesses are interviewed can affect both the amount and the quality of the information retrieved. As has been noted elsewhere:

> "Many police officers will take the view that there are good witnesses and bad witnesses, and that any difference in the quality of their statements can be put down to the individual witness rather than the interviewing technique used." (Ainsworth, 1995a, p. 20)

Police forces traditionally have spent a great deal of time and effort training their officers how to interrogate suspects, but have paid scant attention to the way in which witnesses should be interviewed. Where training has been given, it has generally been concerned with teaching officers how to obtain the necessary evidence needed for a prosecution rather than with using the most appropriate interviewing style (see Malpass, 1996). However, over the last ten years many police forces in Britain, the USA and elsewhere have started to appreciate that different interviewing techniques can produce different results. As a consequence, many of today's police officers will have received some training in the use of appropriate styles of interviewing. This is important, as police officers who are trying to solve crimes rely a great deal on the information which witnesses provide.

As has been highlighted elsewhere in this book, there are many ways in which interviewers can be guilty of influencing the reports which witnesses give. In Chapter 4, for example, we saw that misleading information can all too easily be incorporated into a witness's memory and thus contaminate the original version of events. In Chapter 6 we saw some ways in which investigators may have influenced witnesses to the point where they made mistakes in identifying suspects. In Chapter 8 we will see the dangers of contaminating a witness's memory when hypnosis is used. In Chapter 9 we will see that children can be particularly vulnerable to inappropriate interviewing techniques.

However, simply avoiding the use of techniques which might contaminate memory may not in itself be sufficient. Rather, investigators need to be sure that they are using techniques which will also elicit the maximum amount of (reliable) information from each witness. In other words, police officers must recognise that there are ways in which witnesses can be encouraged to produce all that they know – and ways in which they might be discouraged. In this respect, psychologists have had a great deal to contribute and have been able to develop interviewing techniques which are ethical, appropriate and productive. Whilst traditionally the police service has been reluctant to accept advice from any "outsiders", police officers are likely to adopt techniques which prove to be useful in their day-to-day work. The police service is sometimes described as being "anecdote driven" – if a technique is seen to be useful it will tend to be adopted. This partly explains why interviewing styles have changed in recent years.

Whilst the successful interviewing of witnesses might not be perceived as one of the more glamorous areas of police work, it is a very important one. For, as the Rand Corporation study (1975) showed, the principal determinant of whether or not a case is solved is the completeness and accuracy of the eyewitness accounts. As some sociologists have noted, somewhat cynically, the police are very good at catching criminals, once someone has told them who has done it! The police rarely witness a crime being committed and so of necessity must rely largely on eyewitness accounts. Any technique which claims to improve the amount of information which a witness is likely to produce should thus be greeted warmly.

It must also be borne in mind that the majority of witnesses will have little idea as to what is expected of them. Most people are fortunate enough to witness at worst only one serious crime or one traffic accident in their lifetime. Thus they will rely on the police officer for guidance on what is required. For his or her part, the police officer may be interviewing witnesses almost every day and may forget that, for most witnesses and victims, making statements will be a novel experience. This imbalance in expertise will tend to mean that any suggestions which the officer makes will be accepted readily by the naive witness. Thus most statements will be written down (and reworded) by the police officer rather than by the witness (see Ainsworth, 1995a, ch. 2). Unlike interviews with suspects, witness interviews are not routinely tape recorded. For this reason, it is all but impossible to know the exact words which a witness may have used during the early stages of an interview; rather we have to rely on the statement which is produced following a lengthy interaction between the witness and the investigating officer. In this situation, police officers may inadvertently cue or lead the witness, especially if they already have a suspect in mind or have made a judgement as to who is to blame for a particular incident.

We saw in Chapter 2 that remembering is by no means a simple process. Memory itself is extremely complex and subject to a large number of internal and external influences. However, some psychologists have argued that there are ways in which retrieval from memory might be improved through the use of appropriate techniques. As was noted above, for most witnesses, giving a statement to the police will be a new experience, and so any help with the process will be welcome.

A number of problems can arise when a witness is asked to describe an incident. For example, some witnesses may find the memory of a traumatic event distressing, and so may prefer not to recall the details. Others may believe that some of the information that they have is so trivial as to be worthless in any investigation. In addition, witnesses may not always use appropriate retrieval strategies when trying to recall information. These and many other potential sources of difficulty have been addressed by Fisher and Geiselman in developing the Cognitive Interview Technique. As the technique has generated a great deal of research and practical application, it will be considered in some detail here.

THE COGNITIVE INTERVIEW TECHNIQUE (CIT)

The CIT was developed in the 1980s by two American psychologists, Ronald P. Fisher and R. Edward Geiselman. Unlike a great deal of memory research, the practical applications of the technique were immediately obvious, and the originators were pleased to see it being used by police officers in many different countries. The technique has been revised and refined over recent years, but many of the original notions are retained. The two major areas of emphasis in the technique are *memory* and *communication*. It is recognised that not only must the witnesses retrieve as much information as possible from their memory, but they must also translate their memory into words, and communicate the information to the interviewer. The central core of the process is one of guided retrieval. The interviewer must thus encourage and assist witnesses to access all the relevant information which is already in the memory store. Unlike some more traditional forms of interviewing, in the CIT the witness is put into the dominant role, with the interviewer acting as guide and assistant. This is one aspect that has caused some difficulty for police officers who have become accustomed to regulating and controlling all interview situations.

Fisher and Geiselman (1992) suggest that the interview situation should be seen as a particular type of social interaction. They point out that both interviewer and interviewee will enter the situation with their own agenda and expectations. The first task of the interviewer is to make the witness feel at ease and to encourage his or her active participation in the process. In this way the witness is less likely to be led by the interviewer, and is more likely to give his or her own uncontaminated version of events. When the interviewer does ask questions these should ideally be open-ended, thus allowing the witness to give more expansive answers. If the interviewer starts by asking a series of Yes/No questions, the witness may assume that long, detailed answers are not what is required. As a result, the witness may fail to include many details which could be relevant. Allowing the witness to speak at length without interruption is seen as very important. Interviewers are thus encouraged to adopt an active listening stance in which they let the witness know that he or she has been heard, but do not interrupt immediately by asking for clarification, etc. As was mentioned above, this particular stance is somewhat alien to many police interviewers who are accustomed to asking a series of questions rather than just letting the person give a free narrative account. For example, in one study, Fisher, Geiselman and Raymond (1987) found that police officers on average interrupted the witness a mere 7.5 seconds after they had started to talk. Although it is recommended that the witness be put in the driving seat, the interviewing officer must have some knowledge of the crime, and encourage the witness to report on the more relevant details (see Fisher & MacCauley, 1995).

Fisher and Geiselman recognise that some witnesses who are interviewed, especially victims, will have been traumatised by the incident, and will thus find it difficult or even embarrassing to provide details. In these cases, it is recommended that interviewers spend some time initially in building up rapport and recognising the person's difficulty. In the case of a victim of sexual assault, the provision of an appropriate environment, and an interviewer of the same sex, may also help to make the person feel slightly more at ease. Fisher and Geiselman suggest two ways in which the interviewer can build up a trusting relationship with the witness, i.e. to personalise the interview, and to communicate empathy with the person.

Personalising the interview can involve something as simple as the use of first names, by both victim and interviewer. The aim is to communicate to the victim that he or she is not just another case for the interviewing officer. The reasoning behind the suggestion is that a witness is more likely to try to help the investigator if a good relationship has been built up between them. Communicating empathy is not always easy, but Fisher and Geiselman believe that it is essential if a victim is to provide as much information as possible. Once again the interviewing officer must try to make it clear that he or she understands the trauma the victim is suffering. For this reason it might be considered inappropriate for a male officer to interview a female rape victim. Interviewing officers need to realise that the interview is essentially asking a victim to relive what may well have been the most traumatic incident in that person's life. For this reason patience and understanding are essential during the interview. The interviewer should try to avoid making a judgement about what is said, and should never adopt a confrontational style. It may also be necessary to reassure witnesses that their level of emotional reaction is entirely appropriate given the type of crime which they have experienced. Interviewers must recognise that witnesses may well feel embarrassed by their own show of emotion during the interview and that this will add to stress levels which may already be high.

Thus, what is being advocated is a style which enables a good relationship to be built up between the two people in the interview. The more relaxed a traumatised victim can be made to feel, the more likely he or she is to produce a comprehensive account of events (see Chapter 3). Similarly, the more the victim begins to respect the interviewer, the more effort he or she is likely to put into the task of remembering. The use of the Cognitive Interview Technique with traumatised victims is not without its problems (see Ainsworth & May, 1996). Paradoxically, some of the techniques advocated to enhance memory may actually serve to increase stress levels and so interfere with recall. However, Fisher and Geiselman suggest a number of techniques which might make witnesses feel more relaxed and comfortable in the interview situation. Some of these have already been referred to, but other suggestions include encouraging the person to tell what happened as if it were happening to someone else (see Latts & Geiselman, 1991). It is hoped that this method avoids some of the trauma associated with the victim reliving the experience personally.

Encouraging a witness to relax before the start of the interview may not in itself be enough. Fisher and Geiselman suggest that it may be necessary to get the witness to try to relax again before each new question. This will be particularly appropriate as the interviewer focuses in on the more intimate details of the crime. Simply asking the person to take a few deep breaths, or to imagine a pleasant scene, may be enough to counter mounting anxiety levels. The interviewer must also pay attention to any increase in a victim's anxiety levels, and if necessary give the person a few minutes to regain his or her composure. It may also be helpful for an interviewer to leave the most difficult questions until the end of the session as, by doing so, the person may have been able to provide a great deal of valuable information before stress levels start to interfere with memory retrieval.

It must also be recognised that anxiety can be produced inadvertently by an interviewer who makes the witness feel that he or she is not doing as well as was hoped. Above all, witnesses should be reassured that the interview is not some kind of test on which their performance will be evaluated and perhaps criticised. Throughout the session, the interviewer should seek to reassure witnesses that they are doing fine, and that what they have to say is of genuine interest. Having said that, it is important that the interviewer avoids saying things which might bias a witness's account in future retrievals. As we saw in Chapter 4, it is all too easy for interviewers to interfere with and to alter original memories by the style of questioning.

Fisher and Geiselman offer further advice as to how witnesses might be encouraged to provide information. One such suggestion concerns possible inconsistencies in a person's story. The inconsistency may be a simple error or may arise from a misunderstanding. However, it is suggested that the interviewer should not immediately challenge the person about such inconsistencies as this may put him or her on the defensive. It has long been recognised that humans like to be consistent in their actions and behaviours, and will feel uncomfortable when inconsistencies are pointed out (see Festinger, 1957). For this reason witnesses may seek to justify any inconsistencies by adding spurious details which "explain" the apparent discrepancy.

Other advice which is offered by Fisher and Geiselman includes encouraging the use of relative rather than absolute judgements. Although many police officers may be skilled at providing accurate details of height, weight, etc., most members of the public will not. For this reason, it may be helpful to ask witnesses questions such as, "Was he taller than me or smaller?". On a similar theme, witnesses may be good at recognising things which they have seen but not so good at describing the items verbally. For this reason, Fisher & Geiselman encourage the use of props and suggest that an interviewer might, for example, show the witness a number of different knives and ask, "Was the knife more like this or like that?" Similarly, witnesses may be able to demonstrate something which they have difficulty describing in words. Thus a witness may be able to demonstrate a particular mannerism of a perpetrator but not be able to describe the action verbally.

The main point in much of this advice is that the interview be witness focused. In other words, the interviewer must recognise and respect whatever skills each witness does and does not have, and tailor the interview accordingly. Fisher and Geiselman refer to this as the use of "Witness Compatible Questioning". For example, a witness who is a keen artist may be able to provide a sketch of a suspect, but have difficulty in describing his or her features verbally. For this reason the CIT does not provide a blueprint for each and every interview, but rather encourages flexibility on the part of the interviewer.

Fisher and Geiselman thus offer sound advice on the way in which an interviewer can establish a good relationship with a witness and create an environment in which the witness can feel comfortable and important. The CIT does, however, rely on four main techniques which should aid retrieval, and these will be outlined below.

Recreating the Context

Fisher and Geiselman believe that whenever a person witnesses an event, his or her memory will be affected by the context which existed at the time. Thus things like the person's mood and mental state, what he or she was doing or was with, etc., might all effect the memory trace. Because context appears to play such an important role in the way in which memory is stored, Fisher and Geiselman believe that it is essential to have the witness think about the context in some detail. They suggest that allowing the witness to recall and then recreate the context during the interview will aid memory retrieval considerably. Witnesses might be asked to simply think about the context, or may be asked specific questions about this. Thus the interviewer might ask the witnesses how they were feeling, where they were going, whether they were in a hurry, etc. Fisher and Geiselman recommend that this recreation of the context should be attempted before any specific questions are asked relating to the incident.

This technique has been found to be particularly useful when a witness believes that he or she did once have a detail in their memory, but is unable to retrieve it at the present time. Having the witness think carefully about his or her feelings at the time of the incident appears to aid recovery of elusive detail. The technique is also applied to a situation where a witness knows that he or she has been able to recover the memory on a previous occasion, but is unable to do so now. In such cases

Fisher and Geiselman recommend that the interviewer should get the witness to think back to the occasion when the information could be recalled, i.e. to reinstate the context.

Fisher and Geiselman provide an interesting example of this technique. They cite the case of a witness who at the time of an incident had made a conscious effort to memorise the registration number of a particular vehicle. However, the witness was unable to recall the registration number when later interviewed. The interviewer encouraged the witness to think about why she had tried to memorise the number, and about how she had achieved this. In this instance the witness recalled that the registration number had reminded her of her previous address and that this was how she had tried to remember it. With help from the interviewer she was able to trace back from her old address and recreate the registration number. Recalling the registration number was seen as a great achievement, as the sighting of the car had been almost a year earlier, and all previous attempts at retrieval had been unsuccessful.

Focused Concentration

Fisher and Geiselman believe that witnesses may store both general and highly detailed information in their memory. They believe that there are two different types of coding, and that witnesses store information in both a *concept* code and an *image* code. The interviewer's task is to elicit as much information as possible from the image code. This can best be achieved by encouraging a witness to concentrate as much as possible. In doing so the interviewer tells the witness that although this may be difficult, all the information is stored in the person's memory, and by concentrating very hard he or she should be able to retrieve it. The interviewer encourages the witness to pay attention to the more detailed sensory representations in the visual, auditory, tactile and other sensory systems, rather than just recalling general impressions.

Once focused concentration from the witness has been achieved, the interviewer must try to maintain this level. Interrupting the witness should thus be avoided, and any possible distractions should be eliminated as far as possible. Fisher and Geiselman point out that even inappropriate non-verbal communication can disrupt the process. For this reason interviewers should be trained on how to adopt an unobtrusive style which allows the witness to focus on the task in hand.

Multiple Retrieval Attempts

Fisher and Geiselman compare memory retrieval to a search process. If a person is unable to find a particular object, he or she may start a search by looking in the most likely places. If the item cannot be found, the person may well carry out a further and more thorough search, perhaps covering more ground. Fisher and Geiselman suggest that a similar strategy is appropriate when encouraging witnesses to try to recall details. They acknowledge that witnesses who have failed to retrieve a particular detail may be reluctant to attempt another search. However, it is recommended that they should be encouraged to do so by the interviewer. As we saw in Chapter 2, memory is rarely an "all or nothing" system. Just because a particular piece of information is not immediately accessible, this does not necessarily mean that the item is not in the memory store. Many memory problems can be explained by a failure in retrieval rather than a failure of the storage system itself. However, many witnesses may feel that because they have tried once and failed there is little point in trying again. For this reason Fisher and Geiselman recommend a number of strategies which may encourage the witness to try harder. Such techniques can include obvious verbal encouragement, but may also make use of more subtle non-verbal cues. For example, an interviewer who pauses at the end of a witness's utterance may encourage further effort. One who jumps in immediately may convey to the witness that no further effort is needed.

One word of caution is necessary here. The use of these techniques is entirely appropriate for witnesses who are experiencing a temporary difficulty in retrieving an item from memory. However, if the information was never encoded in the first place, no amount of encouragement will produce the required detail. There is a danger that if a witness is badgered for an answer, he or she may decide to make up a plausible but confabulated response. Those who interview witnesses must thus be cautious that by encouraging a witness to talk they do not inadvertently encourage the witness to fill in details missing from their original memory. An interviewer who uses expressions such as "But you *must* have seen what he looked like" may encourage the witness to produce information for which no actual memory exists. As we will see later in the book, such techniques are inappropriate when interviewing children and hypnotised witnesses, but are also fraught with danger when conducting a cognitive interview. A related point concerns the fact that in the CIT a good relationship between interviewer and witness is seen as desirable. The danger is that the witness will want to please the interviewer, and may do so by inventing some of the details being sought. As we saw in Chapter 3, it may then prove impossible to distinguish original memories from contaminated or confabulated ones.

A final point regarding multiple retrieval attempts concerns the so-called "tip of the tongue" phenomenon. This is the scenario in which a person believes that he or she knows the answer to a question, but cannot quite retrieve it on demand. Most people will have experienced this phenomenon at some time, and may well have learned that if they stop trying so hard to recall the item, it will resurface some time later. For this reason, Fisher and Geiselman recommend that if a witness is experiencing the "tip of the tongue" state, the interviewer should move on and return to the elusive detail later. It should, however, be borne in mind that just because a detail is on the "tip of the tongue" of a witness this does not necessarily prove that the detail is accurate.

Varied Retrieval

When asked to recall details of an incident, witnesses will naturally tend to tell their story from their own perspective, and in chronological order. However, Fisher and Geiselman suggest that some benefit might be gained by asking witnesses to attempt another recall from a different perspective, or in a different order. In particular, asking witnesses for a second recall in reverse order would seem to offer some advantage (see Geiselman *et al.*, 1986). In such cases some peripheral details of actions are often recalled.

The additional suggestion that witnesses be asked to recall from a different perspective is also claimed to offer some benefit. In such cases witnesses are invited to try to describe the incident from another person's perspective (i.e. someone else who was at the scene). The reasoning here is that witnesses may initially only mention those details which affected them directly. When asked to tell the story from the perspective of someone else at the scene they may be able to provide additional details of other aspects of the incident.

This latter suggestion was perhaps one of the most controversial aspects of the original CIT. There is a very real danger that a witness asked to tell the story from another's perspective will simply guess as to what the person would probably have seen. In other words, any new information produced will not be retrieved from an original memory, but rather will be produced by the person's imagination. The technique is certainly fraught with difficulties when used with highly suggestible individuals and with children. Indeed as we will see later, the technique is now considered unsuitable for use with young children and is no longer advocated with such witnesses.

Fisher and Geiselman did come to acknowledge the inherent dangers in the use of this method. They recommend that a witness be told specifically not to guess if the answer is not known. Following some studies with serving police officers, the original CIT was revised in the mid-1980s (see Fisher *et al.*, 1987). The revised version places far less emphasis on asking the witness to use different perspectives and to recall in a different sequence. Rather, interviewers are encouraged to make more extensive use of the repeated recall technique, and to further develop their listening skills. Fisher and MacCauley (1995) have commented that there can be a world of difference between studies carried out under controlled laboratory conditions, and what takes place in the field. As they note:

> "In the real world of crime, the detective interviewer's task is infinitely more complex, as witnesses may be frightened, inarticulate, and unwilling to participate in an extensive investigation." (Fisher & MacCauley, 1995, p. 82)

Another method advocated by Fisher and Geiselman is the probing of different sense modalities in the witness. Although the vast majority of information will be taken in visually, other senses may also have acquired some relevant details (see Chapter 10). When questioned specifically about, say, a perpetrator's voice, the witness may recall that it was distinctive in some way. The witness may also recall that an attacker's hands smelled of oil, or that their breath smelled strongly of garlic. As with other aspects discussed above, the witness may only give information about these details if asked. Recalling some detail from a different sense modality may also provide a trigger for the recall of further visual information. The more details the police have, the easier it will be for them to build up a good profile of a suspect (see Farrington & Lambert, 1997).

A final piece of advice offered by Fisher & Geiselman concerns the recovery of specific details. They suggest that there are two underlying principles to be taken into account when probing for specific information. Firstly, knowledge about an event is represented as a collection of attributes. Secondly, because the various attributes are associated, activating one attribute may stimulate others (Fisher & Geiselman, 1992, p. 113). Thus a witness may recall that one assailant referred to his accomplice by name. The witness may not be able to recall the name itself but, if asked, may remember that it was an unusual or foreign name. Further probing might result in the witness recalling that it was a short name or that it sounded like a nickname, etc. Again, by assisting the witness to probe the different aspects of memory the skilled interviewer may be able to elicit far more information than was initially forthcoming.

Having extracted as much detail as possible, the interviewer should review the information obtained with the witness. This not only allows the witness to confirm the accuracy of the material, but also allows a further opportunity to recall. It is also recommended that witnesses be encouraged to contact the interviewing officer at any time in the future should any further details come to mind.

EVALUATION OF THE COGNITIVE INTERVIEW TECHNIQUE

The development of the CIT has had a dramatic impact on the way in which witnesses are interviewed. Countries such as Britain, Australia and the USA now train many of their police officers in the use of the technique. Great claims have been made for the method and, if nothing else, it has focused attention on the importance of the way in which witnesses should be interviewed. Fisher and Geiselman have not been reticent in extolling the virtues of the technique. They claim that:

> "experimental tests of the Cognitive Interview showed it to increase substantially the amount of information gathered in many different settings. It worked with student and non-student witnesses; it worked with novice and experienced investigators; it worked with criminal and civil investigations; it worked in the laboratory, and more important, in the field, with actual victims and witnesses of crime." (Fisher & Geiselman, 1992, p. 5)

Certainly most studies examining the value of the technique have confirmed that it can produce more information than a more traditional interviewing style. However, many evaluation studies used the original (as opposed to the revised) CIT (see Fisher & MacCauley, 1995, pp. 86–89). One early British study claimed that, after training, detectives were able to elicit up to 55% more information from witnesses (George, 1991). Success of this magnitude is unusual in psychology, and it is not surprising that many police forces were keen to learn more about the technique. However, as we will see later, improvements of the order suggested by George have not always been found.

As with any technique, the CIT does have some limitations. For example, whilst the CIT may prove valuable in assisting cooperative and helpful witnesses to recall more information, it will be of little value with a more reluctant or obstructive witness. A second potential problem is that the CIT does take longer to conduct than a normal interview. In a police service with ever-increasing demands, police officers might not feel that the extra time and effort are justified. In Britain at least, the CIT tends to be used more often in the interviewing of witnesses of more serious crimes. Although all detectives now receive an interviewing handbook (which details the principles of the CIT) they will not necessarily use the technique for the investigation of every offence. Police officers tend to be pragmatists and there may be a feeling that the extra effort which a cognitive interview might involve will not prove to be worth while if the crime is comparatively trivial.

It must also be acknowledged that the CIT requires both greater concentration and greater flexibility on the part of the interviewer. Once again, these skills may not come naturally to many operational police officers. Much police training requires the learning and following of strict procedures (see Ainsworth, 1995a). The CIT does not offer a clearly laid out "How to do it" guide for those wishing to adopt the technique. Indeed, Fisher and MacCauley note:

> "The CI should not be thought of as a formula or recipe for conducting an interview. Rather, it should be regarded as a toolbox of techniques that are selected according to the specific needs of the interview. (Fisher & MacCauley, 1995, p. 85)

Thus the flexibility which the technique demands may frustrate some police officers who are more used to being given a clear set of instructions to follow. This difficulty was highlighted by some recent research which found that police officers do have problems in applying the technique correctly (see Memon, Bull & Smith, 1995). A related problem concerns the fact that even after training, individual police officers do not perform equally well when using the technique (see Fisher, Geiselman & Amador, 1989). This fact can make objective evaluation of the technique somewhat problematic.

Some of the difficulties experienced when applying the technique to police work can be explained by the fact that many police forces tend to make extensive use of in-house training. Thus the training of operational officers in the use of the CIT tends not to be carried out by psychologists with a special expertise in the area. Rather, training is often given by serving officers who may have themselves attended only a short training course and acquired rather limited knowledge. This could prove counter-productive as serving police officers might not use the technique correctly, and so may believe that the results do not justify the extra time and effort on their part.

To return to the evaluation of the technique, Geiselman *et al.* (1984) carried out one study in which the CIT was compared with both a "standard police interview" and a hypnotic interview. In this experiment, student subjects were shown a video of an armed robbery, and then asked a number of questions about the incident. The results showed that the Cognitive Interview and the Hypnotic Interview both produced 35% more accurate information than did the standard police interview. Just as important, though, was the fact that the CIT did not lead to an increase in inaccurate or confabulated information.

Another study (Fisher *et al.*, 1987) using the Revised Cognitive Interview (see above) found similar results. In this study, detectives interviewing crime witnesses were able to obtain on average 45% more accurate information, again without an increase in inaccurate details. In a comprehensive review of 25 CIT studies using over 1,200 subjects, Koehnken *et al.* (1992) reported that all had demonstrated the effectiveness of the technique in eliciting more information when compared to a normal interview. However, it was also found that there was a slight increase in the amount of incorrect information elicited using the CIT. In Britain, a recent field study (Clifford & George, 1995) examined the technique's use by police officers in interviewing real victims and witnesses. This research again demonstrated the effectiveness of the technique and its advantage over other forms of interviewing. Another recent piece of research has shown that the CIT may be more effective with active participants than with passive observers (see Koehnken *et al.* 1992). For this reason, it has been suggested that the CIT may actually lead to better results in the field than have been found in the laboratory.

Despite such evidence, a number of authors have recently questioned some of the claims made for the technique and pointed out some difficulties with its use (see, for example, Memon, Bull & Smith, 1995). One criticism centres around the comparison with a "standard police interview". It has been found that police practice varies widely in different areas, and that there is little standardisation of normal interview techniques. In other words, some so-called standard interview techniques are better than others, and it is thus difficult to make definitive claims as to the exact advantage which the CIT offers. In addition, as was noted earlier, many police officers find that the CIT is not always easy to use. One particular problem that has been identified is the difficulty in communicating instructions to witnesses. Some of the tasks which the CIT asks witnesses to perform may actually be difficult to comprehend and follow.

A further criticism concerns the issue of motivation. Memon *et al.* (1996) suggest that some of the improved performance which CIT witnesses appear to show may in fact be due to increased motivation on the part of the interviewer. Training in the CIT tends to take longer than training in more conventional forms of interviewing, and the interviewer may thus invest more time and effort in order to justify the additional training. In addition, it is not clear whether simply telling a witness to "try harder" will result in an improvement in performance similar to that produced by the CIT.

It is also not entirely clear whether all the four main components of the original CIT are equally useful. As was noted earlier, the Revised Cognitive Interview placed less emphasis on the use of the "changed perspective" and "changed order" components. This change was partly introduced as a result of difficulties experienced in the use of these two components, especially in the field. One recent study has also questioned whether the "change perspective" instruction leads to any improvement in accurate recall (Boon & Noon, 1994).

Perhaps surprisingly the CIT has not generally proved effective when used to try help witnesses to identify suspects (see Fisher *et al.,* 1990). One possible explanation for this is that recognition may involve different memory skills than does recall of details (see Chapter 5). However, the use of the CIT to assist with the construction of facial composites has also met with rather limited success (see Luu & Geiselman, 1993; Koehn, 1993). One interesting study (Smith & Vela, 1990) found that encouraging witnesses to reinstate, mentally, the context where they had first been exposed to a target did not improve facial recognition accuracy. However, subjects whose recognition accuracy was tested in the same location as that in which they had seen the target person earlier, did show an improved performance. This finding suggests that the police may wish to consider interviewing witnesses at the scene of the crime rather than just have them mentally reinstate the context. Such a technique may, however, be inappropriate for a highly traumatised witness where a return to the crime scene may significantly increase anxiety levels, and thus interfere with retrieval.

CONCLUDING COMMENTS

Throughout this chapter, we have talked about the use of the CIT with adult witnesses. However, it has also been used when interviewing children. Some studies have shown an improved performance over conventional interviewing methods, although some aspects of the technique (e.g. the "change perspective" instruction) are unsuitable for use with young children. The complexity of the CIT may mean that it is not always easy to convey instructions to children, especially the very young. Having said that, one recent study showed that the technique can be useful when interviewing children as young as 4 (see Smithson & Ainsworth, in preparation). Other studies have failed to confirm that the CIT does improve recall for child witnesses (see, for example, Memon *et al.,* 1992). However, research by Loohs (1996) has shown that the CIT, when used in conjunction with toy props, can produce significantly more information from 6 year olds.

There is no doubt that the CIT has had a massive impact on the way in which witnesses are interviewed. It is also true to say that in most cases the use of the technique has led to improved recall with little increase in inaccurate information. Although some of the early claims made by Fisher and Geiselman may have been a little too bullish, we should not underestimate the impact that the cognitive interview has had. As we have seen above, applying the technique in the real world of criminal investigations has not always been without its problems. However, there can be few better examples of how applied psychology can assist those charged with the duty of criminal investigation. As such, the advances which stem from the work of Fisher & Geiselman should be applauded. Techniques such as the cognitive interview, when used appropriately, may also mean that the criminal justice system may come to function a little more efficiently and that those guilty of a crime are more likely to be convicted and punished.

CHAPTER 8

The Use of Hypnosis in Witness Recall

As we have seen in previous chapters, human memory can be subjective, fallible and unreliable. It is thus not surprising that any technique which might improve recall should be given serious consideration. The lay person may well ask whether something like a truth drug, or the use of hypnosis, might improve eyewitness memory, making it both more complete and more accurate. In this chapter we will consider whether hypnosis might be of use in eliciting more information from eyewitnesses, and discuss what dangers might be inherent in the use of such techniques.

Hypnosis is shrouded in mystery and misunderstanding. Most people's knowledge of the subject will have been gained from watching a stage or television hypnotist. Such performers appear to have remarkable powers and are often able to persuade members of the public to commit embarrassing acts in front of a large audience. But this public face belies a long history of the use of hypnosis for more laudable purposes. Psychologists and doctors have long used hypnosis in a variety of settings (see Oakley, Alden & Mather, 1996). In modern times, hypnosis is used as a form of therapy, assisting people to stop smoking, gain confidence, etc. In addition, it is used as a form of relaxation training (e.g. for those suffering from dental phobias) and even analgesia, allowing minor operations to be performed without the use of traditional anaesthetics.

Hypnosis is a valuable and powerful tool which is used in a wide range of settings. It is thus perhaps surprising to learn that the scientific community is somewhat split on how exactly hypnosis should be viewed. Some believe that the hypnotic state is an altered state of consciousness which is substantively different from the normal waking or sleeping state (see Hilgard, 1978). Others see it as a "non-state" phenomenon involving the person entering into a relaxed state but one which is merely an extension of the normal conscious state (Wagstaff,

1981). Those who see hypnosis in this way view the interaction between the hypnotist and the subject as similar to any other social psychological interaction. The subject in effect "acts out" the role he or she believes is appropriate for someone who is supposed to be hypnotised. Whichever school one subscribes to, the hypnotic state is accepted to be one where the subject is in a more relaxed and compliant state, and is increasingly responsive to suggestions given by the hypnotist (Hull, 1933).

Early therapists such as Bleuler and Freud used hypnosis in an attempt to recover memories from patients who were suffering from psychiatric problems. Freud's view was that humans had both a conscious and an unconscious mind. He believed that unresolved conflicts and difficulties within the unconscious mind often led to psychiatric disturbance. Freud believed that events which took place in the first few years of life could shape a person's entire personality. However, he believed that memories for such events, especially if they were traumatic, were often repressed, and stored in the unconscious as opposed to the conscious mind. Thus Freud used a number of techniques to tap into the unconscious in order to try to recover what he believed were repressed memories. One such technique was hypnosis. Freud believed that, in a hypnotised state, the patient would be more likely to reveal some "inner secret" from the unconscious mind. One problem with Freud's approach was that he tended to believe that what the patient told him, especially when under hypnosis, "must" be true. As we have seen elsewhere in this book, to make such assumptions is at best naive, and at worst dangerous.

Many modern psychologists have long since dismissed Freud's views as being unscientific and ill conceived. In particular, the notion that many people have repressed, traumatic memories of which they are consciously unaware has been challenged. There is currently a great deal of debate about the so-called "False Memory Syndrome". It does appear that many traumatic "memories" recovered during therapy are in fact fabrications. Problems have arisen when therapists have presumed that everything which a patient says must be true. It also appears that in some cases therapists have led patients to believe that although they have no memory (of say early sexual abuse) the patient's symptoms indicate that such an event "must" have occurred. In situations such as this, it appears likely that at least some patients may confabulate in order to confirm the diagnosis, and in order to comply with the therapist. A detailed discussion of recovered memories and false memory syndrome is beyond the scope of this book; however, the interested reader may wish to consult the *American Psychologist*, Vol. 52, September 1997 for an interesting collection of recent articles on the subject.

However, the notion has persisted that people may have far more information stored in their memory than they can access at any one time. Many early cognitive psychologists recognised that if a person claims to have "completely forgotten" some information, then he or she may in reality be simply experiencing a (temporary) retrieval difficulty (see Chapter 7). Thus the nervous final year student entering the examination room may find that his or her mind has gone blank for the duration of the examination – only to be able to access all the information later the same day. When such "memory loss" is caused by nervousness then the use of hypnosis or some other form of relaxation to reduce anxiety levels may be appropriate and helpful. As we saw in Chapter 4, anxiety can interfere with memory both at the acquisition and the retrieval stage.

If there is disagreement as to the exact nature of hypnosis, then there is also great disagreement as to how and when the technique might be used with eyewitnesses. The opposing camps are best represented in the writings of Martin Reisser and Martin Orne and their views will be considered in some depth here. According to Reisser:

> "... hypnosis can be a valuable investigative aid, and when properly used, it does not require any special actions by the courts in terms of admissibility or special instructions to the jury." (Reisser, 1989, p. 173)

Orne is, however, somewhat more negative stating that:

> "... hypnotically induced testimony is not reliable and ought not to be permitted to form the basis of testimony in court." (Orne, 1984, p. 211)

Both agree that hypnosis is a powerful tool which can be a valuable asset in the recovery of memories. However, disagreements arise when we start to consider how, when, and why hypnosis should be used in the criminal justice setting.

THE USE OF HYPNOSIS TO PRODUCE ADDITIONAL INFORMATION

Orne's view is that hypnotising witnesses can be useful in providing new leads for the police to follow up, especially if the witness or victim has suffered a traumatic event. However, he believes that such information should be seen as just that – a lead to be followed up in the same way that other leads are investigated. One major danger is that police officers may believe that any evidence recovered from a person under hypnosis is somehow "more truthful" than witness statements obtained conventionally. There is a commonly held view (espoused in *The Who* song *We don't get fooled again*) that "the hypnotised never lie". Orne believes that such a view is naive and dangerous. He believes that, under hypnosis, a person may still lie deliberately, but may also confabulate (i.e. make up) details which are missing from his or her memory. The reason for the latter phenomenon lies partly in the interaction which takes place between hypnotist and subject.

It is important to recognise that a hypnotised person will be in a more relaxed, a more compliant and a more suggestible frame of mind. Writers such as Orne believe that there are a number of important consequences of this:

1. The person may well suspend his or her more normal critical judgement and say things of which he or she is unsure.
2. The person may comply with requests from the hypnotist for more information, even if no actual information is available in his or her memory.
3. The hypnotised person may respond to any suggestions made by the hypnotist, and incorporate such information into what the person believes to be his or her original memory.

Orne thus believes that whilst hypnosis can be very useful, the technique is fraught with danger when used on eyewitnesses. As we will see later, the dangers become highlighted when a previously hypnotised witness later gives evidence in court. As Orne (1984, p. 211) points out:

> "'Hypnotically refreshed' memories cannot be used to 'verify' facts for which no adequate evidence exists, especially when subsequent investigation has failed to produce any substantial independent corroboration and the individual did not recall the fact or was not confident of it prior to hypnosis."

Orne makes an interesting point with regard to *pre*-hypnotic beliefs. He suggests that if people believe that their memory *should* get better under hypnosis then they will exhibit this behaviour when they are subsequently hypnotised. In other words, when under hypnosis, people will start to provide more information than they did in their normal state. This could be a positive thing in that people may recall some additional and accurate details which prove to be of value to the police in their investigation. However, it could also have a negative effect in that individuals may so want their memory to be improved whilst under hypnosis that they confabulate information which is plausible, but is not an actual memory.

There are thus potential problems if the hypnotist tells the person that "We always find that people remember much more when under hypnosis". Armed with this information, the subject may well produce the "normal" behaviour and provide more "facts". Whilst many properly trained hypnotists would not bias witnesses in such a way, it is possible that others may inadvertently do so. In the USA it was quite common for police officers who had undergone a short training course to conduct hypnotic interviews, and several thousand did so (see Gilbert, 1980). Their enthusiasm and motivation to solve the crime may have caused them to use methods which a more detached practitioner might avoid.

THE CONDUCTING OF HYPNOTIC INTERVIEWS

There is another point of disagreement between Reisser and Orne. Martin Orne believes that only a properly trained psychiatrist, psychologist or other mental health professional should be employed to conduct hypnotic interviews. One reason for this view is that such professionals are unlikely to put the witness in a position where he or she is harmed by the hypnotic process. If a person becomes very distressed when recalling details of the incident, a therapist is in a position to diagnose post-traumatic stress disorder and, if necessary to advocate treatment (see Gravitz, 1985; McConkey & Sheehan, 1995, ch. 4). Wrightsman makes an interesting point on this issue. He says:

> "The police are trained to investigate; they work 'on' a case. Mental health professionals – psychiatrists and psychologists – work 'with' a victim." (Wrightsman, 1991, p. 155)

Wrightsman further notes that in a mail ballot, 93% of the members of the International Society of Hypnosis were opposed to the use of hypnosis by the police. He also points out that the American Medical Association has advocated that hypnotically induced memories were not accurate enough to be allowed on the witness stand.

In contrast, Martin Reisser believed that police officers themselves were perfectly capable of conducting hypnotic interviews effectively (Reisser, 1989). Reisser conducted training courses for many police officers and felt that after only a few days such people could be taught all the necessary techniques. He dismissed some of Orne's fears and argued that we should trust the trained officers to conduct interviews properly. He supported the views of Cheek and Le Cron (1968) who stated that more harm results from ignorance of hypnosis than from its intelligent use. Reisser also pointed out that mental health professionals will have little knowledge of investigative procedures, and as such will be ill equipped to conduct hypnosis in the police setting (see also Vingoe, 1991).

However, there remains a fear that a police officer, whose primary motivation is to solve a case, might see the welfare of the witness as a secondary consideration to solving the crime. McConkey and Sheehan (1995) provide some interesting and disturbing examples of how problems can arise. Reviewing a number of cases where hypnosis was used, they warn of some possible dangers:

> "it is important to note that no-one is immune to making mistakes and misjudgments, and we recognise that the police and hypnotists involved in these cases did not intend to go amiss. At the same time they perhaps did not fully appreciate that the potential costs of introducing hypnosis into a criminal investigation can be high, and the potential benefits can be low." (McConkey & Sheehan, 1995, p. 19)

The possible negative effects of the use of hypnosis may not cause undue concern to police officers who use the technique regularly. Advocates such as Reisser point to a number of celebrated cases where hypnosis has come to the rescue of police officers struggling to solve what are often serious cases (see Reisser, 1989, 151–152; Watkins, 1989). The most famous and oft-quoted example is that of the Chowchilla kidnapping. In 1976 a group of 26 children and their bus driver were kidnapped and hidden in a quarry in Chowchilla, California. The children and driver did escape their ordeal, but provided the police with little in the way of detailed descriptions of the perpetrators.

The bus driver agreed to be hypnotised and, whilst under hypnosis, recalled most of the registration number of a vehicle used in the kidnapping. This information helped the police to solve the crime, and three men were eventually convicted of the kidnapping. Such high profile cases have led understandably to a keen interest by law enforcement personnel. But, of course, most hypnotic interviews do not result in such dramatic results, and do not even come to the public's attention. We can but speculate as to the number of cases that have resulted in the police wasting valuable time and resources following up inaccurate information. More worryingly, we cannot know how many cases involving hypnotised witnesses may have led to the conviction of an innocent person. Whilst some cases have come to light, there may be others which remain undiscovered and unpublicised.

Reisser always claimed that the hypnotic interview technique is used simply because it works. He drew on his many years of experience with the Los Angeles Police Department in concluding that hypnosis does provide more information in the vast majority of cases where it is used. This view is somewhat at odds with that of an American Medical Association committee which found "no evidence to indicate that there is an increase of only accurate memory during hypnosis" (quoted in

Wrightsman, 1991, p. 157). Reisser termed the supposed improved memory performance "hypnotic hypermnesia" (see Watkins, 1989). As with many areas of eyewitness testimony research, it is not so easy to establish the true facts with regard to the claimed improvement in recall.

One problem stems from the very nature of the cases where hypnosis is typically used. The technique tends to be employed on the more serious cases, often involving traumatic incidents. A psychologist wishing to investigate the usefulness of the technique may find it difficult to conduct experiments in the laboratory which replicate the typical circumstances of criminal cases (see Neisser, 1982). For obvious ethical reasons, psychologists have tended to use less traumatic incidents in their studies. Some research has shown that memory enhancement can occur, whilst other studies have not confirmed this. For example, Yuille and McEwan (1985) found no improvement in memory recall of hypnotised versus non-hypnotised subjects. The authors explain this partly by reference to the fact that the study used an event which was not particularly emotionally disturbing for the participants. They speculate that hypnotic interviews may show more success in dealing with witnesses to, and victims of, crimes which are more personally distressing. For this and other reasons of ecological validity, it may be inappropriate to make direct comparisons between studies in the controlled conditions of the laboratory, and those in the more unpredictable and distressing world of the real investigation.

The typical laboratory-based study allows researchers to test accurately whether memory enhancement does occur, and to test whether the person makes up (i.e. confabulates) any information. Such experiments are able to do this because researchers have an accurate and objective record of what the person did actually see. Outside the laboratory, such control is lost, and it is not possible to prove whether any additional information is truly accurate or merely confabulated. Reisser claimed that in up to 90% of cases valuable new information is provided by hypnotic interviews. Orne argues that although more information may be provided, this does not mean that it is accurate or even useful information. Judging the "success" of hypnotic interviews thus remains a subject of some debate. The issue becomes more difficult to resolve when one considers the important notion of motivation.

MOTIVATION

Because of the nature of hypnosis, a hypnotised person is highly motivated to please the hypnotist. One way in which this might be achieved is by providing more information whilst under hypnosis. However, some have argued that it is the increased motivation rather than the hypnosis itself which leads to enhanced recall (see Wagstaff, 1982). In other words, simply getting a witness to "try harder" may achieve similar results without the use of hypnosis. The way in which all witnesses are interviewed has come under scrutiny recently, and many police forces now recognise that some techniques are better than others (see Ainsworth, 1995a and Chapter 7 of this book). It is not just hypnosis that can show improvement over the so-called standard police interview. As we have seen in the previous chapter, techniques such as the cognitive interview can also result in a witness providing more information, but without an increase in false information. In one relevant study, Geiselman *et al.* (1985) found that both the hypnotic and the cognitive interview technique produced more information than did standard police interviews.

INTERACTIONS BETWEEN THE HYPNOTIST AND THE WITNESS

There is very real concern that even the most well-intentioned police investigator might inadvertently cue or lead a witness during the interview. Thus there is a fear that any theories which the police officer has about the case may well be passed on to the hypnotised witness, and become incorporated into his or her memory of the event. If later asked to testify in court, the witness will find it difficult to separate out the original memory from subsequent information.

This latter problem is one of the main concerns expressed about the use of hypnosis. We saw in Chapter 4 how easy it can be to provide witnesses with misleading information and have them incorporate this into their "original" memory. In a series of experiments, Loftus and her colleagues have shown repeatedly that original memories can be altered by subsequent misleading information. Most of the subjects in the Loftus studies were normal people in a normal state of consciousness. If it is relatively easy to alter the memories of such people, then the problem may be exacerbated if the person has been hypnotised (see Ready, 1986).

It was noted earlier that when under hypnosis, witnesses will tend to be more relaxed, more compliant, and more suggestible. All of these factors will make it even more likely that a witness's memory will be altered by the hypnotic interview itself. Earlier it was suggested that if witnesses feel more relaxed, they will be likely to suspend their critical judgement or at least lower their decision threshold. Thus, when in a normal state, witnesses may well only provide those "facts" of which they are 100% certain. They will choose not to mention information about which they are uncertain, or of which they have only a vague recollection. If pushed by the interviewing officer, their normal critical faculties will surface and they will refuse to speculate about information of which they are unsure. However, when under hypnosis their more relaxed state may well mean that they are more likely to volunteer information about which they are unsure. The relaxed, almost soporific state of many hypnotised subjects can result in the immediate desire to please the hypnotist taking precedence over the possible long-term consequences for an innocent defendant.

The reason that such considerations are important, is that even when the witness is no longer in a hypnotised state, anything that was remembered whilst under hypnosis might be incorporated into the original memory. Whilst under hypnosis a witness might be told "When you awake you will remember everything that you have told me today". Such an instruction is often successful, with the witness subsequently able to recall at will all the details that emerged when under hypnosis. However, such additional information will not necessarily be accurate. The apparent enhancement of memory may be little more than the production of some additional, but inaccurate details. As we will see later, even careful cross-examination on the witness stand might fail to elicit which parts of a witness's statement are drawn from an original, reliable memory, and which are a result of interactions which took place between the witness and the hypnotist.

APPROPRIATE AND INAPPROPRIATE TECHNIQUES

It is not appropriate to consider in depth the vast array of hypnotic techniques that can used, but a consideration of some procedures may be useful. A hypnotised witness will not be told simply to remember as much as possible. Rather, the hypnotist will use techniques such as asking the person to imagine that he or she is watching a videotape of the incident to be recalled. The witness may be instructed to stop the videotape at appropriate points and to examine the scene in more detail. This strategy may be useful, although it may lead the witness to believe that memory works just like a video recorder. However, as was pointed out in the introduction to this book, such an analogy is inappropriate.

Such techniques can obviously be helpful and can encourage a witness to produce more information. However, it is important that the hypnotist does not use inappropriate techniques which might lead to confabulation. For example, a witness may be asked to describe the face of a suspect who was 100 metres away. The witness may be told to zoom in on the person's face as if he or she were using a pair of binoculars or a zoom lens on a video camera. Such a technique can, of course, only be successful if the person has an original memory for the face already stored. If the suspect was so far away that the witness could not physically have seen the face clearly, then no amount of suggestion on the part of the hypnotist will improve recall. However, the hypnotised witness in his or her desire to comply with and please the hypnotist may well produce something. In this case, however, it would be a fabrication or, more accurately, a confabulation. Because of the nature of the hypnotic interaction, witnesses will be less likely to admit that they simply do not know the answer to a question – especially if this meets with the apparent disapproval of the hypnotist. If a witness does claim not to be able to remember, he or she may be told to "try harder". This sort of pressure on a hypnotised subject can lead to "something" being produced whether it is accurate or not.

ORIGINAL MEMORIES AND ADDITIONAL INFORMATION

If the witness were able to separate out the original memory from the confabulated parts, then there would be little problem when he or she appeared in court to give evidence. Unfortunately it appears that witnesses do have great difficulty in separating out these two different sources of memory and the problem may be exacerbated when the witness has been hypnotised (see Orne, 1984).

There is obviously a problem if a hypnotist gives the hypnotised witness certain information or suggests certain possibilities. As we have seen above, such information may become incorporated into the witness's memory. But the influence can be even more subtle. The hypnotised subject who is relaxed and eager to please will be ultra-sensitive to anything the hypnotist does or says. Thus nods of approval, smiles, or vocal reinforcement will tend to encourage the witness to carry on providing information. A cessation of such reinforcement will tend to discourage continuance. Witnesses who produce information which conforms to a police hypnotist's view of events will receive lots of approval and encouragement. By contrast, witnesses who produce versions of events which differ from those held by the police may be discouraged, and perhaps even be encouraged to change their stories in order to win approval. The innocent comment to a witness that he or she "has done really well" may cause an alteration in the confidence that a witness has in the certitude of the information provided.

SAFEGUARDS IF HYPNOSIS IS USED

It is clearly vital that the hypnotist does as little as possible to cue or reinforce the witness. Most interviewers will be aware of this and will try to avoid such mistakes. However, in the heat of the interview, it is possible that interviewers will inadvertently cue the witness or provide inappropriate reinforcement. For this reason, practitioners such as Orne have advocated complete video recording of the entire interview session. It is suggested that this videotaping should include the pre-induction interview as well as the actual hypnotic interview. The video should show both the witness and the interviewer, so that it can be shown that no verbal or non-verbal cuing took place. Those countries that do allow hypnotically refreshed testimony have often insisted that a complete video-recording is made available to the court.

Orne also recommends that only the witness and the person conducting the interview should be present in the room during the hypnosis session. The reason for this is that others in the room, for example police officers investigating the case, may inadvertently cue the witness or give off reinforcement (or disapproval) at certain junctures. If the hypnotist does need to communicate with those investigating the case then short breaks should be introduced to allow for consultation.

Orne also advocates that there should be a post-hypnosis discussion between the hypnotist and the witness. This should cover what took place during the session, and address any fears or worries which the witness may have. It is suggested that this part of the interaction should also be video recorded.

Finally, the witness should be offered a clinical follow-up should he or she appear traumatised by the experience of the hypnotic interview. We should bear in mind that many witnesses will be recalling details of events which they find stressful and disturbing. In some cases, symptoms of post-traumatic stress disorder may emerge, and further counselling may be appropriate (see Ainsworth & May, 1996).

CONCLUDING COMMENTS

As we have seen in this chapter, hypnosis is not necessarily the panacea for the forgetful witness which some authors might claim. It is undoubtedly true that hypnosis can help in the recovery of some memories, especially those involving traumatic incidents. However, hypnosis can also be the proverbial can of worms if it is used inappropriately. If permitted to do so, police forces throughout the world will continue to use hypnosis, because of the reputation which the technique has developed. Being anecdote driven, police officers may be particularly interested to learn about the small number of occasions on which the technique has been used to solve big important cases. Concerns of academics such as Orne and the author of this book may be dismissed as the pressure mounts to solve high-profile cases (see Wagstaff, 1993).

Only relatively recently have courts and the authorities begun to question the value of hypnotically refreshed testimony, and to consider the possible inherent dangers in such evidence. At the time of writing, the admissibility of such evidence varies greatly from one country to another, and, in the case of the USA, from one state to another (see Kebbell, 1997). In some cases, witnesses who have undergone hypnotic memory retrieval are not allowed to give evidence in court later. In other cases, such testimony is allowed with little restriction. Between these two extremes are those countries or states which allow such witnesses to give evidence in court, providing that a number of safeguards are in place. These safeguards may include such things as the complete video recording of the entire hypnotic interview.

Interestingly, a British Home Office circular (Home Office, 1988) considering the use of hypnosis in criminal investigations, contained nothing in the way of procedural guidelines. Although the Home Office does not (at the time of writing) actually ban the use of hypnosis it does not currently encourage its use. Where a witness is known to have been hypnotised, his or her testimony may well face a legal challenge (see Wagstaff, 1993, for one example of such a challenge).

Whilst there remains disagreement about so many aspects of hypnotic memory retrieval, courts should think carefully when considering evidence given by previously hypnotised witnesses. As we have seen in this chapter, hypnosis can offer benefits – but it can also have significant costs. In the previous chapter it was argued that it may be possible to improve the recall of witnesses by using techniques with less inherent dangers than the hypnotic procedures described here. Kebbell (1997) suggests that psychologists would be much better advised to spend their time conducting proper cognitive interviews with witnesses rather than trying to use hypnosis. The present author can only support this viewpoint.

CHAPTER 9

Children as Witnesses

Among all the areas of eyewitness testimony covered in this book, none has received quite so much recent research attention as that concerning children as witnesses. One reason for the massive amount of interest is the increasing number of cases of child sexual abuse which are being recognised. In such crimes, the child victim is often the main or only witness, and as such his or her testimony will be vital to any prosecution.

Traditionally, most Criminal Justice Systems have been reluctant to accept the testimony of young children, believing that they make less reliable witnesses than do adults. However, in recent years, the balance has shifted and the evidence of children is now much more likely to be accepted. As we will see later, legislation in England and Wales has attempted to make it easier for prosecutions to proceed, even when the main evidence is the testimony of a young child. However, there are still many obstacles to be overcome before courts will accept a child's testimony unconditionally.

Prosecutions for child sexual abuse in England were made more difficult following a ruling by Lord Goddard in 1958. In the Appeal Court, he condemned the practice of calling young children to give evidence, and this led to a rule that children under the age of 6 should not be called to give evidence. Following the ruling, most English prosecutors chose not to call children under the age of 8 leading to what one noted writer called "a child molester's charter" (Spencer, 1987).

CHILDREN AND THE LEGAL SYSTEM

The legal system has always been sceptical of the abilities of children as eyewitnesses. This scepticism has been based on three major beliefs:

1. Children's cognitive abilities are not so well developed as those of adults and so their thinking and memory capacities are inferior.
2. Children do not always differentiate between truth and fantasy, and

so their reports cannot be trusted. In addition, they may confabulate or even lie deliberately in court.

3. Children are highly suggestible and so their testimony can be very easily changed by leading questions and suggestion.

Much of the prejudice against children was based not so much on careful research, but more on gut feelings and hearsay. However, one early writer (Whipple, 1911) did cite some evidence in support of some of these prejudices. He reported on the writings of two German doctors who believed that children were the most dangerous of all witnesses, and should, wherever possible, be banned from courts. In contrast, Gross (1910) believed that child witnesses (at least healthy ones) could be as good as adults, especially when recalling simple events. He believed that in some ways children could even be better witnesses than adults, as they did not apportion blame, could control their emotions, and did not get drunk! As we will see later, more recent research has tended to support the views of Gross to some extent, and challenged the notion that children are inevitably poorer witnesses. Indeed, English law has changed in the last ten years to the point where it is now more likely that a child's testimony will be admitted than was previously the case.

Courts in many countries have simply not allowed children below a certain age to give testimony, and have placed restrictions on the testimony given by older children. English law recognised as long ago as 1779 that children could be competent to give evidence, provided that they understood the nature and consequences of the oath (*R* v *Brasier*, 1779). A century ago in the USA, the Supreme Court also held that children could be allowed to give testimony, provided that they were competent (*Wheeler* v *United States*, 1895). This latter case did not specify an absolute age of competence, but rather gave the trial judge discretion. Judges were advised to consider each child individually, bearing in mind factors such as the child's intelligence, his or her understanding of the oath, etc. According to Stafford (1962) the four fundamental elements of competency are:

1. Does the child understand that he or she must speak the truth?
2. At the time of the incident was the child's mental capacity such that he or she could observe and register the event?
3. Is the child's memory sufficiently developed to allow for an independent recollection of the observation?
4. Can the child translate memory for the event into words?

Theoretically, if these competency requirements were met, the child could be allowed to give testimony. However, there were still other formidable obstacles put in the way. English law always maintained that only sworn testimony could be accepted in court. Sworn testimony involves the witness taking an oath to swear to tell the truth. The 1933 Children and Young Persons' Act allowed children to give unsworn testimony provided that the child was reasonably intelligent, and understood his or her duty to tell the truth. However, in such cases the corroboration requirement was invoked. This was a requirement that if a child did give unsworn testimony, it must be corroborated either by other sworn testimony (i.e not just that of another child) or by medical or forensic evidence.

A further problem related to what was known as the "judicial caution". This was a requirement that judges must warn jurors of the dangers of convicting an accused on the basis of the evidence of a child. Judges had no discretion in this matter, and had to issue such a warning during their summing up, irrespective of the quality of any individual child's testimony. As Davies has noted, "This was inevitably discriminatory and might well have raised unnecessary doubts in the minds of the jury" (Davies, 1992, p. 34).

A final but not inconsiderable problem was presented by the hearsay rule. Hearsay evidence is that which a witness has heard another person, not the defendant, say and is not generally allowed in court. One consequence of the hearsay rule was that witnesses were expected to give their evidence in person on the day of the trial and be subject to cross-examination. The effect of the hearsay rule was to exclude from court the evidence of those witnesses to whom a child may have made an initial disclosure. Thus a parent or teacher who may have heard a child make very specific allegations against an accused was not allowed to report these to a court.

RECENT CHANGES IN LEGISLATION AND THE USE OF THE VIDEOLINK

Many of these obstacles were removed, or at least partially dismantled, in England by the introduction of the 1988, 1991 and 1996 Criminal Justice Acts. For example, the requirement that a child's unsworn evidence must be corroborated has now been abolished. Up until very recently the judge was still required to warn the jury of the risk of convicting on the basis of such uncorroborated evidence if the case concerned a sexual offence. However, under the 1996 Criminal Justice Act, judges are no longer required to warn the jury regarding the reliability or otherwise of children's testimony. Judges can still comment upon the reliability of a given witness's statement in individual cases. However, there now appears to be no legal justification for judges to comment automatically on a child's evidence in cases of sexual assault. The case law that had established that children under the age of 7 or 8 were not competent, has also now been challenged by the admission of evidence from 3 and 4-year-olds (see Flin, 1993).

However, one of the most innovative recent changes to the law in England, Wales and Northern Ireland was the introduction of the live videolink in court. Such a system allows the child to give his or her evidence from a room separate from the main courtroom, and to be cross-examined via video cameras and monitors. The system's main purpose was to reduce some of the stress which a child would inevitably feel if asked to appear in the imposing and intimidating atmosphere of the courtroom itself (see Flin, 1993). In addition, the system allowed the child to give evidence without being constantly scrutinised (and perhaps intimidated) by the accused. This can be important as some research has shown that a child's memory is likely to be less accurate when he or she is asked to recall events in the presence of the alleged perpetrator (see Flin, 1993). The live link was first used in the USA in 1983, and by 1990 eight states allowed the use of two-way videolinks, with a further 27 authorising a one-way system (see Small & Melton, 1994). (Two-way links allow the child to both see and be seen by the court, whereas one-way links only allow the child to be seen by those in court). Under English law, the so-called "Live-Link" is available to children under the age of 14 for crimes involving violence, and to those under 17 for crimes involving sexual assault.

Whilst the introduction of the videolink was applauded at the time, there have been some difficulties with the system (see Davies & Noon, 1991, 1993; Flin, 1992). An evaluation of the system in the 23 months following its introduction showed that the majority of court personnel viewed the system positively. In addition, the children themselves (most of whom were victims of sexual assault) were seen to be reasonably happy and effective when giving their testimony via the videolink. Davies and Noon concluded that the system had considerable benefits for children, and that its use should be extended. However, as Kapardis (1997) has noted, the videolink in itself cannot address many of the difficulties faced by many child victims. For example, in Davies and Noon's study, it was found that children had to wait an average of 10 months after an offence before appearing in court to give evidence. On the day of their appearance, children also had to wait on average almost two and a half hours before giving evidence. Perhaps most worrying was the fact that although the videolink was designed to prevent the child having to face the accused directly, few steps were taken to prevent the child bumping into the alleged perpetrator in the environment around the courtroom.

A further difficulty with the videolink system stemmed from the fact that initially its use in court was not an absolute right but rather was at the trial judge's discretion. In some cases trial judges did not allow the use of the system, but instead insisted that a child victim should appear "live" in court. This inevitably led to increased stress for the child, especially if the police or prosecutors had led the child to believe that he or she would be allowed to give evidence via the videolink. Judges' objections to the use of the system appeared to stem from a view that an accuser should be made to face the accused directly if justice is to be seen to be done.

The situation with regard to the use of the videolink has, however, changed recently in England. "Plea and Discretion Hearings" have now been introduced for cases involving children. At these hearings, the judge makes a decision as to the way in which the child will give evidence. At this hearing (if appropriate) a decision is also made as to whether a child's videotaped interview will be shown in court. These decisions are generally binding, although if a child insists that he or she does want to appear in open court, then this request will generally be granted.

Another potential difficulty associated with the videolink surrounds the impact of the child's testimony on the jury. One concern is that the testimony will have less of an impact if it is delivered via a videolink than if it is delivered in open court. Davies *et al.* (1995) conclude that the format of delivery has no effect on jury verdicts. This view would seem to be supported by Swim, Borgida and McCoy (1993). This latter research found that the mode of presentation may make a slight difference if subjects are questioned immediately after the presentation of this evidence. However, Swim and colleagues found that this slight difference disappeared after the jury deliberated on the case. Thus, according to Swim and colleagues, the mode of presentation makes no difference to the proportion of guilty verdicts.

Contrary to this, Ross *et al.* (1994b) found that mock juries are more likely to convict an accused if shown a child giving evidence in open court (as opposed to the child using the videolink). The majority of research does, however, seem to suggest that the mode of presentation may not have a significant impact on the jury's verdict. However, this topic is currently being examined further by the present author and colleagues. (See Pearce & Ainsworth and Lees & Ainsworth, both in preparation.)

There may still be a feeling that a deeply distressed child appearing in open court could have more of an impact on the jury than the same child appearing on a television screen. It is not unheard of for live-link televisions to be switched off temporarily to allow a distressed child to regain his or her composure. Although it has not yet been demonstrated that this action will affect the outcome of a case, it would be somewhat ironic if such attempts to spare the child embarrassment and distress meant that a guilty person was subsequently found not guilty.

THE USE OF VIDEO-RECORDED INTERVIEWS

The relaxation of the rules regarding children's evidence have also resulted in courts now being able to accept video-recorded interviews with children as evidence-in-chief. Such a move is very significant, as it can mean that the child's evidence-in-chief will be accepted in the form of a video-recording, though they may still be cross-examined via a live link. A video-recorded statement by a child has an advantage in that it is usually given shortly after the incident took place. The child's memory will thus tend to be more accurate and detailed than would be the case with an account given in court many months or even years later.

However, as with other recent innovations, there have been some problems associated with video-recorded interviews. A number of cases where recorded interviews were allowed initially in court collapsed when defence counsel challenged the way in which the interviews had been conducted. In some early cases those conducting the interviews with children appeared not to be adequately trained in appropriate interviewing techniques. Specifically, some interviewers were accused of having led child witnesses to the point where the videotaped evidence was ruled inadmissible in court. As a result a number of prosecutions failed, and child victims were left frustrated by their encounter with the justice system.

RECOMMENDATIONS FOR CORRECTLY CONDUCTED INTERVIEWS

The British Home Office has recently devised a Code of Practice designed to help and advise those conducting interviews with child witnesses. This Code of Practice was drawn up after consultation with both legal scholars and psychologists. An excellent review of the proposals has been provided by Bull (1992) and the provisions will be considered in some detail below.

As we saw earlier in this chapter, courts have been reluctant to accept evidence from child witnesses partly because it was thought that all children had poorer memories than adults. However, as we will see later, this presumption has recently been challenged. In particular, it is now generally accepted that children are capable of producing competent accounts of incidents, provided that they are questioned or interviewed in an appropriate manner. At least some of the prejudice against child witnesses stemmed from the results of interviews which had been conducted badly. Provided that children are not pressurised, nor asked leading or suggestive questions, they are perfectly capable of producing accurate accounts. Where problems have arisen these have tended to occur when well-intentioned interviewers have pressurised children for answers, or have suggested their own version of events to the child.

The problem for interviewers is that whilst children often provide fairly accurate accounts of an event, these accounts are usually less detailed than those which an adult might provide. For this reason, interviewers need to be able to ask questions, but without falling into the trap of leading the child, or putting their own ideas to the child. As Bull (1992, p. 5) notes:

> "The skill of questioning is a key issue in effective interviews with children. ... younger children's replies have sometimes been found to be more biassed (than adults) by poor questioning."

Bull makes one important point concerning the child's level of cognitive and intellectual development. Although we know that children's abilities develop chronologically, different children develop at different rates. For this reason a questioning style appropriate for one 8-year-old may be inappropriate for another 8-year-old. Bull advises that, prior to the interview commencing, as much information as possible should be sought concerning the child's level of linguistic, cognitive and communicative development. In addition, information about the child's social, physical and sexual maturity should be sought. Knowledge of an individual child's level in all these areas will help the interviewer to plan the session and to conduct the interview at an appropriate level. Some knowledge as to the child's cultural and religious background may also help in the planning of the interview, as will some rudimentary understanding of child development.

Throughout any interview, it should be borne in mind that almost all children will find the experience stressful. They may be being asked questions of an embarrassing nature, may be making accusations against a person well known to them, and may even have been threatened. For this reason, interviewers should do all they can to reduce the potential sources of further distress. Only relatively recently have British police forces considered it necessary to provide a special area where children and other victims of sexual assault can be interviewed. Any novel surroundings will be potentially stressful to a young child, but the more welcoming and informal the setting, the less stressful will be the situation. As we saw in Chapter 3, stress can interfere with both the encoding and recall of information, so any attempts to reduce stress will be likely to improve memory performance.

The Code of Practice gives advice on the recording equipment used for the interview. Obviously such equipment should be of a high enough standard that persons appearing within it can be both seen and heard clearly. For this reason, a simple home video camera with integral microphone would be unsuitable. Although the primary focus will be on the child's verbalizations, it is important that others in the room can also be both seen and heard. Without this, any court would not be able to tell whether the child was being unduly prompted or led. Thus a camera position which shows both child and interviewer is advised. Alternatively, two cameras can be used so as to allow an inset of the interviewer within a main picture of the child. Ideally, there should be no other people present in the room, but if they are, then their behaviour should also be visible on the video recording. One must bear in mind that the decision of whether or not to admit the recording as evidence is made by the trial judge. After viewing such a tape, he or she may decide to reject all or part of it and this may well seriously affect the prosecution's case.

It has become more common for investigations to be carried out jointly by police officers and social workers. However, it is recommended that only one person should conduct the interview with the child. There are clearly inherent dangers if two different people start firing questions at an already distressed child. The issue of who should carry out the actual interview is perhaps less important than whether that person has received an appropriate amount of training in the art of conducting such interviews. Interviewing children can be difficult at the best of times, but the circumstances surrounding some of the more serious cases of abuse make such interviews both harrowing and disturbing. For this reason, appropriate training should have prepared interviewers for the gamut of emotions and revelations which are likely to surface.

Davies and Wilson (1997) note that, in Britain, more interviews are carried out by police officers than by social workers. This difference is partly accounted for by the fact that many police forces took the decision to train intensively a small number of specialised teams of officers. By comparison, many social work departments chose to spread training "widely but thinly" among staff. As a consequence, many social workers may not have the specialist knowledge and experience which these important interviews might require.

As regards the interview itself, it is recommended that this should pass through a number of phases. The first and in some ways most important phase is the establishment of rapport between the interviewer and the child. This phase is essential in helping the child to relax and feel as comfortable as possible. During this stage, no mention should be made of the allegation itself; rather the interviewer should ask the child to talk about some neutral event from his or her life. Bull suggests that with young children it may be beneficial to use toys or drawings to assist in establishing rapport. This phase will obviously benefit the child, but will also help the interviewer to further establish the child's level of development and plan the most suitable type of interview.

Once rapport has been established, the child should be told about the purpose of the interview. However, it is important that this is done in such a way as not to affect the child's account of events. The child should then be encouraged to give a free narrative account, with only a minimum amount of very general and open-ended prompting. Even at this stage, no direct mention should be made of the allegation. Bull (1992, p. 8) notes that:

> "The main aim of this phase is that children provide an account *in their own words* at their own pace. During this phase the interviewer's role is to act as facilitator and not as an interrogator. ... Every effort should be made to obtain information from the child which is spontaneous and uncontaminated by the interview."

This phase is very important as it allows the child to give a version of events which is free from any influence which the interviewer might bring to bear. The child may well have gaps in his or her memory, though this is likely to cause fewer problems than the use of inappropriate questioning techniques. It is also important to bear in mind that children may feel that they are being questioned because they have done something wrong. If possible, steps should be taken to dismiss this feeling, though again caution needs to be exercised in order to avoid biasing the child's responses.

During this phase the interviewer should try to avoid interrupting the child but should allow the story to unfold naturally. If necessary, open-ended prompts such as "and then what happened" can be used. However, the emphasis should still be on allowing the child to tell his or her story in as natural a way as possible, with the interviewer adopting an "active listening" stance. This involves the interviewer in letting the child know that what he or she has said has been heard and understood, and perhaps repeating the child's words.

In an ideal world the free narrative account should give all the necessary information to decide whether a case should be brought against an accused. However, in most cases the account will be lacking is some detail, and this will mean that further questioning will be needed. For this reason, Bull advocates that a number of different questioning techniques should be considered, starting with open-ended questions. This type of question allows the child to provide additional information but with little danger of contamination by the interviewer. Interviewers should bear in mind that children may be reluctant to admit that they do not know the answer to a particular question and so may be tempted to fabricate one. For this reason it is important that an interviewer lets the child know that if he or she cannot remember, or does not know the answer to a question, then he or she should say so.

One problem with interviewing children has been highlighted by Toglia, Ross and Ceci (1992). These researchers suggest that young children may believe that because one adult (the perpetrator) already knows what happened, then all other adults must also know. For this reason it is important that an interviewer encourages the child to tell as much as possible and to reassure him or her that the real facts are not already known. For most children, this will be an unfamiliar situation, as they normally question adults in order to gather information.

Having obtained as much information as possible through the free narrative account and open-ended questions, it may be necessary to gather further evidence. For this reason, specific but non-leading questions may be asked, provided that these will not cause the child undue stress. This phase allows the interviewer to probe areas which the child may have omitted, or to clarify points which have emerged earlier. The interviewer must bear in mind that the child will not know what is or is not relevant to the investigation. Bull points out that children may be poor at remembering events in chronological order, or at placing events at certain times or on certain days. For this reason, it is recommended that more appropriate questions be used, for example, "Was this before lunch or after lunch?", etc.

Although leading questions would not normally be asked, in some cases they may be necessary. For example, it may be that the child has simply not produced enough detail or evidence without such prompting. It must be borne in mind that evidence obtained by the use of leading questions may well be ruled inadmissible in court. However, two points should be considered. Firstly, children may be more likely to respond to Yes/No questions by saying "Yes". For this reason Bull recommends that any Yes/No questions should be phrased in such a way that they sometimes produce a "Yes" response, and sometimes a "No". Secondly, if a leading question does encourage a child to say more, then the interviewer should revert to the use of non-leading questions to gain further information.

In some cases a child may experience difficulty in putting what happened into words. In such cases, interviewers may wish to consider the use of dolls or other props to help the child. However, the use of such props is not without its own difficulties. It should not be assumed that if a child demonstrates an action using dolls that this proves that this action took place. For example, Bruck and Ceci (1995) suggest that 3-year-old children interviewed using anatomically detailed dolls may report having been touched even when this is not the case. They may even go so far as to insert their fingers into the anal or genital cavities, even if this has never been done to them.

Bull suggests that dolls might prove useful in allowing the child to demonstrate actions to which they have already referred verbally. Alternatively, dolls may be helpful in allowing a child with a poor vocabulary to show the interviewer just what happened. However, dolls and other prompts should only be introduced once the general substance of a complaint has been established. When introduced, the interviewer should also be careful not to lead or prompt the child by suggesting certain actions.

Having obtained as much information as possible, the interviewer must then ensure that the session is closed in an appropriate manner. In particular, it is important that the child is left in a positive frame of mind, and is not made to feel that he or she has failed in any way. The child should be thanked for his or her help, and be asked whether he or she wishes to say anything else, or has any questions of the interviewer. It may be useful to give the child or guardian a name and contact telephone number should either wish to discuss the matter further.

Adherence to all the guidelines outlined above will make it more likely that a child's video-recorded evidence will be accepted in court. However, it is by no means certain that the recording of a well-conducted interview will be accepted unconditionally. As was noted earlier, the admission of such evidence is not automatic.

The evidence contained within the videotape may, however, prove valuable in a slightly different way. Some of those accused of a crime may be shown parts of the videotaped interview during their questioning by the police. When confronted with such evidence, a number of alleged perpetrators choose to admit the offence and thus save the child the trauma of having to actually appear in court. Indeed, in one study in the USA, Liposvky et al. (1992) found that in only 16.8% of cases involving child witnesses did the child actually have to appear in court.

Davies and Wilson (1997) note that the Memorandum of Good Practice has gained wide acceptance among most professionals working in the area – with the exception of many barristers. Davies and Wilson are wholly supportive of its provisions and note that:

"The Memorandum provides safeguards for the child, the interviewers and the accused which are unlikely to be surrendered. The research demonstrates that the memorandum is a useful tool in the legitimate prosecution of child sex offenders. It is in the interests of all parties to refine and develop its recommendations to ensure that it is more widely and effectively employed in the interests of justice and children." (Davies & Wilson, 1997, p. 10)

CHILDREN'S MEMORY PERFORMANCE

It was noted earlier that much of the suspicion of child witnesses stems from a belief that a child's memory is inevitably inferior to that of an adult. It is true to say that children's memory ability does improve with age, and that younger children do tend to provide less information than older children and adults (see, for example, Clifford, 1993; Leippe, Romanczyk & Mannion, 1991). However, much recent research has suggested that the inferior performance of young children is not inevitable and that what is provided is not necessarily inaccurate. Fivush (1993) provides a review of a great deal of recent research and concludes that even pre-school children can provide an accurate account of an event which they themselves have experienced, and are capable of retaining information over a period of time. Having said that, it has also been found that younger children's recall tends not to be as detailed or as exhaustive as that provided by older children. In other words, although younger children do tend to provide less information than older children, what they do provide tends to be accurate.

Fivush also makes the point that whilst younger children tend to provide less detail spontaneously, they can usually provide more information when cues or prompts are used by the interviewer. It is also suggested that in some cases children remember different aspects of an event than adults or older children. Fivush makes the point that a child who can only recall details after a great deal of prompting may be seen as a poor witness, and his or her story may be challenged by defence counsel in court. As was noted earlier, there is an additional danger that any prompts may be seen as leading the child and so lead to the exclusion of evidence. This is thus something of a Catch 22 situation. If the young child gives only a brief free narrative account, his or her testimony may be seen as vague and unconvincing. However, if the child is prompted to give more details, the prompting itself may be attacked by defence counsel and the testimony may be ruled inadmissible.

One should also bear in mind that young children tend to be less consistent in their answers than older children and adults. This is partly due to the fact that their memory skills are somewhat undeveloped. Thus, whilst they may take in a great deal of information, they may have difficulty in recalling the same details across different retrieval attempts. A child asked a number of different questions about the same incident may also appear confused and provide different answers. Such lack of consistency is likely to be pounced on by defence counsel as proof of a child's inaccuracy (see Fivush *et al.*, 1991).

SUGGESTIBILITY AND THE CHILD WITNESS

Earlier in this chapter we drew attention to the fact that children are often thought to be more suggestible than adults and, as such, are more likely to be affected by leading and suggestive questioning. Bruck and Ceci (1995) have provided an extensive review of research on suggestibility and have provided a list of potential sources of error. Some of these will be summarised briefly below.

If an interviewer starts with the presumption that a child has been sexually abused, then the interview may be seen as a way of confirming this hypothesis rather than as a way of establishing the truth. Consequently, investigators should be encouraged to approach each case with an open mind rather than just as a way of confirming a blinkered view. This point was highlighted in a number of cases in Britain (e.g. in Cleveland) in which interviewers were criticised for adopting such a posture. Interviewers should also be aware that repeating a question will tend to invite younger children to change their story over time. Having changed their original story, children may then repeat the revised version in any subsequent interviews (see Chapter 4).

Bruck and Ceci make an important point with regard to the emotional tone which interviewers might adopt. They point out that an interviewer who adopts an accusatory stance (e.g. by suggesting to the child that he or she is afraid of telling the truth) may encourage the child to confabulate or to change the original story. In a similar vein, Bruck and Ceci suggest that it is entirely inappropriate for interviewers to invoke peer pressure as a way of encouraging a child to provide certain information. It would thus be unfair to tell a child that friends have already indicated that he or she has been the victim of abuse. Children, especially younger ones, may be particularly susceptible to this type of pressure and may not wish to be seen to be going against their friends.

Because children tend to be intimidated by authority figures, interviewers should be aware that some of those interviewed may seek to please the interviewer as much as possible. Children may see this as being more important than telling the truth, and so may fabricate a story which they believe the authority figure wishes to hear. Most children are not particularly assertive, and so would find it difficult to stand up to an adult who is encouraging them to change their original story.

Similarly, if a child is told by an interviewer that an alleged perpetrator has done bad things, the child may incorporate this information into any subsequent reports about interactions with the accused person. It has also been demonstrated that 6-year-old children easily confuse what they have experienced with other information that has been suggested to them. As a consequence, young children may later be unable to separate out the original memory from subsequent additional (and perhaps misleading) information. This can be a particular problem as children who have been interviewed in a suggestive way may still appear to be highly credible even to professionals.

The above considerations may help to identify those cases where a child is likely to have been led by unsuitable questioning techniques. However, it would be inappropriate to conclude that all children will be susceptible to such dubious practices. Although a number of studies have demonstrated the suggestibility effect, others have shown that in some cases children as young as 4 are able to resist the influence of leading questions (see, for example, Siegal & Peterson, 1995). Similarly, Davies (1993) has suggested that although younger children tend to perform less well than older children when asked to describe another person, they can and often do perform well on simple identification tasks. In common with many other writers, Davies argues that the way in which children are interviewed is perhaps more important than a simple consideration of their age.

We can thus see that it would be naive to assume, as have some legal scholars, that all children are suggestible and should therefore be treated with suspicion. It would also be inappropriate to conclude that children are always more suggestible than adults. In the same way that some children may be more able to resist pressure than others, some adults will be more easily led than others (see Gudjonsson, 1992). Although age is an important factor in determining the probable precision of eyewitness testimony, it is only one of a number of variables which will affect the likely accuracy.

Most psychologists would thus want to argue that it is inappropriate for children to be excluded from the criminal justice process simply because of their age. The vast majority of recent research has brought into question the belief that children's memory performance is inevitably poorer than that of adults. However, few psychologists would be so bold as to suggest that there are no differences between testimony given by young children and that given by adults. Clifford (1993) has commented on the fact that most books published prior to 1984 argued that children did make poorer witnesses. However, many subsequent publications suggest that this pessimistic view is not entirely appropriate and that, in some cases and on some tasks, children can be as good as the average adult.

CONCLUDING COMMENTS

If nothing else, the massive amount of research on the subject has served to focus attention on the way in which child witnesses should and should not be interviewed. Whilst the Criminal Justice System may retain some of its scepticism, it is now more likely that a child's voice will be heard and that those guilty of abuse will be punished. No doubt psychologists will continue to argue that more should be done to help and protect those children who make well-founded allegations against adults. However, the progress over the last 15 years should be acknowledged. In the area of child witnesses, psychologists have had a significant impact on both policy and practice. This is no small feat and deserves to be both recognised and applauded.

CHAPTER 10

Identification via Other Sense Modalities

Throughout this book we have referred to witnesses as *eye*witnesses. This terminology is commonplace in the literature and perhaps reflects the fact that the vast majority of information which witnesses take in is via the eyes. This focus is reflected in most books on perception which devote far more space to visual perception than to other forms. If the overemphasis on visual perception is understandable, this should not be taken to mean that perception via other sense modalities is irrelevant. A police officer interviewing a witness may well ask him or her to "tell me what you *saw*", but will of course be interested in what the witness heard, or perhaps smelled, tasted or felt. Witnesses to a bank robbery may recount details of what they actually saw, but other inputs may well have registered and have been recorded in their memory. It is interesting to note that in the Cognitive Interview Technique (see Chapter 7) witnesses are encouraged to check their memories for any information which may have been taken in via other sense modalities. Fisher and Geiselman believe that a significant amount of non-visual information is often encoded and that a skilled interviewer may be able to encourage the witness to recall such details.

In reality, visual cues often interact with verbal cues to produce an overall impression. Thus a witness who describes a robber as very aggressive may have formed this impression by watching the robber's behaviour and listening to what he or she said. Thus visual and verbal cues may interact to form an impression, and it is not always possible to identify exactly which sense modality originally produced which impression. In Chapter 5 we saw how verbally presented misleading information can interfere with material which was originally presented visually (see Loftus & Green, 1980). Witnesses may thus have difficulty in recalling whether the memory which they possess comes from material which was originally presented visually or aurally. As with eyewitnesses, earwitnesses may also experience difficulty if exposed to subsequent misleading information (see Thompson, 1985a), or if faced with more than one to-be-recognised voice (see Goldstein & Chance, 1985). It should also be noted that, like faces, voices can elicit stereotypes which can affect memory. It has been found that there is often a high degree of consensus in the attributions which people make about voices, but such consensus does not necessarily equate with accuracy (see Aronovitch, 1976).

A witness who notices that a male perpetrator has a particularly high-pitched voice, for example, may believe that he will have an effeminate appearance. If the person's face is seen, the memory of it may be subsequently distorted by the voice stereotype. Yarmey (1994) has suggested that whether the voice is believed to be that of a "criminal type" or a "non-criminal type" may affect memory. He found that subjects tended to associate particular traits with particular vocal attributes. This occurred both with targets who were labelled as "good guys" and those labelled as "bad guys". Yarmey's research led him to the following conclusion:

> "These results suggest that good guys are given greater attention and deeper processing than are bad guys ... more false identifications would be expected for those persons who evoke bad guy stereotypes than for good guy stereotypes." (Yarmey, 1994, p. 111)

This is an interesting finding which suggests that perpetrators who fit the stereotype of a "typical" criminal are less likely to be identified correctly than are those who do not evoke such a stereotype.

There will be a large number of incidents in which the witness can produce very little information about a suspect's appearance and can draw only upon knowledge gained via other sense modalities. For example, a witness who sees a robber wearing an effective disguise will be able to provide little information about his or her appearance. The witness may, however, recall that the person's voice was distinctive, or that he or she smelled strongly of B.O. There will be other cases where witnesses have never seen the perpetrator at all, but have formed an impression of him or her via what they heard. In cases such as ransom demands, bomb hoaxes and abusive phone calls, the witness may never have viewed the perpetrator but may be able to provide some information about the person's voice. For example, the witness may be able to describe the person's accent, pitch and normal tone. Having said that, it has been recognised that witnesses will often have difficulty in recalling specific details of a perpetrator's voice (see Kunzel, 1990). Information about the person's speech will rarely lead to a positive identification, but may help the police to eliminate a number of possible suspects. In some cases, the witness may actually be asked to listen to a so-called "voice parade" and to try to identify which was the voice he or she heard earlier. This procedure may serve a useful purpose, but, as we will see later, may also be fraught with potential problems. It should also be noted that the rules governing the conduct of voice parades are less well developed than those governing the conduct of visual ID parades (see Yarmey, 1994).

The voice of a perpetrator may also be broadcast by the media in the hope that a member of the public may recognise it. One such case involved the kidnapping of a female estate agent in England. The kidnap victim could provide little information about the perpetrator and he remained at large for some time. The police had, however, been able to tape record the kidnapper's voice when he phoned the woman's employer with a ransom demand and instructions for payment. Unfortunately, the police failed to arrest the man when he collected the ransom money. Some weeks after the crime, a decision was made to broadcast the recording of the voice on *Crimewatch UK*. Following the programme, a woman phoned in to say that she recognised the voice as being that of her ex-husband. The police subsequently arrested the man and he was convicted of the kidnapping. This dramatic example suggests that identification by voice can be achieved in certain circumstances. However, the recognition of a familiar voice may be somewhat easier than the identification of a voice heard only once before. As we will see later, under such conditions, successful identification will invariably prove to be extremely difficult.

IDENTIFICATION BY VOICE

In Chapter 6 we considered some of the difficulties of facial identification. Identification of a suspect via other sense modalities may prove to be even more difficult and may bring its own problems. Whilst most people may have little difficulty in recognising the voice of someone whom they know well, they may find it much more difficult to identify the voice of a relative stranger which they may have heard only once (see Yarmey, 1995). Identification of voices by humans may be difficult and some writers have advocated that identification might be better tested by the use of voiceprints (see Hammersley & Read, 1996). These allow voices to be analysed and examined by machine, and then compared for likeness. The issue of voiceprints is rather beyond the scope of this chapter though the reader may wish to note the apparent lack of consensus on the topic. Writing in 1981, Bull concluded that identification by voiceprint was no better than identification by humans. However, Hammersley and Read (1996) suggest that machines may be significantly better than humans at voice identification tasks. This difference of opinion may be partially accounted for by the increasing sophistication of voiceprint machines and associated software.

Impetus for research on voice identification in Britain came from the publication of the Devlin Report (1976). This report had noted that, as far as its members were concerned, no scientific research had been conducted on the topic (see Clifford, 1980, for a review of early work). The report did, however, recommend that research into voice identification should proceed quickly and that the possibility of using "voice parades" for identification purposes should be examined. Although the Devlin Committee was essentially correct in their assessment of the state of research, courts both in England and the USA did already accept identification by voice in certain cases. For example, a witness may claim that she "heard the neighbours arguing in the street" and accept that the voices did indeed come from the said neighbours. Hollien, Bennet and Gelfer (1983) note that the admission of voice identification by courts in England goes back as far as 1660. In the USA, a court accepted evidence of voice identification in 1935 following the baby Lindberg kidnapping case. In this instance, the baby's father claimed to have recognised the kidnapper's voice some three years after it was originally heard.

Writing in 1984, Bull and Clifford acknowledged the dearth of research on the topic of voice identification but suggested that:

> "research into human abilities to recognize voices should not be neglected but rather be rapidly pursued. (Bull & Clifford, 1984, p. 92)

They acknowledged that although some progress had been made in understanding voice identification, much of the work was at a rudimentary level and lacked ecological validity (i.e. the results might not be valid outside the laboratory). Their approach was to consider many of the variables which were relevant to *eye*witnesses and to assess whether the same factors might be relevant when considering *ear*witnesses. That this approach might be appropriate was confirmed by Kapardis (1997, p. 258) who noted that:

> "The existing literature shows a remarkable degree of similarity between visual and voice identification. ... Earwitnesses, like eyewitnesses, are equally prone to error and thus potentially unreliable.

Bull and Clifford first considered age as a possibly important variable in earwitnessing. They noted that voice recognition appears to develop at a very early age and that babies in their first few months quickly learn to differentiate between the voice of their mother and that of a stranger. Drawing on their own and others' research, Bull and Clifford concluded that voice identification skills do appear to develop with age up to the middle to late teens. Abilities generally stay at this optimum level until about age 40, and then start to show a decline with increasing age. It should be noted, however, that these are tendencies rather than absolutes. It is certainly not the case that all 45-year-olds and 14-year-olds are inferior to all 25-year-olds. However, Bull and Clifford make an important point concerning the applicability of voice identification research findings. Many experiments in psychology use undergraduate students as subjects. The average age of these subjects is around 20, and as such they may as a group perform better than many real life middle-aged witnesses.

Bull and Clifford also considered whether the gender of the listener might have an effect on voice recognition accuracy. Their own studies suggested that females tended to perform slightly better than males, although they caution that this slight superiority may not be found under more stressful earwitnessing conditions. There was also some slight evidence for a same-sex effect in that females tended to perform marginally better when trying to identify a female (as opposed to a male) voice. Bull and Clifford's conclusions on gender differences have not, however, always been supported by other researchers (see, for example, Thompson, 1985b; Yarmey, 1986).

In Chapter 5 we considered the problem of cross-racial visual identifications. In that chapter we reported that there was a fairly well-established tendency for the identification of faces from another race to be more difficult than the identification of same-race faces. The limited amount of research by Bull and Clifford and by Goldstein *et al.* (1981) suggests that cross-racial identification by voice may not pose such a difficulty. However, once again we must be aware that this conclusion is based on a very small amount of research evidence, and so this should not be seen as the definitive view on the subject.

One interesting line of enquiry has been to consider the voice identification powers of those who are visually impaired. A completely unsighted person may be a victim of a crime but be unable to provide any information about the visual appearance of the perpetrator. There is something of a common assumption that blind people learn to cope with their blindness partly by developing greater sensitivity in their other sense modalities. Thus a blind person may learn to differentiate between visitors on the basis of the sound of their footsteps, or even on the basis of their individual smell. This so-called compensation hypothesis may be a fairly widely held belief, but, as Bull and Clifford note, there has not been universal support for the idea from psychological research. Those studies which did find differences between sighted and unsighted subjects often used tests which would appear to have little applicability to earwitness identification tasks.

Bull and Clifford's own research using voice recognition tests found that there was a statistically significant difference between the performance of blind and sighted subjects. This would tend to offer some support for the compensation hypothesis. However, before accepting this conclusion some notes of caution are appropriate. Firstly, whilst the difference between the two groups was statistically significant, it was not a particularly large one – blind subjects were accurate on 67% of the trials compared to 52% for the sighted subjects. (Both these were significantly greater than chance). Secondly, it should be noted that those who were completely blind performed no better that those who had some limited sight. In addition, those who had been blind for many years performed no better than those whose blindness had a more recent onset. These latter two findings are difficult to explain from the perspective of the compensation hypothesis. It would surely have been predicted that those who had been totally blind for many years would show more evidence of compensation than those whose visual impairment was less severe, and/or had developed more recently.

It would thus appear that although visually impaired witnesses may perform slightly better than sighted witnesses on voice recognition tasks, the difference cannot be totally explained by a simple compensation hypothesis. The difference in performance does, however, raise the question as to whether it might be possible to train sighted people to develop their voice recognition skills. Unfortunately, the small amount of work in this area suggests that, as with visual identification, such training has little if any effect (see Bull and Clifford, 1984, p. 104). The reader may also be interested to note that trained phoneticians (voice experts) do not necessarily perform better than other listeners in voice recognition tasks (see Ladefoged, 1981).

Another aspect of earwitnessing considered by Bull and Clifford concerned the length of the speech sample that a witness may have heard. Common sense would suggest that the longer the sample of speech, the more likely it is that the witness will be able to later recognise the voice. As we saw in Chapters 3 and 5, length of exposure to a stimulus can be an important factor in eyewitnessing recognition tasks. Bull and Clifford reviewed a number of studies on sample size, including some of their own experiments. They concluded, perhaps surprisingly, that the length of the speech sample appears to make little difference to later identification – provided that at least one sentence was heard originally. However, it is noted that this finding only applies to adults – children seem to show improved recognition accuracy when larger speech samples are used. Bull and Clifford also caution that their research is not definitive and that further research is needed before we can draw firm conclusions as to the length of speech samples which would produce optimum performance (see also Yarmey, 1994, p. 114).

As a footnote to the studies reviewed by Bull and Clifford, other authors suggest that hearing a voice for several short periods may lead to better recognition than hearing the voice sample all at once (see Yarmey & Matthys, 1992). Yarmey (1992) also found that although increased familiarity with a voice did lead to more correct identifications, it also led to an increase in the rate of false identifications. Yarmey explains this curious finding by reference to the fact that increased exposure may lead the witness to believe that he or she *should* be able to pick out the suspect. As a consequence, the witness guesses rather than admit that he or she is unsure.

A related point concerns the fact that, in most laboratory studies, witnesses listen passively to a tape-recorded voice. It has been suggested that such passive listening may produce different results when compared with the situation in which a witness verbally interacts with a perpetrator. In one of the few studies to consider this point, Hammersley and Read (1985) found that passively heard voices were less likely to be identified than those in which there was interaction between the target and the subject witness. This result may have implications for witnesses in real cases, many of whom will have had a vocal interaction with the perpetrator. By comparison, most subjects in laboratory studies will have listened passively to the voice. It should, however, be noted that if the interaction was particularly stressful, this may result in poorer memory (see Chapter 3).

If attempts are to be made to identify a suspect from his or her voice, then it is possible that some kind of voice parade will be used. Such a procedure will be in some ways similar to a traditional (visual) ID parade (see Chapter 6). There will, however, be one important difference. In visual ID parades the witness generally has the opportunity to scan all the faces on the parade simultaneously. However, with a voice parade, the witness hears the voices sequentially and has to make a decision about each one in turn. This fact means that it becomes less like a multiple choice test, and more like a normal decision-making task. In such circumstances it is less likely that the witness will simply guess or will pick out the voice which most resembles that originally heard (see Chapter 6).

As with visual ID parades, consideration may need to be given to the composition of the parade, both in terms of the total number of voices on the parade, and the similarity of the target voice to that of the distracters. Bull and Clifford suggest that fair results can be achieved if six distracters are used on voice parades – an increase in this number may not be necessary to achieve a valid result. Once again, though, Bull and Clifford caution that these results may hold only for situations where speech samples of one sentence are used, where there is little stress in the task, where no disguise is used, and where subjects are tested immediately.

As we saw with visual ID parades (Chapter 6), the actual size of the voice parade may be less important than its functional size (see Wells, Leippe & Ostrom, 1979). A voice parade containing the suspect plus five foils may not necessarily be fair. If, for example, three of the foils are so completely different from the suspect that it is unthinkable that they might be picked out, then the functional size of the line-up may be more correctly thought of as three rather than six. This point is made by Yarmey (1994, p. 102). Yarmey was asked to appear as an expert witness for the defence in a case in which a voice parade had been used by the police. Yarmey believed that the procedure in this case was flawed and that the identification of the suspect by the witness was not necessarily accurate. Yarmey replicated the procedure used by the police and was able to show that the chances of the suspect being picked out from a six-person parade were significantly greater than one in six. In this particular case the voices of the five foils were quite similar to each other (they were all police officers) but were all considerably different from that of the suspect. Given this fact it would appear that most people would be likely to select the odd one out, and come to believe that this was the voice of the perpetrator.

Bull and Clifford also considered whether the target voice's position in the test array might make any difference to recognition accuracy. They found that in general it did not. However, if the target voice was the first one heard in the parade, there was a significantly greater chance that the voice would be recognised. In some experiments where the target voice was the first in the array, the chances of correct identification were almost doubled. These findings are interesting, though it may not be possible to make direct comparisons with earwitnessing tasks outside the laboratory. In real criminal cases it is extremely unlikely that witnesses' voice recognition abilities would be tested immediately after exposure to a suspect's voice. As such the apparent recency effect (see Chapter 2) found by Bull and Clifford in the laboratory may not be mirrored in "real world" voice recognition tests.

One important consideration in both eyewitnessing and earwitnessing identification tasks is the effect of disguise. It has been well established that the disguise of important facial features reduces significantly the chances of correct visual identification (See Chapter 5). It also appears from the limited amount of research in the area that the same is true of earwitnessing tasks. Any deliberate attempt to disguise the voice's normal sound tends to lead to a reduced likelihood of correct identification.

There is, however, an additional complication when considering vocal identifications. The human voice is not constant, but varies according to the topic of conversation, the speaker's mood and other factors. Some forms of disguise may be deliberate in that the speaker makes a conscious effort to change some characteristics of his or her voice. However, disguise may also be less intentional – for example, where a person's voice changes naturally as a response to differing conditions. Thus a person committing an armed robbery may be in an extremely agitated state. This may result in his or her voice changing in significant ways. It might, for example, become more highly pitched and be louder. The robber may also tend to speak more rapidly than normal and to issue short staccato commands to those in the bank. It may thus prove extremely difficult for a witness to later identify the voice when the suspect is speaking in a more normal way.

This latter point is important when considering the results of laboratory-based studies of earwitness identification. In these experiments, subjects invariably have to listen to a voice whose characteristics are not altered at all from original presentation to testing. In many cases, subjects will have listened to the exact same recording with which they were presented earlier. Given this, it appears likely that many laboratory-based studies of earwitnessing may have overestimated the likelihood of correct identification in the real world. In one of the few studies to examine the effect of voice disguise in the laboratory (Clifford & Denot, 1982) it was found that the rate of correct identifications fell significantly for subjects who heard a voice in an altered state from that originally presented.

In addition to the disguise discussed above, a voice may also appear different when it is heard over the telephone. Although some people do deliberately speak differently when using the telephone, the machine itself also causes some alterations in the voice's characteristics. In many of the cases which might involve earwitnessing (e.g. bomb hoaxes, obscene phone calls) the voice may only ever be heard over the telephone. As such, it is important to know whether this factor is likely to reduce recognition accuracy. Drawing on a limited amount of research, Bull and Clifford conclude that the use of the telephone does indeed reduce voice identification accuracy, but not to the level of chance.

In cases where a suspect's voice was originally heard over the telephone the police may choose to conduct a voice parade by having the witness listen to the array of voices over the telephone. Such a strategy would appear to be appropriate as it should mean (at least theoretically) that the suspect's voice will be more similar than if it was subsequently heard in a different form. However, Bull and Clifford found that subjects who had originally heard a voice over the telephone still showed poor recognition accuracy even when the voice was subsequently again heard over the telephone. Rathborn, Bull and Clifford (1981) also showed that a voice originally heard over the telephone need not be tested over the telephone on a subsequent identification attempt. These authors found that witnesses who heard the voice on a tape recorder on second presentation performed no worse than those who reheard the voice over the telephone.

Two final points raised by Bull and Clifford concern the effects of delay, and the effects of expectancy. Although definitive answers are still some way off, it does appear that, as with visual identifications, the longer the time interval between the original hearing of a voice and subsequent recognition testing, the less likely it is that the voice will be correctly identified. Having said that, Bull and Clifford do add that the effects of delay are far from catastrophic and in some experiments voices have been correctly identified several weeks or months after their original hearing. On the television programme *This is Your Life*, old friends of each week's guest are first heard speaking rather than appearing visually. In most cases, such voices are immediately recognised and named by the week's guest. It should, however, again be acknowledged that the recognition of a very familiar voice is somewhat different from the recognition of a perpetrator's voice, perhaps heard only once.

More recent studies suggest that whilst the retention interval might be important, it is not possible to specify an exact point at which identifications will become completely unreliable (see Hammersley & Read, 1996, p. 138). As was the case with faces, it appears that some voices are more distinctive (and thus more memorable) than others. One need only think of different voices heard on the radio – some such voices leave a lasting impression while others are forgotten almost instantly. For this reason, time delay will tend to have less of an effect on memory for distinctive voices than it would on memory for less memorable ones (see Yarmey, 1994, p. 106). Similarly, a voice that was an important part of a salient and vivid event in which the witness was involved may be better recognised than one with less significance.

Bull and Clifford also suggest that expectancy and preparedness can play a role in vocal identification rates. As might be predicted, subject witnesses who are forewarned that their voice recognition memory will be later tested tend to perform better than those who are given no such warning. This finding again suggests that laboratory-based research studies may have overestimated the likely accuracy of real-life vocal identification. Most witnesses and victims will have no advance warning that they may be about to witness a crime, let alone that their memory will be later tested.

It would thus appear that whilst voice identification is possible there are a large number of factors which will affect the likely accuracy of any such identifications. As has been noted extensively above, issues of ecological validity lead one to question the applicability of some laboratory-based studies. In some cases, laboratory studies may have led to an over-estimation of the likely accuracy of earwitnesses in real criminal cases. However, Hammersley and Read (1996), in their recent comprehensive review of earwitnessing studies, suggest that the opposite might be true. They point out that many laboratory-based studies have employed particularly difficult voice recognition tasks and thus may have underestimated the likely accuracy of witnesses in real cases. Perhaps the conclusion to be drawn is that laboratory-based studies have helped to identify many of the important variables in understanding earwitness identification tasks. However, as with visual identification, it is not possible to make absolute predictions as to the probable accuracy of earwitness identifications. Nevertheless psychologists can and do testify as to the fairness or otherwise of earwitness identification tests and can have an influence on verdicts (see Yarmey, 1994, p. 102).

Identification by voice remains a comparatively under-researched subject and as such it is hard to draw firm conclusions. Hammersley & Read (1996, p. 118) caution that:

> "it is unlikely that people can reliably identify by voice strangers whom they have heard once briefly."

However, the same authors also suggest that, providing certain criteria are met, evidence of voice identification should not necessarily be completely dismissed. They state (p. 118):

> "... we see no reason to exclude evidence of identification from voice altogether, as long as the recognition procedures followed are fair and allow witnesses to fail to identify anyone."

OTHER SENSE MODALITIES

If research on voice identification is still at a rudimentary stage then that on identification via the remaining senses has barely made it out of the starting blocks. Whilst acknowledging this fact, there are still some cases where an identification via, say, smell may be attempted. In one episode of the acclaimed fictional British television series *Cracker*, a rape victim recalls that her assailant wore a strong and distinctive aftershave. The victim (herself a police officer) then made several trips to perfume counters and eventually believed that she had identified the aftershave worn by her attacker. The woman suspected that one particular colleague may have committed the rape and a search of his belongings dramatically revealed that he did use the aftershave which she had identified earlier. This convinced the policewoman of her colleague's guilt, though it is perhaps unlikely that such unscientific identification evidence would be accepted in a court of law.

Although this example is taken from a fictional television series, there will be some cases in which such evidence may help the police to pinpoint a suspect. Unfortunately, psychologists would be able to say very little about the likely accuracy of this type of identification. We do have some knowledge concerning the perception of, and memory for, odours, but much of this work appears to have little direct relevance to witness identification. A recent edited work dealing with memory for odours (Schab & Crowder, 1995) contains no explicit reference to the identification of people via the olfactory sense. However, interestingly, the book does cover some material which could be of relevance to eye-witnessing research. For example, within the book, Herz and Eich (1995) draw our attention to the fact that there are some fairly well-established individual differences in odour perception abilities. Specifically, females invariably perform better on odour recognition tests than men. In addition, in common with visual identification accuracy rates, performance tends to decrease with advancing age (see Murphy, 1995).

Human olfactory abilities appear to have declined during recent evolutionary history, perhaps because such skills are less in demand today than are those which rely on other sense modalities. Checking visually to see if the supermarket meat is past its sell-by date may have more survival value than checking whether it smells rancid! However, some authors believe that almost all humans still possess the faculties and abilities needed to become more expert in their olfactory abilities. Evidence suggests that perfumers develop remarkable abilities to differentiate between slightly different odours. Similarly, expert wine tasters become highly skilled and are able to differentiate between different wine odours and tastes. Even more impressively, such experts are often able to identify and name a wine smelled and tasted perhaps months or even years earlier (see Ainsworth, 1988a, 1988b).

It would thus appear that it would be inappropriate to dismiss entirely the prospect of identification via the sense of smell. For some witnesses who may have special skills in this area, identification via smell may be a realistic possibility. We should also note that recent developments in the use of gas chromatography may in future make it possible to identify suspects via their distinctive smell profile.

Before scoffing at such a suggestion, the reader may wish to note that police forces in some countries already take a smell sample from the scene of a crime and attempt to match this to the smell of a suspect. In Holland, the police use specially trained dogs for this attempted identification. In a typical case, the police may find some item which the suspect has touched at the scene of the crime. A sterile but absorbent cloth will be wrapped around the item, and then transferred to a sealed container. If the police arrest a suspect, a dog may be brought in to provide evidence that the suspect did indeed handle the item at the scene. The dog will typically smell the cloth and then go along a line which includes the suspect and a number of foils. In many cases, the dog is able to indicate which of the people on the parade matches the odour emanating from the cloth. Courts in Holland have now accepted that, subject to a number of important safeguards, identification by this means can be accepted as evidence. Interestingly, the police in Holland are now starting to take smell samples from many of those arrested, in the same way that fingerprints might be routinely taken. Smell samples can then be stored in a library, and used to match future crimes with known suspects (see de Bruin, 1996; van Koppen, 1995).

Thus there would appear to be some potential for using smell as a method of identification. As machines become more sophisticated, it is possible that smell profiles might be built up and used as an additional way of identifying perpetrators. Such machines are already being used to try to detect changes in bodily odours when a person is lying (see Coghlan, Kiernan & Mullins, 1995) and may have many other forensic applications.

It is not obvious whether identification via the remaining senses might also be possible. There can be few instances where it would be appropriate to attempt the identification of a suspect by taste. However, there may be other cases (e.g. a rape) where a disguised attacker comes into close physical contact with his victim, allowing her to feel some aspects of his physical make-up. The victim may recall that the man felt very muscular, that he had small hands or was distinctive in some other way. Once again, such details may help the police to narrow down a range of suspects, but are unlikely to allow a firm identification of the perpetrator. One possible exception to this rule might be identification by the visually impaired. For example, a blind rape victim may have had the opportunity to explore her attacker's face with her hands. This may have allowed her to form a very vivid impression of the man's face, and even enable her to pick the face out from an ID parade. Whether such evidence would be accepted would, of course, ultimately be up to the individual court.

CONCLUDING COMMENTS

It can be seen from this chapter that identification might be possible via other sense modalities. Although most identifications will continue to be made visually, the other senses may still take in valuable information which will be of value to investigators. Future research will need to establish the exact conditions under which identifications via other senses may or not be accurate. Once such research has been carried out, investigators should be encouraged to tap the potentially rich sources of information which other sense modalities might provide.

CHAPTER 11

The Psychologist as Expert Witness

From all that has been written in the preceding chapters it can be seen that psychologists have made valuable contributions to our understanding of eyewitness performance. It has been argued from the outset that courts may have unrealistic expectations as to the ability of eyewitnesses to provide accurate and objective testimony. Given these facts, one might want to argue that in certain cases eyewitness testimony should be excluded altogether, or, if accepted, be treated with extreme suspicion. The reality is that a large proportion of criminal cases could never be brought to court without the evidence provided by eyewitnesses.

Not only do courts need the testimony of eyewitnesses, but jurors appear to welcome eyewitness testimony when deciding a case (see Loftus, 1984b). Whilst other forms of evidence may be considered more scientific, much of this is of a technical nature and not easily understood by members of the jury. There can be little more compelling evidence than when a confident, competent eyewitness describes having seen the accused actually commit the crime (see Loftus, 1979). However, as we have seen throughout this book, such evidence does not necessarily prove that the defendant did indeed commit the crime of which he or she stands accused.

Given what we know about the reliability of eyewitness testimony, it might be reasonable to presume that it would be quite common for psychologists to appear as expert witnesses, especially in cases which rely heavily on such testimony. Whether because of a suspicion of the value of psychological research, or because courts would prefer jurors to make up their own minds, the number of occasions on which psychologists are called as expert witnesses remains relatively small and it is still unusual for psychologists to be called upon in this way. However, as we will see later, the number of occasions on which psychologists do appear as experts is increasing over time. Gudjonsson (1996) notes that there are a large number of different areas in which forensic psychologists are now called to give evidence, including that of eyewitness testimony. However, he also points out that the number of appropriately qualified experts, at least in Britain, is very small.

Psychologists are often prompted to appear as expert witnesses by a desire to prevent a possible miscarriage of justice (see Cutler & Penrod, 1995). In cases where eyewitness testimony is the sole or main evidence against an accused, a psychologist may well be called by the defence in an attempt to warn jurors of the dangers of relying too heavily on eyewitness testimony. Gudjonsson (1993) has suggested that psychologists have a unique contribution to make to judicial proceedings and this view has been echoed by many other practitioners.

Before moving on we must bear in mind that most of the comments in this chapter apply to cases where the expert is called by one side or the other. In some countries (e.g. many of those in central Europe) experts are appointed by the court itself. It is interesting to note that psychologists appointed by the court appear to have higher status than those appointed by the defence or prosecution (see Nijboer, 1995).

Many psychologists believe that jurors (and other "triers of fact") may make one of two different types of error when considering eyewitness testimony. Firstly, it is thought that jurors are prone to over-believe eyewitnesses' testimony and to give it more credence than is perhaps justified. Secondly, it has been argued that jurors find it difficult to distinguish between witnesses who are likely to be accurate, and those who are not. As we will see later, much of the testimony given by psychologists is aimed at challenging these possible errors.

THE ADMISSIBILITY OF EXPERT EVIDENCE ON EYEWITNESS RELIABILITY

Much of the debate on the role of psychologists as expert witnesses has taken place in the USA. As Kapardis (1997) observes, psychologists in the USA have been appearing as experts more frequently and in a greater range of cases than in most other countries (see also Landsman, 1995; Davies, 1995). A number of landmark rulings have been made in respect of the admissibility of expert testimony, and whilst these rulings often apply only to the particular state in which they were made, they do highlight the main issues in the debate as regards eyewitness expert testimony. For this reason we will next review some of the more important rulings from the American courts and examine the reasoning behind them. (The interested reader may wish to consult Nijboer (1995) for a review of other countries).

According to Fulero (1993; in Cutler & Penrod, 1995), the first American case in which the defence tried to call a psychologist as an expert witness was that of *Criglow* v *State* (1931). In this case (involving a man charged with robbery) the defence sought to call a psychologist to testify as to the powers of observation and recollection of two eyewitnesses. The court chose to reject the testimony, and this decision was upheld by the Arkansas Supreme Court. The main reason offered for the rejection of the expert testimony was that such testimony would "invade the province of the jury". In other words, the court believed that it was up to jurors to decide whether eyewitnesses were or were not likely to be accurate, and that jurors did not need any help in reaching such a decision. Whether or not expert testimony does invade the province of the jury is one of the major issues in the debate, and we will return to this topic later.

In another American case (*People* v *Collier*, 1952), the defence attempted to introduce a psychologist to provide evidence as to the effects of stress on eyewitness testimony. The court rejected this testimony, and again stated that such evidence would invade the province of the jury. The court in the Criglow case also considered that the testimony of a psychologist was not necessary, as such information would be "within the field of common knowledge and experience" (Cutler & Penrod, 1995, p. 19). This is another important consideration which, as we will see later, recurs in later rulings.

Cutler and Penrod note that testimony in these early cases was somewhat different from testimony give by psychologists today. In many such former cases psychologists would give an opinion as to whether a particular witness was or was not likely to be mistaken. In these cases psychologists could provide little in the way of empirical evidence to support their view. In more recent cases, psychologists tend not to talk about such specific factors, but are more likely to provide general information as to the factors effecting eyewitness reliability. Juries may also be told that they can choose to accept or reject the testimony of the expert in reaching a decision. Cutler and Penrod (1995) note that this factor makes it less likely that the testimony will be judged to be invading the province of the jury.

If expert testimony by psychologists is to be accepted then it needs to fulfil some purpose and help jurors in their decision making. In one ruling in the USA (*United States* v *Amaral*) the court decided upon a number of admissibility criteria, i.e.:

1. The expert must be qualified to testify about the subject matter.
2. The expert must testify about a proper subject.
3. The testimony must conform to a generally accepted explanatory theory.
4. The probative value of the testimony must outweigh its prejudicial effect.

The Amaral court drew upon the Frye test which had been developed many years earlier (*Frye* v *United States*, 1923). Although concerned with the admissibility of lie detection evidence, the Frye case had established some important criteria by which expert testimony in general might be judged.

Interestingly, the court in the Amaral case rejected the testimony of the expert because it was considered not to be of "a proper subject matter". The court again ruled that it should be up to the jury to decide what weight to give to the testimony of eyewitnesses. It also expressed the view that jurors could be trusted to do this without the help of an expert.

Cutler and Penrod note that the situation in the USA changed following the introduction in 1975 of the new Federal Rules of Evidence. Although the rules were not binding in non-federal cases, many American courts adopted rules similar to those spelled out in the new federal rules. These included the notion that the expert must be qualified; that the testimony must assist the triers of fact; and that the expert's testimony should be sufficiently reliable. The ruling that the testimony need only "assist" the jury is in contrast to the rule established in the Amaral case where it was stated that such testimony must offer "appreciable help". The federal rules also suggested that the probative value of expert testimony must outweigh its prejudicial impact. This latter point is interesting. Given that many psychologists believe that eyewitnesses can and often do make mistakes, such experts may well wish to bring this fact to the attention of the jury. However, it might be ruled that such testimony is inadmissible because it could have a prejudicial effect on the jury's decision.

Cutler and Penrod observe that following the introduction of the new rules, courts were much more likely to accept expert testimony than had previously been the case. In one important appeal case (*United States* v *Downing*, 1985) Judge Becker ruled that expert eyewitness testimony should *not* be presumed to invade the province of the jury and that much of what an expert has to say *is* beyond the common knowledge held by most jurors. This important ruling challenged a number of earlier decisions as to the admissibility of expert testimony. It is however interesting to note that when the district court reconsidered the admissibility issue in the Downing case it still chose to reject the testimony of the expert called by the defence. The grounds for this rejection were that the testimony may have been unreliable, and so may have misled the jury.

The rules on the admissibility of expert testimony in the USA were fully explored in the case of *Daubert* v *Merrell Dow Pharmaceuticals Inc.* (1993). Although this case did not involve eyewitness testimony, it laid down many important rules and has been seen by many as a land-mark decision in relation to expert testimony. The judges in the Daubert case rejected the rigid notion that expert testimony can only be accepted if it is based on a "generally accepted" theory. The judges also ruled that whilst the expert's testimony must be based on "scientific knowledge" such knowledge need not be irrefutable. The judges accepted that there can be no absolute certainties in science. However, they also felt that any expert opinion must be based upon knowledge obtained using the scientific method of investigation. The judges thus ruled that any expert testimony must be based upon scientific knowledge and that it must assist triers of fact to understand or determine a fact at issue. Thus when deciding whether or not to accept such expert testimony, judges needed to establish whether the evidence was scientifically valid and whether the reasoning could be applied to the facts at issue.

Judges in the Daubert case went even further in spelling out what they believed should be accepted as "scientific methodology". They noted that the scientific method is based upon the generation and testing of appropriate hypotheses. They also noted that attempts to falsify such hypotheses are crucial to the scientific method and are what distinguishes science from other fields. The judges also recognised another important criterion, i.e. whether or not the theory or technique had been subject to peer review and publication.

The Daubert ruling was thus seen as a landmark decision in the USA and established some important criteria for deciding upon the admissibility of expert evidence (see Faigman, 1995; Landsman, 1995; Duncan, 1996). Although the rules did allow some flexibility, they established the importance of scientific validity in any proposed submission. Nevertheless, it should be noted that in all cases the decision as to whether or not to accept such testimony still rested with the trial judge.

Cutler and Penrod note that although the rules allowed considerable discretion, a number of appeals were lodged on the basis that a trial judge had excluded expert testimony by a psychologist. Whilst many such appeals failed, a number were successful, and the cases further established the criteria under which American judges might accept or reject expert testimony by a psychologist. For example, in 1983 the Arizona Supreme Court ruled that the trial judge in the case of *State* v *Chapple* had been wrong to exclude expert testimony by a psychologist. In this case, the psychologist wished to give evidence on a number of matters including unconscious transference, the effects of post-event information, and the relationship between confidence and accuracy. Interestingly, unlike in previous cases, the appeal judges ruled that knowledge of such factors was *not* within the general knowledge of jury members. This ruling was supported by judges in the case of *People* v *McDonald* (1984). In this case, judges ruled that it would be an error to exclude expert testimony if the case against an accused was based mainly on uncorroborated eyewitness evidence.

Notwithstanding these rulings, Cutler and Penrod (1995, p. 26) note that:

> "Despite these generally favourable recent developments, the overall position of the courts is still somewhat negative with respect to admitting eyewitness expert testimony."

Cutler and Penrod also note that there is considerable variation between one court and the next. Many decisions apply only to the particular circuit or state in which the case was tried. Thus it is not easy to present an overall picture as to the current admissibility of expert testimony in the USA. (See Cutler & Penrod, 1995, ch. 3 for some examples of the wide variation).

Debates in the American courts have served to highlight the main issues in any discussion of expert eyewitness testimony though the rulings have no authority outside the United States. Many other countries are currently debating this issue, but the legal position does vary from one country to another (see Kapardis, 1997, pp. 178–182). In England and Wales, for example, courts have traditionally been somewhat reluctant to accept expert testimony from psychologists (see Sheldon & MacLeod, 1991; Canter, 1997). In a landmark decision (*R* v *Turner*, 1975) the court ruled that for expert testimony to be admitted it must provide information which is "beyond the common knowledge and experience of the jury". Note that this is similar, but not identical, to one of the rulings in the American courts (see above).

Whilst the decision in the Turner case would seem to preclude much of the testimony offered by psychologists in England and Wales, critics have argued that human behaviour is not always a simple matter of common sense (see Colman & Mackay, 1993). Thornton (1995) points to a number of recent encouraging signs with regard to the admissibility of expert testimony in England and Wales. One such example is the case of *R* v *Sally Loraine Emery and Another* (1993). This case did not involve eyewitness testimony, but was concerned with post-traumatic stress disorder, learned helplessness and battered woman syndrome. The court decided that it would admit evidence on these matters from a psychiatrist and a psychologist. The appeal court upheld the original court's decision, suggesting that the evidence was complex and not known by the general public. As such, the expert testimony would help the jury to determine the facts of the case. The ramifications of this decision are that English courts are now more likely to accept expert evidence in the field of eyewitness testimony. Whilst the "common knowledge" rule has not been completely abandoned, it would appear that the Emery case has allowed the rule to be interpreted more broadly (see Colman & Mackay, 1995).

In the last few years two leading British experts on eyewitness testimony (Graham Davies and Ray Bull) have each been allowed to provide expert testimony in a number of cases. However, Davies points out that it may be easier for psychologists in the UK to give evidence in child witness cases, most of which are civil (as opposed to criminal) hearings. He notes that:

> "... the role of the psychologist in Britain is solely one of providing reports, typically for the defence, and advising on lines of questioning: 'a second in the corner' rather than a contestant." (Davies, 1995, p. 187)

However, if the rise in demand continues, there may be a shortage of experts with the appropriate qualifications and expertise to appear as experts in Britain (see *New Scientist*, 23 August 1997)

ISSUES SURROUNDING THE ADMISSION OF EXPERT TESTIMONY ON EYEWITNESSES

Most of the recent debate as to whether or not to admit expert testimony has focused on four main areas, i.e.

1. The scientific reliability of such testimony.
2. The relevance of the testimony to the facts of the particular case being considered.
3. The effectiveness of traditional safeguards in reducing the danger of misidentifications.
4. Whether such testimony does actually assist the jury to help to understand or determine a fact in issue.

With regard to the first of these, concerns have included the lack of an explanatory theory, the lack of reliability of research findings, the methodology used in the research, and the lack of agreement among experts. Some of these concerns were addressed in the Downing case discussed earlier. Cutler and Penrod (1995, p. 51) also point out that the Downing case was one of the first in which opposing experts gave evidence as to the likely reliability of eyewitness testimony. Thus, whilst the defence called an expert to give evidence regarding the fallibility of eyewitness memory, the prosecution called a number of experts to refute this testimony. We will return to this later in the chapter.

In respect of the second point, courts may rule that whilst expert testimony is interesting it is not relevant to the circumstances of the case before them. Thus, although an expert may need to provide an overview of recent relevant psychological research, he or she needs also to be clear as to how the findings relate to the case under consideration. As was noted in Chapter 6, courts may not always share the psychologist's view as to the relevance of research findings.

When one considers the third point, the particular circumstances of any identification will need to be taken into account. As was noted in Chapter 6, different countries have different rules as to the conduct of any identification tests. However, most western societies have some degree of commonality in the rules, which should be adhered to (see Wagenaar, 1988, ch. 3). Although the lawyers themselves may challenge the admissibility of evidence on the basis that rules were not observed, psychologists may be able to provide further evidence as to the likelihood of a mistaken identification. Psychologists can, of course, also be influential in formulating rules which should ensure the fair conduct of identification procedures (see Wells *et al*., 1994). Having said that, courts may not always accept that a breach of the rules will make any identification completely unreliable. In one case involving a man accused of being a Nazi war criminal, a psychologist called by the defence stated that a total of 37 rules had been directly or indirectly broken by investigators (see Wagenaar, 1988, p. 145). Despite this, the trial court accepted the identification evidence and convicted John Demjanjuk of war crimes.

Turning to the fourth point highlighted above, it is not easy to determine whether or not expert testimony does actually assist the jury in their deliberations, or has an effect on the eventual outcome of the case. Some light has been cast on the question by Loftus (1984b). Loftus describes one interesting case in which two brothers, Thomas and Patrick Hanigan, were charged with beating and torturing three Mexicans. The case was highly unusual in that two juries sat in the same courtroom, one to decide the fate of Thomas, and one to decide that of Patrick.

The evidence against the two brothers was virtually identical and consisted mainly of eyewitness identifications by the three victims. Expert evidence about eyewitnessing was offered in the case of Thomas, but not in the case of Patrick. (The latter's jury sat in another room whilst the expert testimony was presented). One jury found Patrick guilty of the crimes, but surprisingly the second jury found his brother Thomas not guilty. Loftus suggests that this bizarre result may be due partly to the fact that expert testimony was offered in the case of one defendant but not the other. Whilst the result was fascinating, it would be inappropriate to try to generalise from a single case such as this. Loftus does, however, note that interviews with jurors involved in other cases suggest that expert testimony does affect the deliberation process of the jury (see Loftus, 1984b, p. 281). In addition, studies using mock juries (see below) show that jurors who are exposed to expert testimony spend more time discussing eyewitness accounts than do those who are not presented with such information.

Interviews with jurors in criminal cases can provide interesting insights, but such interviews rely on the jurors being able to provide accurate and unbiased recollections. Many may not be able to do this, and so the method might not be particularly reliable. An alternative is to use mock juries, which hear (or read) evidence and then deliberate on their verdict, as would a real jury. This method allows psychologists to study deliberations in great detail and to draw conclusions as to the important variables in any particular case. Although the method has its disadvantages (for example, the fact that mock jurors' decisions do not have consequences for a defendant) it does provide valuable insights into decision-making processes. Loftus reviews a number of studies which have used mock juries to assess the impact of expert testimony. She concludes that these studies generally show that:

> "exposure of jurors to an expert reduces the effect of eyewitness testimony, perhaps by causing jurors to scrutinize the testimony more carefully." (Loftus, 1984b, p. 281)

Loftus reviews some of her own and others' experiments and concludes that mock juries who are exposed to expert testimony on eyewitnesses are less likely to convict than juries who are not exposed to such information. This may be applauded by many who are concerned about wrongful convictions, and be seen as evidence that, in relevant cases, juries should hear expert testimony. However, it might be inappropriate to see a lower rate of conviction as a wholly positive move. Egeth and McCloskey (1984) acknowledge that expert testimony may serve to make jurors more sceptical of eyewitness accounts and thus less likely to convict. In cases where an accused is innocent this would, of course, be a wholly positive outcome. However, in cases where the accused is in fact guilty, this increase in scepticism may lead to the jury reaching the wrong decision and finding the perpetrator not guilty. This raises the question of whether psychologists should be involved in juries' decision-making processes and raises a number of ethical questions (see later).

Egeth and McCloskey have been largely critical of the increase in the number of psychologists providing expert testimony. They state quite forcefully that:

> "contrary to the claims of several psychologists and lawyers the available evidence fails to demonstrate the general usefulness of expert psychological

testimony and, in fact, does not even rule out the possibility that such testimony may have detrimental effects." (Egeth & McCloskey, 1984, p. 284)

A few psychologists have supported this view (e.g. Elliot, 1993), though most have not. However, it would be inappropriate to ignore completely the concerns expressed by Egeth and McCloskey. They argue that the two main justifications advanced for the introduction of expert testimony (i.e the over-belief rationale, and the discrimination rationale) have not always been supported. For example, they suggest that jurors are not completely naive and are not necessarily too willing to believe everything that eyewitnesses say. Further, they argue that jurors are often capable of deciding which witnesses are likely to be telling the truth and which are likely to be mistaken. Egeth and McCloskey's main premise is thus that jurors do not necessarily need help in evaluating testimony, and, even if they do, psychological testimony may not be able to provide this help. Their conclusion is quite worrying in that they claim that:

"expert testimony about eyewitness behaviour has not been shown to be either safe or effective." (Egeth & McCloskey, 1984, p. 301)

As was noted earlier, this pessimistic view has not always found favour with other psychologists, especially those who appear regularly as expert witnesses in court (see Leippe, 1995). One has to say that the increase in the number of cases in which psychologists are appearing in court suggests that most in the legal profession do not share the concerns of Egeth and McCloskey. However, as Davies (1995, p. 186) notes:

"In retrospect, the turmoil stirred up by McCloskey & Egeth can be seen to have had a generally positive impact on the quality and relevance of research in the field."

Wells (1984) addressed many of the points raised by Egeth and McCloskey and concluded that whilst these writers do make some interesting points, they have not proved their case. Wells argues that whilst over-belief is not necessarily inevitable, there are some conditions under which jurors do over-believe eyewitnesses. In addition, he argues that jurors are often incapable of discriminating accurate from false identification testimony. Wells makes a valid point in saying:

"Regardless of whether or not expert testimony can correct all these problems, it is difficult to justify simply sitting back and ignoring an attorney's plea for guidance on the issues." (Wells, 1984, pp. 313–314)

It is difficult not to agree with Wells' point. Nevertheless, the reader may wish to note that in one of the cases discussed earlier in this chapter (United States v. Downing) Michael McCloskey challenged the testimony to be given by another psychologist (Robert Buckout) and was successful in having that testimony excluded!

THE RELATIONSHIP BETWEEN LAW AND PSYCHOLOGY

Frazzini (1981) has suggested that the legal profession's reluctance to accept expert testimony by psychologists may be based on "a fear of the novel". Grano puts the point well when he states:

"The legal profession always has been wary of turning to other disciplines for the resolution of legal questions, and psychological studies calling into question the law's very method of determining guilt and innocence undoubtedly hardened resistance." (Grano, 1984, p. 316)

The point is made even more eloquently by Allen and Miller, who say:

'The law is a hostage to the knowledge possessed by others; it needs data, good data. It can well do without the biasses and prejudices of related disciplines – it has enough of its own to deal with." (Allen & Miller, 1995, p. 337)

Whilst professionals such as psychiatrists may be routinely called upon to give expert testimony, the status and expertise of the psychologist may be a little more ambiguous. As was noted above, the law is not renowned for its speed or enthusiasm in accepting new ideas and so may be reluctant to acknowledge that this new breed of expert has something of value to offer. Frazzini, however, believes that expert testimony can be extremely useful:

"... expert psychological testimony is the best way for jurors to learn about the unreliability of eyewitness testimony. ... For innocent men and women, wrongly accused because of mistaken identifications, expert psychological testimony still offers a beacon of hope." (Frazzini, 1981, p. xx)

Despite this, Frazzini notes that because eyewitness testimony is often a proven formula for conviction, few people want to interfere with or challenge such evidence. Grano (1984) supports this point and highlights the difficulty which prosecutors already face in trying to obtain a conviction. It should also be acknowledged that psychology as a science is in its early stages of development and may not yet have accumulated the body of knowledge which might make its general acceptance more likely.

Psychological research does not always lend itself easily to the requirements of the law (see Davies, 1995). To take one example, researchers often carry out experiments to establish whether there are statistically significant differences between different conditions. In reporting their results psychologists may state that "the difference was significant at the .05 level". What psychologists mean by this is that it is very unlikely that the result occurred by chance. However, most lawyers, let alone jurors, would have little understanding as to what "significant at the .05 level" actually meant. The legal profession tend to use expressions such as "on the balance of probabilities" (in civil cases) or "beyond reasonable doubt" (in criminal cases). Whilst there may be some overlap between the terms used by psychologists and lawyers, they are not identical. As Davies (1995, p. 184) notes:

> "Technical vocabulary is always a barrier to collaboration between professionals, but when the two use the same terms in rather differing ways then this can frequently lead to misunderstanding."

A psychologist who establishes that a statistically significant difference does exist can honestly say that it is unlikely (or extremely unlikely) that this occurred by chance. However, he or she could not state that such a possibility does not exist (see Maass, 1996). This is not the place to debate the finer points of statistical significance, but psychologists need to be aware that their own measures of proof are not necessarily identical to those required by the law (see Cutler & Penrod, 1995, ch. 4). We should also note that the law tends to want "facts" rather than probabilities. However, psychological research may not yet be at the stage where the provision of "facts" is possible (see Davies, 1995, p. 183).

We should also be aware of one of the recurring themes throughout this book, i.e the issue of external or ecological validity. The vast majority of eyewitness studies have been carried out within the confines of the psychology laboratory, invariably using psychology undergraduate students as subjects. Whilst the results of such studies are relevant to real eyewitnesses and real crimes, a simple and complete extrapolation from one to the other is not always justified. (See Maass, 1996, for an excellent review of these points.) Tollestrup, Turtle and Yuille (1994) have argued that a concentration on laboratory research has in some cases left psychologists with a potentially distorted view of eyewitnesses. They argue that a more comprehensive picture would emerge if a wider variety of research methods was employed. This point has been echoed by Cutshall and Yuille (1989) who suggest that we need far more field studies examining eyewitness accuracy.

Davies (1995) has highlighted a number of different methods which might be used in eyewitness research. Interestingly, he identifies a number of studies in which the results of laboratory-based studies have not been replicated in the field. The concern over external validity may be seized upon by lawyers keen to challenge the relevance and applicability of experiments conducted exclusively in the lab. This point is also relevant to the earlier debate concerning the scientific nature of psychological research.

Research is generally carried out in the laboratory in order that the researcher can control all the relevant variables. By doing this, the experiments may come to be perceived as more scientific than studies which do not permit such control. However, this control may paradoxically make it less likely that the results are applicable to specific cases in the "real world". It has been generally accepted that internal and external validity are often inversely related. This means that the results of those studies which have exerted the maximum amount of control may be the most difficult to apply outside the laboratory. Control is nonetheless important, as a badly conducted study which produces ambiguous results is of little use inside or outside the laboratory.

Psychologists should be prepared to acknowledge that there are potential differences between subjects in the laboratory and witnesses outside. For example, there will be different consequences for experimental subjects and real witnesses when trying to identify a suspect. Such a fact may mean that there are significant differences in identification rates when comparing real witnesses and experimental subjects (see Malpass & Devine, 1984). In addition, real witnesses, especially victims, may experience more stress than a subject witness when faced with an identification test (see Ainsworth & King, 1988). Although some studies do involve a greater amount of realism than others (see, for example, Koehnken & Maass, 1988), even the most carefully planned experiment may differ significantly from the situation experienced by those involved in actual crimes. For example, as was noted in Chapter 3, it is impossible (for ethical reasons) to simulate much of the fear and anxiety experienced by victims of violent crime. Thus, although psychologists can give evidence on this matter they cannot draw on laboratory-based studies which have replicated such conditions.

One recurring theme in the debate over admissibility is whether or not jurors are able to distinguish between eyewitnesses who are likely to be accurate and those who are not. The law has often ruled that jurors should be able to make this distinction by scrutinising the witness's testimony and his or her performance under cross-examination. Courts have sometimes ruled that such matters are simply a question of common sense (see above). However, research suggests that this may be a naive assumption. We may, for example, take the issue of the relationship between confidence and accuracy. The commonsense view would be that the more confident a witness appears to be, the more likely it is that he or she will be accurate. However, as we saw in Chapter 3, there is often little relationship between eyewitness confidence and accuracy. Wells (1984) suggests that although some jurors' intuitions about eyewitness accuracy may be appropriate, this is not the case with the confidence-accuracy link. He notes:

> "I am willing to argue that there is at least one important aspect of eyewitness testimony that is misunderstood by the trier of fact. All four methods of assessing people's intuitions converge on the conclusion that confidence and accuracy are perceived to be strongly related. ... When we compare human intuition with scientific data ... we must conclude that intuition is inadequate on this matter." (Wells, 1984, pp. 271–272)

Wells goes on to suggest that there are other areas in which intuition may not be accurate. For example, most jurors will not be aware that witnesses often overestimate the length of time that an incident took. Consequently, jurors may erroneously believe that the amount of time that a witness had to take in information was sufficient for him or her to form an accurate picture of a suspect. Similarly, jurors may not be aware that the perusal of a large number of mugshots may lead to an increase in the likelihood of false identifications (see Chapter 6). Wells also highlights the fact that many jurors will believe that police officers make superior witnesses and that they are more likely to be accurate in their testimony. However, research suggests that this assumption may not be accurate. There are other areas in which Wells believes that intuition may be inaccurate. He cites examples such as crime seriousness, the effects of hypnosis, and biased line-up instructions. Wells acknowledges that further research is needed on these latter factors before we can reach firm conclusions, but he asserts that:

> "... the evidence might be sufficient already to suggest that the lay person, as trier of fact, be counselled on these matters." (Wells, 1984, p. 272)

As we saw earlier, such a view has not always been mirrored by legal rulings. For example, in the case of United States v. Dyas (1977) the court wrote:

> "... we are persuaded that the subject matter of the proffered testimony is not beyond the ken of the average layman nor would such testimony aid the tried in a search for the truth. (Quoted in Loftus, 1984b, p. 279)

Recent research by Lindsay (1994) has broadly offered support for Wells's earlier conclusions. In a series of experiments, Lindsay found that jurors may have little insight into the factors that influence their decisions about eyewitness testimony. However, Lindsay also points out that jurors have little idea as to how they should evaluate the probable accuracy of eyewitness identifications. Lindsay's research also led him to conclude that jurors routinely underestimate the importance of many relevant variables, and apply significantly wrong expectations in respect of other variables (see Lindsay, 1994, p. 381). Lindsay's conclusions are, however, tempered by his view that in some cases expert testimony by a psychologist may not necessarily assist a jury to make better decisions. He suggests that whilst psychologists may prove useful in the courtroom, their talents might be better used in developing more appropriate interviewing techniques (see Chapter 7) and in improving identification procedures (see Chapter 6). This view is supported by Doyle (1989, p. 146) who suggests that a focus on investigative professionalism offers the best hope for the future. Lindsay's rather pessimistic conclusion is that:

> "The best way to reduce the tragedy of wrongful convictions based on eyewitness errors is to prevent those errors from occurring. Once the case is before courts it is probably too late!" (Lindsay, 1994, p. 382)

ETHICAL CONSIDERATIONS

As with many other issues discussed in this chapter, there will no doubt be further debate on the question of whether jurors are already able to make sound judgements as to the probable accuracy of eyewitness accounts. There will undoubtedly be some courts in which expert testimony is admitted, and some where it is not (see Lipton, 1996, p. 19). There will also continue to be discussions among psychologists as to whether they should be appearing as expert witnesses. We have already witnessed a number of cases in which one psychologist appears for the prosecution and one for the defence. Many fear that this "battle of the experts" can serve only to damage the reputation of psychology as a scientific discipline (see Turnstall *et al.*, 1982). It is certainly one of the more important factors which psychologists will need to consider when deciding whether or not to appear as expert witnesses.

Wrightsman observes that psychology aims to be a profession which stands for objectivity and accuracy in its procedures. He further notes that:

> "Even though expert witnesses are usually hired (and paid) by one side, it is their responsibility to report all their conclusions, whether those favor the side paying them or not." (Wrightsman, 1991, p. 43)

These are worthy sentiments but one has to wonder whether the pressures put on an expert witness will always permit total objectivity. In deciding whether or not to employ a particular expert, defence counsel will no doubt pay some attention to the previous success rate of the expert. In reality, defence counsel might be unwilling to employ an expert whose wish to be totally fair and objective has resulted in a client's conviction. It is certainly not being suggested that psychologists cannot be trusted to provide accurate and objective testimony. Indeed, a survey by Kassin, Ellsworth and Smith (1989) suggested that although "hired guns" exist in the field of psychology, bias is not a common feature in eyewitness experts. Nevertheless, as Wrightsman (1991) points out, psychologists will tend to sympathise with the side that employs them. This sympathy may not be conscious, but may result in a selective filtering of information through a desire to be helpful to the client. Kapardis (1997) notes that forensic psychologists in the USA have recently been given formal guidelines in an attempt to ensure that they behave in appropriate ways. Davies (1995) suggests that the reputation of psychologists in Britain might best be served by the rigorous enforcement of codes of practice and the registration of qualified experts.

A psychologist's wish to appear unbiased and objective may prove to be difficult. For example, Horgan (1988) points out that the expert psychologist is often perceived by the jury as an advocate rather than an unbiased scientist. More worryingly, Allen and Miller (1995) have suggested that the more that fact-finders defer to experts, the more likely they are to come up with irrational verdicts. (An interesting discussion of such points is also provided by Doyle, 1989.) One need only look at other professionals (e.g. psychiatrists) to realise that experts are quite often perceived as providers of opinion, rather than fact (see Ainsworth, 1995a, p. 108).

CONCLUDING COMMENTS

We can thus see that whether or not psychologists should be allowed to give expert testimony on eyewitness matters is a very complex question. As we have seen above, there are a whole range of legal and personal considerations to be taken into account. (The reader may wish to consult Wagenaar (1988, ch. 6) for an interesting discussion of the personal dilemmas facing expert witnesses.) If courts do permit such testimony, then psychologists will need to decide for themselves whether they are able to help or hinder the court's decision-making processes. We can only hope that the reputation of psychology as a scientific discipline will be enhanced rather than besmirched by the appearance in court of more psychologists in the future.

Conclusion

The starting point for this book was that courts may have unrealistic expectations as to the ability of eyewitnesses to produce objective and reliable information. One example of this expectation is found in the oath taken by witnesses in which they swear to "tell the truth, the whole truth and nothing but the truth". From all the research reviewed in this book it would appear almost impossible for even the most well-intentioned witness to meet this requirement. We have seen in Chapters 1 and 2 that the processes of perception and memory often edit and distort recollections to the point where witnesses produce a subjective and selective version of "the truth".

This, however, is not to suggest that eyewitnesses should be excluded from giving their version of events in court. As was noted in Chapter 11, a significant number of cases would never reach court if eyewitnesses were completely banned. However, what is needed is a greater understanding of the processes which affect perception and memory. As we saw in Chapters 3 and 4, there are a large number of variables which will affect whether or not a witness is likely to be accurate. Consideration of these factors is vital if we are to be able to differentiate between accurate and inaccurate witnesses. We are certainly not yet at the stage at which psychologists can make totally reliable predictions as to the likely accuracy of individual witnesses. However, by identifying some of the relevant factors, psychologists are in a position to provide information which should allow juries to make a more realistic assessment of the likely truthfulness of individual witnesses.

As we saw in Chapter 11, the relationship between psychology and law has often been an uneasy one. Having said that, great strides have been made over the last 20 years and psychologists are now in a position where they can and do influence law. If we take the example of children's testimony (Chapter 9) we can see that there have been a number of significant changes in legislation which now make it more likely that children will be allowed to be heard in court. Many of these changes have taken place at least partly as a result of research evidence produced by psychologists (see Davies, 1996.) Child victims are now much more likely to be given a fair hearing than was the case only ten years ago. Courts do now recognise that children are capable of producing accurate testimony – provided that they are interviewed in appropriate ways. Once again psychologists have been able to offer constructive advice on how interviews with children might best be conducted. Psychologists were also instrumental in the introduction of the live videolink and in arguing for the acceptance of videotaped evidence in court. Consequently, it is now more likely that those who commit crimes against children will be punished. This example suggests that psychologists have a great deal more to offer than simply advising courts on possible errors in eyewitness identifications (see Chapter 11).

Another major contribution which psychologists have made is the development of more appropriate interviewing techniques. As was noted in Chapter 7, police officers may previously have believed that the way in which witnesses were interviewed was irrelevant – people either could remember or they could not. However, from all the research produced to date it does appear that techniques such as the cognitive interview can have a major impact on the amount of information that a witness can provide. The significance of this fact should not be underestimated. Given that the police rely heavily on information obtained from eyewitnesses, any technique that can improve accurate recall should be greeted warmly. However, as we saw in Chapter 7, the police may still need some persuading that the extra time which the cognitive interview may take is justified. Most of the evidence points to the fact that the Cognitive Interview Technique leads to an increase in the amount of reliable information that a witness can produce. This fact means that the guilty may be more likely to be convicted and punished.

On the subject of improving witness recall, we must also mention the use of hypnosis. At a time when the cognitive interview is being used more and more widely, hypnosis is being used less and less frequently. Once hailed as a major breakthrough in the fight against crime, the use of hypnosis is now treated with considerable suspicion. We saw in Chapter 8 that while hypnosis may assist in the recovery of some memories, its use can also create major problems. Foremost of these problems are cases where a previously hypnotised witness later appears in court to give evidence. Research has shown that in these circumstances the witness will find it all but impossible to separate out the original memory from any subsequent information. A hypnotised subject is particularly vulnerable to contamination and can all too easily be misled. For this reason, a number of states in America have banned previously hypnotised witnesses from later appearing in court. Other states allow such witnesses to appear, provided that agreed safeguards have been observed. As was pointed out in Chapter 8, problems are perhaps most likely to arise when the police themselves conduct the hypnotic interview. The pioneering work by Beth Loftus showed how easy it can be to alter memory through the introduction of misleading information. For a witness in the hypnotised state, the problem can only be exacerbated.

The decline in the acceptance of hypnosis as an investigatory tool is in part due to campaigning by psychologists, notably Martin Orne. Orne's research did much to persuade psychologists and the legal profession that there are significant dangers involved in the use of hypnosis. Here again we have an example of how psychology and law can come together in a constructive way, and how psychology can even produce change in one of the most conservative of institutions.

Perhaps the most researched area in the field of eyewitness testimony is that of identification evidence. Here, psychologists have been able to study procedures and to identify ways in which mistakes might be made. Through many hours of experiments in the laboratory, psychologists have been able to highlight biases in procedures which may contribute to an unacceptably high rate of mistaken identifications.

Psychologists have also been able to offer constructive advice on the way in which procedures might be improved. Unfortunately, a number of these suggestions have still not been incorporated into legal practice, and mistaken identifications continue to occur. Perhaps in the future, legislators will acknowledge the fundamental flaws in many eyewitness identification procedures, and incorporate some of the changes advocated by psychologists.

We saw in Chapter 10 that research into identification via other sense modalities is still at an early stage. However, it is an important area of research in which there is great potential for new discoveries (see Hammersley & Read, 1996). It will be interesting to see how the courts treat such identifications in the future. Whether they choose to accept or reject identification via sense modalities other than sight will depend partly on the available psychological research evidence at the time.

We can thus see that psychologists have made some major contributions to our understanding of eyewitness testimony, and in some cases have influenced policy. However, it would be inappropriate to paint a completely positive picture. There remains a major debate around the issue of ecological validity (see Chapter 11). The fact that the vast majority of eyewitness testimony experiments are still carried out in the laboratory is cause for some concern. The dilemma was highlighted in Chapter 11 where it was acknowledged that the heavy emphasis on scientific methodology may blind us to differences between subject witnesses in the laboratory and "real" witnesses in the outside world. The limited number of studies which have looked at actual witnesses and victims have shown that whilst some laboratory-based findings do apply equally outside the lab, others do not (see Yuille, 1993; Davies, 1995). Future researchers will need to use a wider range of research methods if their findings are to achieve greater acceptance. Psychologists have accumulated a massive amount of data on the behaviour of undergraduate psychology students in the laboratory. The extent to which many of these findings translate to other subjects and other settings remains to be seen.

Research into eyewitness testimony shows no sign of slowing down. This is partly due to the fact that it is an area in which psychologists can easily demonstrate the significance and applicability of their findings. Unlike some areas of psychological research, eyewitness testimony studies have an obvious and immediate relevance in the "real world". Every day, hundreds of witnesses and victims step into the witness box and swear to "tell the truth, the whole truth and nothing but the truth". On hearing those words, a wry smile may appear on the face of any psychologist who happens to be in court at the time!

The criminal justice system would virtually grind to a halt without eyewitnesses who are willing to appear and testify in court. Let us hope that future psychological research will allow us to further distinguish between those witnesses whose testimony should be believed, and those whose should not. Let us also hope that research findings will be accepted more widely, and that, when appropriate, changes in legislation will occur.

Considerable progress has been made in the last 20 years, but much more needs to be done. Psychologists and lawyers will no doubt continue to interact in the future and, in some cases, may be able to produce changes in both procedures and legislation. Witnesses will continue to appear in court and will no doubt continue to make mistakes. However, psychological research may at least allow us to understand and perhaps even predict these errors. Psychologists may thus be able to have some impact on the rate at which miscarriages of justice occur. If their efforts achieve a reduction in the number of such mistakes, then the countless hours of research will not have been in vain.

References

Ainsworth, P.B. (1981) Incident perception by British police officers. *Law and Human Behavior,* **5**, 231–236.

Ainsworth, P.B. (1988a) Psychology and wine appreciation: Unlikely bedfellows? Paper presented to the *British Psychological Society London Conference*, 19 December.

Ainsworth, P.B. (1988b) "I know it's familiar but I can't quite put a name to it." Sensory evaluation and wine tasting. Paper presented to the *British Psychological Society London Conference*, 19 December.

Ainsworth, P.B. (1995a) *Psychology and Policing in a Changing World.* Chichester: Wiley.

Ainsworth, P.B. (1995b) Turning heroes into villains: The role of unconscious transference in media crime reporting. Paper presented to the *5th European Conference on Law and Psychology*, Budapest, 2 September.

Ainsworth, P.B. (1995c) Police folklore and attributions of guilt: Can psychology challenge long held assumptions? Paper presented to the *5th European Conference on Law and Psychology*, Budapest, 2 September.

Ainsworth, P.B. & King, E. (1988) Witnesses' perceptions of identification parades. In M.M. Gruneberg, P.E. Morris & R.N. Sykes (Eds), *Practical Aspects of Memory: Current Research and Issues*, Volume 1. Chichester: Wiley.

Ainsworth, P.B. & May, G. (1996) Obtaining information from traumatized witnesses through the Cognitive Interview Technique. Paper presented to the *Trauma and Memory International Research Conference*, Durham, NH, 27 July.

Allen, R.J. & Miller, J.S. (1995) The expert as educator: Enhancing the rationality of verdicts in child sex abuse prosecutions. *Psychology, Public Policy and Law,* **1**, 323–338.

Allport, D.A., Antonis, B. & Reynolds, P. (1972) On the division of attention: A disproof of the single channel hypothesis. *Quarterly Journal of Experimental Psychology,* **24**, 225–235.

Allport, G.W. & Postman, L. (1947) The basic psychology of rumor. *Transactions of the New York Academy of Sciences,* **8**, 61–81.

Aronovitch, C. (1976) The voice of personality: Stereotyped judgements and their relation to voice quality and sex of speaker. *Journal of Social Psychology,* **99**, 207–220.

Atkinson, R.C. & Shiffrin, R.M. (1971) The control of Short Term Memory. *Scientific American*, **225**, 82–90.

Baddeley, A.D. (1986) *Working Memory*. Oxford: Oxford University Press.

Baddeley, A.D. (1990) *Human Memory: Theory and Practice*. Hove: Lawrence Erlbaum.

Baddeley, A.D. (1995) Memory. In C.C. French & A.M. Colman, *Cognitive Psychology*. New York: Longman.

Bahrick, H.P., Bahrick, P.O. & Wittlinger, R.P. (1975) Fifty years of memory for names and faces: A cross-sectional approach. *Journal of Experimental Psychology: General*, **104**, 54–75.

Bartlett, F.C. (1932) *Remembering: A Study in Experimental and Social Psychology*. London: Cambridge University Press.

Bekerian, D.A. & Bowers, J.M. (1983) Eyewitness testimony: Were we misled? *Journal of Experimental Psychology (Learning, Memory & Cognition)*, **9**, 139–145.

Belli, R.F. (1989) Influences of misleading post-event Information: Misinformation, interference and acceptance. *Journal of Experimental Psychology (General)*, **118**, 72–85.

Bond, N.W. & McConkey, K.M. (1995) Information retrieval: Reconstructing faces. In N. Brewer & C. Wilson (Eds), *Psychology and Policing*. Hillsdale, NJ: Lawrence Erlbaum.

Boon, J. & Davies, G. (1988) Attitudinal influences on witness memory: Fact and fiction. In M.M. Gruneberg, P.E. Morris & R.N. Sykes (Eds), *Practical Aspects of Memory: Current Research and Issues,* Volume 1. Chichester: Wiley.

Boon, J. & Davies, G. (1996) Extra-stimulus effects on eyewitness perception and recall: Hastorf and Cantril revisited. *Legal and Criminological Psychology*, **1**, 153–164.

Boon, J. & Noon, E. (1994) Changing perspectives in cognitive interviewing. *Psychology, Crime and Law*, **1**, 59–69.

Bothwell, R.K. (1991) Trait anxiety and facial recognition. Review manuscript cited in D.J. Narby, B.L. Cutler & S.D. Penrod (1996).

Bothwell, R.K., Brigham, J.C. & Malpass, R.S. (1989). Cross-racial identification. *Personality and Social Psychology Bulletin*, **15**, 19–25.

Brandon, R. & Davies, C. (1973) *Wrongful Imprisonment: Mistaken Convictions and their Consequences*. London: George Allen & Unwin.

Brigham, J.C. & Cairns, D.L. (1988) The effect of mugshot inspections on eyewitness identification accuracy. *Journal of Applied Social Psychology*, **18**, 1394–1410.

Brigham, J.C. & Pfeiffer, J.E. (1994) Evaluating the fairness of line ups. In D.F. Ross, J.D. Read & M.P. Toglia (Eds), *Adult Eyewitness Testimony: Current Trends and Developments*. Cambridge: Cambridge University Press.

Brown, E., Deffenbacher, K.A. & Sturgill, W. (1977) Memory for faces and the circumstances of encounter. *Journal of Applied Psychology*, **62**, 311–318.

Brown, R. (1986) *Social Psychology* (2nd edition). New York: Free Press.

Bruce, V. (1988) *Recognising Faces*. Hove: Lawrence Erlbaum.

Bruce, V. & Young, A. (1986) Understanding face recognition. *British Journal of Psychology*, **77**, 305–327.

Bruck, M. & Ceci, S.J. (1995) Amicus Brief for the case of New Jersey v Margaret Kelly Michaels presented by committee of concerned social scientists. *Psychology, Public Policy and Law*, **1**, 272–322.

Buckhout, R. (1980) Nearly 2000 witnesses can be wrong. *Bulletin of the Psychonomic Society*, **16**, 307–310.

Bull, R. (1980) Voice identification by man and machine: A review of research. In S. Lloyd-Bostock (Ed.), *Psychology in Legal Contexts: Applications and Limitations*. London: Macmillan.

Bull, R. (1992) Obtaining evidence expertly: The reliability of interviews with child witnesses. *Expert Evidence*, **1** (1), 5–12.

Bull, R. & Clifford, B.R. (1984) Earwitness voice recognition accuracy. In G.L. Wells & E.F. Loftus (Eds), *Eyewitness Testimony: Psychological Perspectives*. Cambridge: Cambridge University Press.

Canter, D. (1997) The status of the expert in legal proceedings. *Forensic Update*, **51**, 29–35.

Chance, J.E. & Goldstein, A.G. (1996) The other-race effect and eyewitness identification. In S.L. Sporer, R.S. Malpass & G. Koehnken (Eds), *Psychological Issues in Eyewitness Identification*. Hillsdale, NJ: Lawrence Erlbaum.

Cheek, D.B. & Le Cron, L.M. (1968) *Clinical Hypnotherapy*. San Francisco: Grune & Stratton.

Christiaansen, R.E. & Ochalek, K. (1983) Editing misleading information from memory: Evidence for the coexistence of original and post-event information. *Memory and Cognition*, **11**, 467–475.

Clifford, B.R. (1980) Voice identification by human listeners: On earwitness reliability. *Law and Human Behavior*, **4**, 373–394.

Clifford, B.R. (1993) Witnessing: A comparison of adults and children. *Issues in Criminological and Legal Psychology*, **20**, 15–21.

Clifford, B.R. & Bull, R. (1978) *The Psychology of Person Identification*. London: Routledge & Kegan Paul.

Clifford, B.R. & Denot, H. (1982) Visual and verbal testimony and identification under conditions of stress. Unpublished manuscript. North East London Polytechnic.

Clifford, B.R. & George, R. (1995) A field evaluation of training in three methods of witness/victim investigative interviewing. *Psychology, Crime and Law*, **2**, 1–18.

Clifford, B.R. & Hollin, C (1981) Effects of type of incident and the number of perpetrators in eyewitness testimony. *Journal of Applied Psychology*, **66**, 352–359.

Clifford, B.R. & Richards, V.J. (1977) Comparison of recall by policemen and civilians under conditions of long and short durations of exposure. *Perceptual and Motor Skills*, **45**, 503–512.

Coghlan, A., Kiernan, V. & Mullins, J. (1995) Nowhere to hide. *Technoscopy* (*New Scientist* Supplement, 4 November), 4–7.

Colman, A.M. & Mackay, R.D. (1993) Legal issues surrounding the admissibility of expert psychological and psychiatric testimony. *Issues in Criminological and Legal Psychology,* **20,** 46–50.

Colman, A.M. & Mackay, R.D. (1995) Psychological evidence in court: Legal developments in England and the United States. *Psychology, Crime and Law,* **1,** 261–268.

Craik, F.I.M. & Lockhart, R.S. (1972) Levels of processing: A framework for memory research. *Journal of Verbal Learning and Verbal Behavior,* **11,** 671–684.

Criglow v. State. (1931) 36 S.W. 2d 400.

Cutler, B.L., Berman, G.L., Penrod, S. & Fisher, R.P. (1994) Conceptual, practical and empirical issues associated with eyewitness identification test media. In D.F. Ross, J.D. Read & M.P. Toglia (Eds), *Adult Eyewitness Testimony: Current Trends and Developments.* Cambridge: Cambridge University Press.

Cutler, B.L. & Penrod, S.D. (1995) *Mistaken Identification: The Eyewitness, Psychology and the Law.* Cambridge: Cambridge University Press.

Cutler, B.L., Penrod, S.D. & Martens, T.K. (1987) The reliability of eyewitness identifications: The role of system and estimator variables. *Law and Human Behavior,* **11,** 223–258.

Cutshall, J. & Yuille, J. (1989) Field studies of eyewitness memory of actual crimes. In D.C. Raskin (Ed.), *Psychological Methods in Criminal Investigation and Evidence.* New York: Springer.

Daubert v. Merrell Dow Pharmaceuticals Inc. 1993, Ed. 2d 469, 113 S Ct. 2786.

Davies, G.M. (1992) Protecting the child witness in the courtroom. *Child Abuse Review,* **1,** 33–41.

Davies, G.M. (1995) Evidence: Psychological perspective. In R. Bull & D. Carson (Eds), *Handbook of Psychology in Legal Contexts.* Chichester: Wiley.

Davies, G.M. (1996) Children's identification evidence. In S.L. Sporer, R.S. Malpass & G. Koehnken (Eds), *Psychological Issues in Eyewitness Identification.* Hillsdale, NJ: Lawrence Erlbaum.

Davies, G.M., Ellis, H.D. & Shepherd, J.W. (1981) *Perceiving and Remembering Faces.* London: Academic Press.

Davies, G.M., Kurvink, A., Mitchell, R. & Robertson, N. (1996) Memory for cars and their drivers: A test of the interest hypothesis. In D.J. Hermann, C. McEvoy, C. Hertzog, P. Hertel & M.K. Johnson (Eds), *Basic and Applied Memory Research: Practical Applications,* Volume 2. Hillsdale, NJ: Lawrence Erlbaum.

Davies, G.M. & Noon, E. (1991) *An Evaluation of the Live Link for Child Witnesses.* London: Home Office.

Davies, G.M. & Noon, E. (1993) Video links: Their impact on child witness trials. *Issues in Criminological and Legal Psychology,* **20,** 22–26.

Davies, G.M., Shepherd, J. & Ellis, H.D. (1979) Effects of interpolated mugshot exposure on accuracy of eyewitness identification. *Journal of Applied Psychology,* **64,** 232–237.

Davies, G.M., Stevenson-Robb, Y. & Flin, R. (1988) Tales out of school: Children's memory for an unexpected incident. In M.M. Gruneberg, P.E. Morris & R.N. Sykes (Eds), *Practical Aspects of Memory: Current Research and Issues,* Volume 1. Chichester: Wiley.

Davies, G.M. & Wilson, C. (1997) Implementation of the memorandum: An overview. In H. Westcott & J. Jones (Eds), *Perspectives on the Memorandum: Policy, Practice and Research in Investigative Interviewing*. London: Arena.

Davies, G.M., Wilson, C., Mitchell, R. & Milsom, J. (1995) *Videotaping Children's Evidence: An Evaluation*. London: Home Office.

de Bruin, J. (1996) *The Detection Dog and Science*. Rotterdam: Rotterdam Police Dog Section publication.

Deffenbacher, K.A. (1989) Forensic facial memory: Time is of the essence. In A.W. Young & H.D. Ellis (Eds), *Handbook of Research on Face Recognition*. Amsterdam: North Holland.

Devlin Report (1976) *Report to the Secretary of State for the Home Department of the Departmental Committee on Evidence of Identification in Criminal Cases*. London: HMSO.

Diges, M. (1988) Stereotypes and memory of real traffic accidents. In M.M. Gruneberg, P.E. Morris & R.N. Sykes (Eds), *Practical Aspects of Memory: Current Research and Issues*, Volume 1. Chichester: Wiley.

Dolan, R.J., Fink, G.R., Rolls, E.T., Booth, M., Holmes, A., Frakowiak, R.S.J. & Fritson, K.J. (1997) How the brain learns to see objects and faces in an impoverished context. *Nature*, **389**, 596–599.

Doyle, J.M. (1989) Legal issues in eyewitness identification. In D.C. Raskin (Ed.), *Psychological Methods in Criminal Investigation and Evidence*. New York: Springer.

Dritsas, W.J. & Hamilton, V.L. (1977) Evidence about evidence: Effects of pre-suppositions, item salience, stress, and perceiver set on accident recall. Unpublished manuscript, University of Michigan.

Duncan, B.L. (1976) Different social perceptions and attribution of intergroup violence: Testing the lower limits of stereotyping of blacks. *Journal of Personality and Social Psychology*, **34**, 590–598.

Duncan, K.L. (1996) "Lies, damned lies and statistics?" Psychological syndrome evidence in the courtroom after Daubert. *Indiana Law Journal*, **7**, 753–771.

Egeth, H.E. & McCloskey, M. (1984) Expert testimony about eyewitness behavior: Is it safe and effective? In G.L. Wells & E.F. Loftus (Eds), *Eyewitness Testimony: Psychological Perspectives*. Cambridge: Cambridge University Press.

Elliot, R. (1993) Expert testimony about eyewitness identification: A critique. *Law and Human Behavior*, **17**, 423–437.

Ellis, H.D. (1984) Practical aspects of face memory. In G.L. Wells & E.F. Loftus (Eds), *Eyewitness Testimony: Psychological Perspectives*. Cambridge: Cambridge University Press.

Ellis, H.D., Deregowski, J.B. & Shepherd, J.W. (1975) Descriptions of white and black faces by white and black subjects. *International Journal of Psychology*, **10**, 119–123.

Ellis, H.D., Shepherd, J.W., Shepherd, Flin, R. & Davies, G. (1989) Identification from a computer-driven retrieval system compared with a traditional mugshot album search: A new tool for police investigations. *Ergonomics*, **32**, 167–177.

Faigman, D.L. (1995) The evidentiary status of social science under Daubert: Is it scientific, technical or other knowledge? *Psychology, Public Policy and Law*, **1**, 960–979.

Farrington, D.P. & Lambert, S. (1997) Predicting offender profiles from victim and witness descriptions. In J.L. Jackson & D.A. Bekerian (Eds), *Offender Profiling: Theory, Research and Practice*. Chichester: Wiley.

Festinger, L. (1957) *A Theory of Cognitive Dissonance*. Evanston, IL: Row, Peterson.

Fisher, R.P. & Geiselman, R.E. (1992) *Memory Enhancing Techniques for Investigative Interviewing*. Springfield, Ill: Charles C. Thomas.

Fisher, R.P., Geiselman, R.E. & Amador, M. (1989) Field test of the cognitive interview: Enhancing the recollection of actual victims and witnesses of crime. *Journal of Applied Psychology*, **74**, 722–727.

Fisher, R.P., Geiselman, R.E. & Raymond, D.S. (1987) Critical analysis of police interview techniques. *Journal of Police Science and Administration*, **15**, 177–185.

Fisher, R.P., Geiselman, R.E., Raymond, D.S., Jurkevitch, L.M. & Warhaftig, M.L. (1987) Enhancing enhanced eyewitness memory: Refining the cognitive interview. *Journal of Police Science and Administration*, **15**, 291–297.

Fisher, R.P. & MacCauley, M.R. (1995) Information retrieval: Interviewing witnesses. In N. Brewer & C. Wilson (Eds), *Psychology and Policing*. Hillsdale, NJ: Lawrence Erlbaum.

Fisher, R.P., Quigley, K., Brock, P., Chin, D. & Cutler, B.L. (1990) The effectiveness of the Cognitive Interview in description and identification tasks. Paper presented at the *Biannual Meeting of American Psychology and Law Society*, Williamsburg, VA.

Fivush, R. (1993) Developmental perspectives on autobiographical recall. In G.S. Goodman & B.L. Bottoms (Eds), *Child Victims, Child Witnesses: Understanding and Improving Testimony*. New York: Guilford Press.

Fivush, R., Hammond, N.R., Harsch, N., Singer, N. & Wolf, A. (1991) Content and consistency in early autobiographical recall. *Discourse Processes*, **14**, 373–88.

Flin, R.H. (1992) Child witnesses in British courts. In F. Losel, D. Bender & T. Bleisener (Eds), *Psychology and Law: International Perspectives*. New York: Walter de Gruyter.

Flin, R.H. (1993) Hearing and testing children's evidence. In G.S. Goodman & B.L. Bottoms (Eds), *Child Victims, Child Witnesses: Understanding and Improving Testimony*. New York: Guilford Press.

Frazzini, S.F. (1981) Review of eyewitness testimony. *The Yale Review*, **70**, 18–20.

Fruzzetti, A.E., Toland, K., Teller, S.A. & Loftus, E.F. (1992) Memory and eyewitness testimony. In M. Gruneberg & P. Morris (Eds), *Aspects of memory. Vol 1: The Practical Aspects* (2nd edition). London: Routledge.

Frye *v.* United States. (1923) 293 F. 1013 (D.C. Cir. 1923).

Fulero, S.M. (1993) Eyewitness expert testimony: An overview and annotated bibliography, 1931–1988. Unpublished manuscript, Sinclair College. Quoted in Cutler & Penrod (1995).

Geiselman, R.E., Fisher, R.P., Cohen, G., Holland, H. & Surtes, L. (1986) Eyewitness responses to leading and misleading questions under the cognitive interview. *Journal of Police Science and Administration*, **14**, 31–39.

Geiselman, R.E., Fisher, R.P., Firstenberg, I., Hutton, L.A., Sullivan, S.J., Avetissian, I.V. & Prosk, A.L. (1994) Enhancement of eyewitness memory: An empirical evaluation of a cognitive interview. *Journal of Police Science and Administration*, **12**, 74–80.

Geiselman, R.E., Fisher, R.P., MacKinnon, D.P. & Holland H.L. (1985) Eyewitness memory enhancement in the police interview: Cognitive retrieval mnemonics versus hypnosis. *Journal of Applied Psychology*, **70**, 401–412.

George, R. (1991) A field and experimental evaluation of three methods of interviewing witnesses/victims of crime. Unpublished manuscript, Polytechnic of East London.

Gilbert, J.N. (1980) *Criminal Investigation*. Columbus, Ohio: Merrill.

Goldstein, A.G. (1979) Race related variation of facial features: Anthropometric data I. *Bulletin of the Psychonomic Society*, **13**, 187–190.

Goldstein, A.G. & Chance, J.E. (1981) Laboratory studies of face recognition. In G.M. Davies, H.D. Ellis & J.W. Shepherd (Eds), *Perceiving and Remembering Faces*. London: Academic Press.

Goldstein, A.G. & Chance, J.E. (1985) Voice recognition: the effects of faces, temporal distribution of "practice", and social distance. Paper presented to *The Midwestern Psychology Association Meeting*: Illinois, USA.

Goldstein, A.G., Knight, P., Bailiss, K. & Conover, J. (1981) Recognition memory for accented and unaccented voices. *Bulletin of the Psychonomic Society*, **17**, 217–220.

Gonzalez, R., Ellsworth, P.C. & Pembroke, M. (1993) Response biases in lineups and showups. *Journal of Personality and Social Psychology*, **64**, 525–537.

Gorenstein, G.W. & Ellsworth, P. (1980) Effect of choosing an incorrect photograph on a later identification by an eyewitness. *Journal of Applied Psychology*, **65**, 616–622.

Grano, J.D. (1984) A legal response to the inherent dangers of eyewitness identification testimony. In G.L. Wells & E.F. Loftus (Eds), *Eyewitness Testimony: Psychological Perspectives*. New York: Cambridge University Press.

Gravitz, M.A. (1985) Resistance in investigative hypnosis: Determinants and management. *American Journal of Clinical Hypnosis*, **28**, 76–83.

Greene, E., Flynne, M.B. & Loftus, E.F. (1982) Inducing resistance to misleading information. *Journal of Verbal Learning and Verbal Behavior*, **21**, 207–219.

Gregory, R.L. & Colman, A.M. (1995) *Sensation and Perception*. Harlow: Longman.

Gross, H. (1910) Zur Frage Der Zeugenaussage. H. Gross' Archiv, **36**, 372–382.

Gudjonsson, G. H. (1992) *The Psychology of Interrogations, Confessions and Testimony*. Chichester: Wiley.

Gudjonsson, G.H. (1993) The implications of poor psychological evidence in court. *Expert Evidence*, **2**, 120–124.

Gudjonsson, G.H. (1996) Forensic psychology in England: One practitioner's experience and viewpoint. *Legal and Criminological Psychology*, **1**, 131–142.

Hall, D.F., Loftus, E.F. & Tousignant, J.P. (1984) Postevent information and changes in recollection for a natural event. In G.L. Wells & E.F. Loftus (Eds), *Eyewitness Testimony: Psychological Perspectives*. New York: Cambridge University Press.

Hammersley, R. & Read, J.D. (1985) The effect of participation in a conversation on recognition and identification of the speakers' voices. *Law and Human Behavior*, **9**, 71–81.

Hammersley, R. & Read, J.D. (1996) Voice identification by humans and computers. In S.L. Sporer, R.S. Malpass & G. Koehnken (Eds), *Psychological Issues in Eyewitness Identification*. Hillsdale, NJ: Lawrence Erlbaum.

Hastorf, A.A. & Cantril, H. (1954) They saw a game: A case study. *Journal of Abnormal and Social Psychology*, **97**, 399–401.

Herz, R.S. & Eich, E. (1995) Commentary and Envoi. In F.R. Schab & R.G. Crowder (Eds), *Memory for Odors*. New Jersey: Lawrence Erlbaum.

Hilgard, E.R. (1978) States of consciousness in hypnosis: divisions or levels? In F.H. Frankel & H.S. Zamansky (Eds), *Hypnosis at its Bicentennial: Selected Papers*. New York: Plenum.

Hollien, H., Bennet, G. & Gelfer, M.P. (1983) Criminal identification comparison: Aural versus visual identifications resulting from a simulated crime. *Journal of Forensic Sciences*, **28**, 208–221.

Home Office (1988) Circular No 66/1988: *The Use of Hypnosis by the Police in the Investigation of Crime*. London: Home Office.

Horgan, D.D. (1988) The ethics of unexpected advocacy. Paper presented at the meeting of the *American Psychological Association*, Atlanta, August.

Hosch, H. (1994) Individual differences in personality and eyewitness identification. In D.F. Ross, J.D. Read & M.P. Toglia (Eds), *Adult Eyewitness Testimony: Current Trends and Developments*. Cambridge: Cambridge University Press.

Houts, M (1956) *From Proof to Evidence*. Springfield, Ill: Charles C. Thomas.

Huff, C.R. (1987) Wrongful convictions: Societal tolerance of injustice. *Research in Social Problems*, **4**, 99–115.

Hull, C.L. (1933) *Hypnosis and Suggestibility*. New York: Appleton Century Crofts.

Kapardis, A. (1997) *Psychology and Law: A Critical Introduction*. Cambridge: Cambridge University Press.

Kassin, S.M., Ellsworth, P.C. & Smith, V.L. (1989) The "general acceptance" of psychological research on eyewitness testimony: A survey of experts. *American Psychologist*, **44**, 1089–1098.

Kebbell, M. (1997) Should we use hypnosis to interview eyewitnesses? *Forensic Update*, **50**, 10–13.

Koehn, C. (1993) Improving Mac-A-Mug Composites with the Cognitive Interview. Unpublished manuscript, Florida International University, Miami.

Koehnken, G. & Maass, A. (1988) Eyewitness testimony: False alarms or biased instructions. *Journal of Applied Psychology*, **73**, 363–370.

Koehnken, G., Milne, R., Memon, A. & Bull, R. (1992) A meta-analysis of the effects of the cognitive interview. Paper presented to the *Third European Conference on Psychology and Law*, Oxford, England.

Kunzel, H.J. (1990) *Phonetische Untersuchungen zur Specherkennung durch linguistisch naive Personen.* Stuttgart: Franz Steiner Verlag. Cited in Yarmey (1994).

Ladefoged, P. (1981) Expectation affects identification by listening. Paper presented to *The Acoustical Society of America, 94th Meeting*, New York, April.

Landsman, S. (1995) Of witches, madmen and products liability: An historical survey of the use of expert testimony. *Behavioural Sciences and Law,* **13**, 131–157.

Latane, B. & Darley, J.M. (1970) *The Unresponsive Bystander: Why Doesn't He Help?* New York: Appleton Century Crofts.

Latts, M.G. & Geiselman, R.E. (1991) Interviewing survivors of rape. *Police and Criminal Psychology,* **7**, 8–17.

Leippe, M.R. (1994) The appraisal of eyewitness testimony. In D.F. Ross, J.D. Read & M.P. Toglia (Eds), *Adult Eyewitness Testimony: Current Trends and Developments.* New York: Cambridge University Press.

Leippe, M.R. (1995) The case for expert testimony about eyewitness memory. *Psychology, Public Policy and Law,* **1**, 909–959.

Leippe, M.R., Romanczyk, O. & Mannion, A.P. (1991) Eyewitness memory for a touching experience: Accuracy differences between child and adult witnesses. *Journal of Applied Psychology,* **76**, 367–379.

Light, L.L., Kayra-Stuart, F. & Hollander, S. (1979) Recognition memory for typical and unusual faces. *Journal of Experimental Psychology Human Learning and Memory,* **5**, 212–228.

Lindsay, D.S. (1990) Misleading suggestions can impair eyewitnesses' ability to remember event details. *Journal of Experimental Psychology (Learning, Memory & Cognition),* **16**, 1077–1083.

Lindsay, D.S. (1994) Memory source monitoring and eyewitness testimony. In D.F. Ross, J.D. Read & M.P. Toglia (Eds), *Adult Eyewitness Testimony: Current Trends and Developments.* Cambridge: Cambridge University Press.

Lindsay, R.C.L. (1994a) Biassed line-ups: where do they come from? In D.F. Ross, J.D. Read & M.P. Toglia (Eds), *Adult Eyewitness Testimony: Current Trends and Developments.* Cambridge: Cambridge University Press.

Lindsay, R.C.L. (1994b) Expectations of eyewitness performance: Jurors' verdicts do not follow their beliefs. In D.F. Ross, J.D. Read & M.P. Toglia (Eds), *Adult Eyewitness Testimony: Current Trends and Developments.* Cambridge: Cambridge University Press.

Lindsay, R.C.L., Nosworthy, G.J., Martin, R. & Maartynuck, C. (1994) Using mugshots to find suspects. *Journal of Applied Psychology,* **79**, 121–130.

Lindsay, R.C.L. & Wells, G.L. (1983) What do we really know about cross-race eyewitness identification? In S.M.A. Lloyd-Bostock & B.R. Clifford (Eds), *Evaluating Witness Evidence: Recent Psychological Research and New Perspectives.* New York: Wiley.

Liposvky, J.A., Tidwell, R., Crisp, J., Kilpatrick, D., Saunders, B.E. & Dawson, V.L. (1992) Child witnesses in criminal courts: Descriptive information from three Southern States. *Law and Human Behavior,* **16**, 635–650.

Lipton, J.P. (1996) Legal aspects of eyewitness testimony. In S.L. Sporer, R.S. Malpass & G. Koehnken (Eds), *Psychological Issues in Eyewitness Identification.* Hillsdale, NJ: Lawrence Erlbaum.

Loftus, E.F. (1975) Leading questions and the eyewitness report. *Cognitive Psychology,* **7**, 560–572.

Loftus, E.F. (1976) Unconscious transference in eyewitness identification. *Law and Psychology Review,* **2**, 93–98.

Loftus, E.F. (1977) Shifting human color memory. *Memory and Cognition,* **5**, 696–699.

Loftus, E.F. (1979) *Eyewitness Testimony.* Cambridge, MA.: Harvard University Press.

Loftus, E.F. (1984a) Eyewitnesses: Essential but unreliable. *Psychology Today.* February, 22–26.

Loftus, E.F. (1984b) Expert testimony on the eyewitness. In D.F. Ross, J.D. Read & M.P. Toglia (Eds), *Adult Eyewitness Testimony: Current Trends and Developments.* Cambridge: Cambridge University Press.

Loftus, E.F. & Burns, H.J. (1982) Mental shock can produce retrograde amnesia. *Memory and Cognition,* **10**, 318–323.

Loftus, E.F., Donders, K., Hoffman, H. & Schooler, J.W. (1989) Creating new memories that are quickly assessed and confidently held. *Memory and Cognition,* **17**, 607–616.

Loftus, E.F. & Greene, E. (1980) Warning: Even memories for faces can be contagious. *Law and Human Behavior,* **4**, 323–334.

Loftus, E.F. & Hoffman, H. (1989) Misinformation and memory: The creation of new memories. *Journal of Experimental Psychology (General),* **118**, 100–104.

Loftus, E.F. & Ketcham, K. (1991) *Witness for the Defense.* New York: St Martin's Press.

Loftus, E.F., Loftus, G.R. & Messo, J. (1987) Some facts about weapon focus. *Law and Human Behavior,* **11**, 55–62.

Loftus, E.F., Miller, D.G. & Burns, H.J. (1978) Semantic integration of verbal information into visual memory. *Journal of Experimental Psychology (Human Learning and Memory),* **4**, 19–31.

Loftus, E.F. & Palmer, J.C. (1974) Reconstructions of automobile destruction: An example of the interaction between language and memory. *Journal of Verbal Learning and Verbal Behavior,* **13**, 585–589.

Loftus, E.F., Schooler, J.W., Boones, S.M. & Kline D. (1987) Time went by so slowly: Overestimation of event duration by males and females. *Applied Cognitive Psychology,* **1**, 3–13.

Logie, R.H., Baddeley, A.D. & Woodhead, M.M. (1987) Face recognition: Pose and ecological validity. *Applied Cognitive Psychology,* **1**, 53–69.

Loohs, S. (1996) Mnemonic aids in questioning children: misleading useless or helpful? Paper presented to the *6th European Conference on Law and Psychology*, Sienna, Italy.

Luu, T.N. & Geiselman, R.E. (1993) Cognitive retrieval techniques and order of feature construction in the formation of composite facial images. *Journal of Police and Criminal Psychology,* **9**, 34–39.

Maass, A. (1996) Logic and methodology of experimental research in eyewitness psychology. In S.L. Sporer, R.S. Malpass & G Koehnken (Eds), *Psychological Issues in Eyewitness Identification.* Hillsdale, NJ: Lawrence Erlbaum.

Maass, A. & Koehnken, G. (1989) Eyewitness identification: Simulating the weapon effect. *Law and Human Behavior,* **13**, 397–408.

Malpass, R.S. (1981) Training in face recognition. In G. Davies, H. Ellis & J. Shepherd (Eds), *Perceiving and Remembering Faces*. London: Academic Press.

Malpass, R.S. (1996) Enhancing eyewitness memory. In S.L. Sporer, R.S. Malpass & G Koehnken (Eds), *Psychological Issues in Eyewitness Identification*. Hillsdale, NJ: Lawrence Erlbaum.

Malpass, R.S. & Devine, P.G. (1983) Measuring the fairness of eyewitness identification line-ups. In S.M.A. Lloyd-Bostock & B.R. Clifford (Eds), *Evaluating Witness Evidence: Recent Psychological Research and New Perspectives*. New York: Wiley.

Malpass, R.S. & Devine, P.G. (1984) Research on suggestion in lineups and photospreads. In D.F. Ross, J.D. Read & M.P. Toglia (Eds), *Adult Eyewitness Testimony: Current Trends and Developments*. Cambridge: Cambridge University Press.

MacLeod, M.D. & Shepherd, J.W. (1986) Sex differences in eyewitness reports of criminal assaults. *Medicine, Science and Law*, **26** (4), 311–318.

McCloskey, M. & Zaragoza, M. (1985) Misleading postevent information and memory for events: Argument and evidence against memory impairment hypotheses. *Journal of Experimental Psychology (General)*, **114**, 1–16.

McConkey, K.M. & Sheehan, P.W. (1995) *Hypnosis, Memory, and Behavior in Criminal Investigation*. New York: Guilford Press.

McKenzie, I. (1995) Psychology and legal practice: Fairness and accuracy in identification parades. *Criminal Law Review*, 200–208.

McNeil, J.E. & Warrington, E.K. (1993) Prosapagnasioa: A face specific disorder. *Quarterly Journal of Experimental Psychology*, **46A**, 1–10.

Memon, A., Bull, R. & Smith, M. (1995) Improving the quality of the police interview: Can training in the use of cognitive techniques help? *Policing and Society*, **5**, 53–68.

Mcmon, A., Cronin, O., Eaves, R. & Bull, R. (1996) An empirical test of the mnemonic components of the Cognitive Interview. In G. Davies, S. Lloyd-Bostock, M. McMurran & C. Wilson (Eds), *Psychology, Law and Criminal Justice: International Developments in Research and Practice*. Berlin: Walter de Gruyter.

Memon, A., Cronin, O., Eaves, R. & Bull, R (1992) The cognitive interview and child witnesses. In *Children Evidence and Procedure*. British Psychological Society DCLP Occasional Paper No. 19.

Morton, J., Hammersley, R.H. & Bekerian, D.A. (1985) Headed records: A model for memory and its failures. *Cognition*, **20**, 1–23.

Moscovitch, M., Winocut, G. & Behrmann, M. (1997) What is special about face recognition? Nineteen experiments on a person with visual object agnosia and dyslexia but normal face recognition. *Journal of Cognitive Neuroscience*, **9**, 555–604.

Munsterberg, H. (1909) *On the Witness Stand*. New York: Doubleday.

Murphy, C. (1995) Age associated differences in memory for odors. In F.R. Schab & R.G. Crowder (Eds), *Memory for Odors*. Hillsdale, NJ: Lawrence Erlbaum.

Narby, D.J., Cutler, B.L. & Penrod, S.D. (1996) The effects of witness, target, and situational factors on eyewitness identifications. In S.L. Sporer, R.S. Malpass & G Koehnken (Eds), *Psychological Issues in Eyewitness Identification*. Hillsdale, NJ: Lawrence Erlbaum.

Neisser, U. (1967) *Cognitive Psychology*. New York: Appleton Century Crofts.
Neisser, U. (1982) *Memory Observed: Remembering in Natural Contexts*. San Francisco: W.H. Freeman & Co.
New Scientist (1997). 23 August: Dearth of an expert witness, pp. 16–18.
Nijboer, H. (1995) Expert Evidence. In R. Bull & D. Carson (Eds), *Handbook of Psychology in Legal Contexts*. Chichester: Wiley.
Nosworthy, G.J. & Lindsay, R.C.L. (1990) Does nominal line-up size matter? *Journal of Applied Psychology,* **75**, 358–361.
Oakley, D., Alden, P. & Mather, M.D. (1996) The use of hypnosis in therapy with adults. *The Psychologist,* **9**, 502–505.
Orne, M. (1984) Hypnotically induced testimony. In G.L. Wells & E.F. Loftus (Eds), *Eyewitness Testimony: Psychological Perspectives*. New York: Cambridge University Press.
Pease, K. (1996) Repeat Victimization and Policing. Unpublished paper, University of Huddersfield.
People *v*. Collier (1952), 249, P. 2d 72 (Cal).
People *v*. McDonald (1984), 37 Cal. 3d 351, 690 P. 2d 709,716, 208 Cal. Rptr. 236, 245.
Perrett, D.K., Mistlin, A.J., Potter, D.D., Smith, P.A.J., Chitty, A.J., Broenimann, A.J., Milner, R. & Jeeves, M.A. (1986) Function organization of visual neurones processing facial identity. In H. Ellis, M. Jeeves, F. Newcombe & A. Young (Eds), *Aspects of Face Processing*. Dordrecht: Martinus Nijhoff.
Pigott, M.A. & Brigham, J.C. (1985) Relationship between accuracy of prior description and facial recognition. *Journal of Applied Psychology,* **70**, 547–555.
Powers, P.A., Andriks, J.L. & Loftus, E.F. (1979) Eyewitness accounts of females and males. *Journal of Applied Psychology,* **64**, 339–347.
R *v*. Brasier (1779) 1 Leach 199, 168 Eng. Rep. 202.
R *v*. Sally Loraine Emery and Another (1993) 14 Cr. App. R. (S) 394.
R *v*. Turner (1975). QB 834. Quoted in Kapardis (1997), p. 178.
Rand Corporation (1975) *The Criminal Investigation Process,* Volumes 1–3. Santa Monica, CA: Rand Corporation.
Rathborn, H.A., Bull, R.H. & Clifford, B.R. (1981) Voice recognition over the telephone. *Journal of Police Science and Administration,* **9**, 280–284.
Read, J.D. (1994) Understanding bystander misidentification: The role of familiarity and contextual knowledge. In D.F. Ross, J.D. Read & M.P. Toglia (Eds), *Adult Eyewitness Testimony: Current Trends and Developments*. Cambridge: Cambridge University Press.
Ready, D.J. (1986) The Effects of Hypnosis and Guided Memory on Eyewitness Recall and Suggestibility. Unpublished Doctoral Dissertation. Florida State University, Tallahassee.
Reisser, M. (1989) Investigative hypnosis. In D.C. Raskin (Ed.), *Psychological Methods in Criminal Investigation and Evidence*. New York: Springer.
Rogers (1993) *Criminal Law Review* 386: cited in Kapardis (1997).
Ross, D.F., Ceci, S.J., Dunning, D. & Toglia, M.P. (1994a) Unconscious transference and lineup identification: Toward a memory blending approach. In

D.F. Ross, J.D. Read & M.P. Toglia (Eds), *Adult Eyewitness Testimony: Current Trends and Developments*. Cambridge: Cambridge University Press.

Ross, D.F., Hopkins, S., Hanson, E., Lindsay, R.C.L., Hazen, K. & Eslinger, T. (1994b) The impact of protective shields and videotape testimony on conviction rates in a simulated trial of child sexual abuse. *Law and Human Behavior*, **18**, 553–566.

Ross, D.F., Read, J.D. & Toglia, M.P. (1994), *Adult Eyewitness Testimony: Current Trends and Developments*. Cambridge: Cambridge University Press.

Rumelhart, D.E. (1975) Notes on a schema for stories. In D.G. Bobrow & A. Collins (Eds), *Representation and Understanding*. New York: Academic Press.

Schab, F.R. & Crowder, R.G. (Eds), (1995) *Memory for Odors*. Hillsdale, NJ: Lawrence Erlbaum.

Schooler, J.W. & Engst-Schooler, T.Y. (1990) Verbal overshadowing of visual memories: Some things are better left unsaid. *Cognitive Psychology*, **22**, 36–71.

Schooler, J.W., Ryan, R.S. & Reder, L. (1996) The costs and benefits of verbally rehearsing memory for faces. In D.J. Hermann, C. McEvoy, C. Hertzog, P. Hertel & M.K. Johnson (Eds), *Basic and Applied Memory Research: Practical Applications*, Volume 2. Hillsdale, NJ: Lawrence Erlbaum.

Shapiro, P.N. & Penrod, S.D. (1986) Meta-analysis of facial identification studies. *Psychological Bulletin*, **100**, 139–156.

Sheftel, Y. (1996) *Defending Ivan the Terrible: The Conspiracy to Convict John Demjanjuk as Ivan the Terrible*. Washington, DC: Regnery Publishers Inc.

Sheldon, D.H. & MacLeod, M.D. (1991) From normative to positive data: Expert psychological evidence reexamined. *Criminal Law Review*, 811–820.

Shepherd, J.W. (1981) Social factors in face recognition. In G. Davies, H. Ellis & J. Shepherd (Eds), *Perceiving and Remembering Faces*. London: Academic Press.

Shepherd, J.W. (1983) Identification after long delays. In S.M.A. Lloyd-Bostock & B.R. Clifford (Eds), *Evaluating Witness Evidence: Recent Psychological Research and New Perspectives*. New York: Wiley.

Shepherd, J.W., Davies, G.M. & Ellis, H.D. (1978) How best shall a face be described? In P.M. Morris & R.N. Sykes (Eds), *Practical Aspects of Memory*. London: Academic Press.

Shepherd, J.W. & Ellis, H.D. (1973) The effect of attractiveness on recognition memory for faces. *American Journal of Psychology*, **86**, 627–623.

Shepherd, J.W. & Ellis, H.D. (1996) Face recall – methods and problems. In S.L. Sporer, R.S. Malpass & G. Koehnken (Eds), *Psychological Issues in Eyewitness Identification*. Hillsdale, NJ: Lawrence Erlbaum.

Shepherd, J.W., Ellis, H.D. & Davies, G.M. (1982) *Identification Evidence*. Aberdeen: Aberdeen University Press (Pergamon).

Siegal, M. & Peterson, C.C. (1995) Memory and suggestibility in conversations with children. *Australian Journal of Psychology*, **47**, 38–41.

Small, M.A. & Melton, G.B. (1994) Evaluation of child witnesses for confrontation with criminal defendants. *Professional Psychology: Research and Practice*, **25**, 228–233.

Smith, S.M. & Vela, E. (1990) Environmental context-dependent eyewitness recognition. *Applied Cognitive Psychology,* **6**, 125–139.

Spencer, J. (1987) Child abuse: The first steps to justice. *The Times,* 3 October, p. 8.

Sporer, S.L. (1992) An archival analysis of person descriptions. Paper presented to the Biennial Meeting of the *American Psychology-Law Society,* San Diego, California.

Sporer, S.L., Malpass, R.S. & Koehnken, G. (Eds), (1996) *Psychological Issues in Eyewitness Identification.* Hillsdale, NJ: Lawrence Erlbaum.

Stafford, C.F. (1962) The child as a witness. *Washington Law Review,* **37**, 303–324.

State *v.* Chapple (1983), 135 Ariz. 281, 660 P. 2d 1208, 1221.

Steblay, N.M. (1992) A meta-analytic review of the weapon focus effect. *Law and Human Behavior,* **16**, 413–424.

Stern, L.B. & Dunning, B. (1994) Distinguishing accurate from inaccurate eyewitness identifications: A reality monitoring approach. In D.F. Ross, J.D. Read & M.P. Toglia (Eds), *Adult Eyewitness Testimony: Current Trends and Developments.* Cambridge: Cambridge University Press.

Sternberg, R.J. (1996) *Cognitive Psychology.* Orlando, FL: Holt, Rinehart & Winston.

Swim, J.K., Borgida, E. & McCoy, K. (1993) Videotaped versus in-court witness testimony: Does protecting the child witness jeopardize due process? *Journal of Applied Social Psychology,* **23**, 603–631.

Thompson, C.P. (1985a) Voice identification: Attempted recovery from a biassed procedure. *Journal of Practical Research and Applications,* **4**, 213–224.

Thompson, C.P. (1985b) Voice identification: Speaker identification and a correction of the record regarding sex effects. *Journal of Practical Research and Applications,* **4**, 19–28.

Thompson, J., Morton, J. & Fraser, L. (1997) Memories for the Marchioness. *Memory,* **5**(5), 615–638.

Thomson, D.M. (1995) Eyewitness testimony and identification tests. In N. Brewer & C. Wilson (Eds), *Psychology and Policing.* Hillsdale, NJ: Lawrence Erlbaum.

Thornton, P. (1995) The admissibility of expert psychiatric and psychological evidence: judicial training. *Medicine, Science and the Law,* **35**, 143–149.

Tickner, A.H. & Poulton, E.C. (1975) Watching for people and actions. *Ergonomics,* **18**, 35–51.

Toglia, M., Ross, D. & Ceci, S. (1992) The suggestibility of children's memory. In M. Howe, C. Branerd & V. Reyna (Eds), *The Development of Long Term Retention.* New York: Springer Verlag.

Tollestrup, P.A., Turtle, J.W. & Yuille, J.C. (1994) Actual victims and witnesses to robbery and fraud: An archival analysis. In D.F. Ross, J.D. Read & M.P. Toglia (Eds), *Adult Eyewitness Testimony: Current Trends and Developments.* Cambridge: Cambridge University Press.

Turnstall, O., Gudjonsson, G., Eysenck, H. & Howard, L. (1982) Professional issues arising from psychological evidence presented in court. *Bulletin of the British Psychological Society,* **35**, 329–331.

Tversky, B. & Tuchin, M. (1989) A reconciliation of the evidence on eyewitness testimony: Comments on McCloskey & Zaragoza. *Journal of Experimental Psychology (General)*, **118**, 86–91.

United States *v*. Downing (1985) 753 F 2d 1224 (3rd Cir. 1985).

van Koppen, P. (1995) Sniffing experts: theory and practice of scent line-ups. *Expert Evidence*, **3**, 103–108.

Vingoe, F.J. (1991) The truth and nothing but the truth about forensic hypnosis. *The Psychologist*, **4**, 395–397.

Wagenaar, W.A. (1988) *Identifying Ivan: A Case Study in Legal Psychology*. Hemel Hempstead: Harvester Wheatsheaf.

Wagenaar, W.A. & Veefkind, N. (1992) Comparison of one-person and six-person line-ups. In F. Losel, D. Bender & T. Bleisener (Eds), *Psychology and Law: International Perspectives*. New York: Walter de Gruyter.

Wagstaff, G.F. (1981) *Hypnosis, Compliance and Belief*. Brighton: Harvester Press.

Wagstaff, G.F. (1982) Recall of witnesses under hypnosis. *Journal of the Forensic Science Society*, **22**, 33–39.

Wagstaff, G.F. (1993) What expert witness can tell courts about hypnosis: A review of the association between hypnosis and the law. *Expert Evidence*, **2**, 60–70.

Watkins, J.G. (1989) Hypnotic hypermnesia and forensic hypnosis. *American Journal of Forensic Hypnosis*, **32**, 71–83.

Weingardt, K.R., Toland, H.K. & Loftus, E.F. (1994) Reports of suggested memories: Do people truly believe them? In D.F. Ross, J.D. Read & M.P. Toglia (Eds), *Adult Eyewitness Testimony: Current Trends and Developments*. Cambridge: Cambridge University Press.

Wells, G.L. (1984) How adequate is human intuition for judging eyewitness testimony? In G.L. Wells & E.F. Loftus, (Eds), *Eyewitness Testimony: Psychological Perspectives*. New York: Cambridge University Press.

Wells, G.L. (1988) *Eyewitness Identification*. Toronto: Carswell.

Wells, G.L., Leippe, M.R. & Ostrom, T.M. (1979) Guidelines for empirically assessing the fairness of a line-up. *Law and Human Behavior*, **3**, 285–293.

Wells, G.L., Seelau, E.P., Rydell, S.M. & Luus, C.A.E. (1994) Recommendations for properly conducted line-up identification tasks. In D.F. Ross, J.D. Read & M.P. Toglia (Eds), *Adult Eyewitness Testimony: Current Trends and Developments*. Cambridge: Cambridge University Press.

West, R.L., Crook, T.H. & Baron, K.L. (1992) Everyday memory performance across the lifespan: Effects of age and noncognitive individual differences. *Psychology and Ageing*, **7**, 72–82.

Wheeler *v*. United States (1895) 159 U.S. 526.

Whipple, G.M. (1911) The psychology of testimony. *Psychological Bulletin, 8*, 307–309.

Woodhead, M.M., Baddeley, A.D. & Simmonds, D.C.V. (1979) On training people to recognise faces. *Ergonomics, 22*, 333–343.

Worden, R.E. & Shepherd, R.L. (1996) Demeanour, crime and police behavior: A re-examination of the police services study data. *Criminology, 34* (1), 83–105.

Wrightsman, L.S. (1991) *Psychology and the Legal System* (2nd edition). Pacific Grove, CA: Brooks/Cole.

Yarmey, A.D. (1986) Verbal, visual and voice identification of a rape suspect under different conditions of illumination. *Journal of Applied Psychology*, **71**, 363–370.

Yarmey, A.D. (1992) Accuracy of eyewitness and earwitness showup identifications in a field setting. Poster presented at the *American Psychology-Law Society Conference*, San Diego, California, March.

Yarmey, A.D. (1994) Earwitness evidence: Memory for a perpetrator's voice. In D.F. Ross, J.D. Read & M.P. Toglia (Eds), *Adult Eyewitness Testimony: Current Trends and Developments*. Cambridge: Cambridge University Press.

Yarmey, A.D. (1995) Earwitness and evidence obtained by other senses. In R. Bull & D. Carson (Eds), *Handbook of Psychology in Legal Contexts*. Chichester: Wiley.

Yarmey, A.D. (1996) The elderly witness. In S.L. Sporer, R.S. Malpass & G. Koehnken (Eds), *Psychological Issues in Eyewitness Identification*. Hillsdale, NJ: Lawrence Erlbaum.

Yarmey, A.D. & Matthys, E. (1992) Voice identification of an abductor. *Applied Cognitive Psychology*, **6**, 367–377.

Yuille, J.C. (1984) Research and teaching with the police: A Canadian example. *International Review of Applied Psychology*, **33**, 5–24.

Yuille, J.C. (1993) We must study forensic eyewitnesses to know about them. *American Psychologist*, **48**, 572–573.

Yuille, J.C., Cutshall, J.L. & King, M.A. (1986) Age related changes in eyewitness accounts and photo-identification. Unpublished manuscript: University of British Columbia.

Yuille, J.C. & McEwan, N.H. (1985) Use of hypnosis as an aid to eyewitness memory. *Journal of Applied Psychology*, **70**, 389–400.

Index